MICHELLE OBAMA

ELIZABETH LIGHTFOOT

Guilford, Connecticut

An imprint of The Rowman & Littlefield Publishing Group, Inc.
4501 Forbes Blvd., Ste. 200
Lanham, MD 20706
www.rowman.com

Distributed by NATIONAL BOOK NETWORK

British Library Cataloguing in Publication Information available

Library of Congress Cataloging-in-Publication Data
Names: Lightfoot, Elizabeth.
Title: Michelle Obama / Elizabeth Lightfoot.
Description: Revised edition. | Guilford, Connecticut : Lyons Press, an
  imprint of the Rowman & Littlefield Publishing Group, 2019. | Includes
  bibliographical references and index.
Identifiers: LCCN 2018026932 (print) | LCCN 2018030938 (ebook) | ISBN
  9781493041336 (e-book) | ISBN 9781493038831 (pbk. : alk. paper)
Subjects: LCSH: Obama, Michelle, 1964– | Presidents' spouses—United
  States—Biography. | Legislators' spouses—United States—Biography. |
  African American women lawyers—Biography. | African American
  women—Biography. | African American lawyers—Biography. | Chicago
  (Ill.)—Biography.
Classification: LCC E909.O24 (ebook) | LCC E909.O24 L54 2019 (print) | DDC
  973.932092 [B]—dc23
LC record available at https://lccn.loc.gov/2018026932

Printed in the United States of America

For Nick, Graeme, Isabel, Alastair, and Honor
With love and hope

CONTENTS

PREFACE

How This Book Came to Be

Still the First Lady of Hope (and Why, Ten Years On, the Title Still Fits)

IT's HARD TO BELIEVE NOW, A FULL DECADE LATER, BUT IN EARLY 2008 relatively few Americans knew the name Michelle Obama. We knew about Barack Obama, her husband, the junior senator from Illinois who had been catapulted into the spotlight after delivering a stirring keynote address at the 2004 Democratic National Convention, because he now found himself one of two final contenders for the Democratic nomination for president of the United States. We knew the rough outline of his life story from his 2004 speech and his autobiographical books, *Dreams from My Father* and *The Audacity of Hope*, but we knew very little about the life story of his life partner. Who was Michelle LaVaughn Robinson Obama, the would-be First Lady?

That was the question posed to me by Tom McCarthy, an editor from Lyons Press, when he contacted me in the late winter of 2008, as the primary race was heating up. The Connecticut publishing house was looking to publish books about the two potential First Ladies, Michelle Obama and Cindy McCain. (At that point, Hillary Clinton was very much still in the race for the Democratic nomination, but they figured no one really needed an introduction to her husband, Bill, the former president and would-be First Man or First Gentleman or whatever he would have been called, had his wife won.) Would I be interested in writing about Michelle?

Of course I was. Michelle and Barack Obama stood to be the first African-American First Lady and president of the United States. Regardless of the end result, the 2008 presidential election would be historic. For this former newspaper and wire service reporter, what could be a better story to witness and recount?

Like most of the world at that stage, I knew very little about the would-be First Lady. I had caught my first glimpse of her only a few days earlier, when I happened to turn on the TV and saw an interview she did with Larry King. Like everyone else who was watching CNN that night, I saw an attractive, articulate woman who was clearly comfortable in front of the camera. She was measured and funny, engaging in easy banter with her host but not shying away from the big questions. She spoke eloquently, and a bit teasingly, about her husband, and she was clearly a committed and dedicated mom. In short, she seemed every bit as purposeful, thoughtful, well spoken, magnetic, and intriguing as her increasingly famous spouse.

The part of the interview that really spoke to me was when Larry King asked her about the issue of race in the 2008 election. While not denying that race was a factor, Michelle said what her husband was really doing was bringing people together, from all different backgrounds and all regions of the country. "I mean, you know, he's touched on every element of this country—every race, every political party," she said. "And I think . . . he is uniting people not around race, but around hope. And I say this race is just the rejuvenation of hope."[1]

Both her delivery and her message spoke to me, inspiring me to do a little digging. I discovered that Michelle Obama and I were the same age, that we had degrees from the same school, and that we grappled with some of the same issues: how to balance family and career, how to balance personal dreams with those of our loved ones, how to make a difference in the world while also attending to the mundane, never-ending, day-to-day responsibilities.

An e-mail I received out of the blue piqued my interest further. Having signed up to receive information about the Obama campaign after seeing the would-be president speak at a rally several weeks earlier, I had turned on my computer in late February to discover an e-mail waiting in my inbox. "Elizabeth," it read. "A friend sent me this video over the weekend. After nearly a year on the campaign trail, I've seen a lot of things that have touched me deeply, but I had to share this with you." The writer shared a link to *Yes We Can*, the will.i.am video featuring a Barack Obama campaign speech set to music with an array of celebrity performers, from Scarlett Johansson to Kareem Abdul-Jabbar. The e-mail asked recipients to share the video with friends and family. It was signed, simply, "Michelle."[2]

The video, which of course went viral, underscored the poetic nature of the candidate's words, to say nothing of the almost musical cadence of his oratory. And then there was the message itself. "It was a creed, written into the founding documents that declared the destiny of a nation, Yes We Can," the video began. "It was whispered by slaves and abolitionists as they blazed a trail toward freedom through the darkest of nights. Yes we can." It went on to talk about immigrants, workers who organized, women who won the right to vote, a president who "chose the moon as a frontier, and a King who took us to the mountaintop and pointed the way to the Promised Land." It ended with a rousing call to say "Yes" to justice, equality, opportunity, and prosperity, with will.i.am and company, all the while, singing, "Yes we can."[3]

How could anyone not be moved? How could anyone not want to learn more about the e-mail's author, the would-be First Lady? So, yes, I was excited about the book project, but before signing a contract I felt I needed to run the idea by my husband and four children, then ages nine, thirteen, fifteen, and sixteen. "What do you think? Should I—can I—do this?" I asked them. "Are you nuts?" they responded. "Yes you can!" (The fact that their words echoed the would-be president's message was not lost on me.)

And so with their blessing, I said Yes. For the next few months, as my children ate cereal, pasta, or peanut butter and jelly for every meal, I was ensconced in all things Michelle. My waking hours were spent scouring newspapers, magazines, websites, blogs, social media, and books; trolling TV news, radio talk shows, and YouTube; and reaching out to anyone and everyone who could tell me more about Michelle Obama. What was her childhood like? What was her profession? How did she and Barack make time for each other and for their daughters with everything else they had going on? What issues were most important to her? How was she likely to spend her time as First Lady? And what would it mean, for the Obamas, for our country, and for the world, to have the first African-American family take up residence in the White House?

There was a lot to sift through and then a lot to pull together into some sort of cohesive story. The interesting thing was, after I had compiled boxes and boxes of notes about everything from her favorite fashion designers to her senior thesis at Princeton, when I sat down to write, the words came pouring out. It was as though this story and I had been waiting to meet.

I met the deadline, pulling eleven chapters together and making revisions by early August so the manuscript could be ready for publication just after the election. And then, on the evening of November 4, 2008, I sat down in front of the television with my laptop, waiting for the returns to come in so I could write the final chapter, "Crossing the Finish Line."

Around 11:00 p.m., it became clear that our country would have a beautiful, young, new First Family: Barack, Michelle, Malia, and Sasha Obama. I recorded my impressions, not without a few tears splashing down onto my keyboard as I watched our new president, his wife and children, and that remarkable, happy, hope-filled crowd in Chicago's Grant Park. The next morning, while the rest of the world absorbed the news, I typed up my notes and sent the last chapter off to the publisher. I was done, or so I thought.

Fast-forward ten years. In March 2018 an e-mail appeared in my inbox from Tom McCarthy, the editor who had contacted me all those years ago. A full decade after the first edition had come out, the publishing house was looking to reissue *Michelle Obama: First Lady of Hope* with a new preface and new chapters about the First Lady's major initiatives while she was in the White House, her legacy, and what we might expect going forward. Would I be interested?

Truth be told, I hesitated. My life has grown very busy, inspired, in part, by political events in our country and also, if I really think about it, by Michelle Obama's example. In addition to my ongoing work at a school, where I tell stories about how education has changed lives, I have grown increasingly active supporting people and causes I care about, most of which have to do with expanding opportunities to those who are marginalized. I don't have a lot of free time.

Beyond that, though, I had a more philosophical question. Who was I to tell Michelle Obama's story? It was one thing to write an exploratory book back in 2008, when I was just one of millions of Americans who wanted to know more about our would-be First Lady; it was quite another now that we'd been living with her, watching her, learning from her, for nearly ten years. Our world had grown so complex in that time, too. The political divisions have grown so wide. How could I add anything to that conversation?

And yet, maybe that was the point. We all need to be having these conversations in all of our communities. If I believe, as Michelle and Barack Obama so often said early in the campaign, that together we can work to build "a world as it should be," then we all need to engage. Part of "taking your seat at the table," another favorite phrase of Michelle Obama, is literally sitting down.

And so, I decided to sit, re-immersing myself in our former First Lady, trying to figure out what she meant to us as a country. As I researched information for a new edition, I found myself inspired and uplifted once again by her example as a woman, wife, and mother; by her marriage, which, by all accounts and appearances, is a true partnership of equals, based on love and mutual respect; by the Obamas' scandal-free decade in the world spotlight (no small thing, in the climate in which I write today). I am inspired and energized by her commitment to service and the public good and by her remarkable list of accomplishments during the White House years as her husband tackled the issues we heard more about: reviving a tanking economy, revamping health care, combatting terrorism, and trying to unwind wars in Iraq and Afghanistan. I marvel at her insistence that we do the right thing—that "when they go low, we go high"—and that she never seems to veer from that creed, no matter what is going on in the world around her. Most of all, I remain inspired by her unwavering belief that, in the end, working together, we can build a country that will be "worthy of our children's promise."

It has been fascinating to watch the world respond to Michelle Obama, whose iconic voice and image are now known across the globe. She has been photographed—and shown to be equally comfortable—on international stages alongside world leaders, royalty, and pop stars and in everyday settings with everyday citizens. For me, two images convey her essence as First Lady. One, from 2009, is the view of the statuesque Michelle Obama standing alongside the diminutive Queen Elizabeth, each with an arm around the other. It was called a "breach of protocol" at the time, the two touching each other, but it also conveyed honest human connection, warmth, and affection. The other, which also has a "queen" theme, comes from the postpresidential life. About a year after the Obamas had left the White House, the president's and First Lady's official portraits were unveiled and hung at the Smithsonian's National Portrait Gallery. A few days later, a two-year-old girl from Washington, DC, visited the gallery with her mother. Tiny, wearing a red and pink raincoat, Parker, the little girl, couldn't take her eyes off Amy Sherald's portrait of Mrs. Obama. She stood in front of the painting, her mouth agape, as her mom tried unsuccessfully to get her to turn her way and smile so she could capture a photo of her child, who is African-American, in front of the portrait of the first African-American First Lady. But Parker wouldn't budge—she just kept staring at the former First Lady, whom she later described as "a queen." Another visitor witnessed the scene, snapped a photo of Parker looking at Michelle, posted it, and of course it went viral, ultimately reaching Mrs. Obama herself.

Eventually Parker was invited to visit "the queen," and a video of the tiny two-year-old dancing to "Shake It Off" with the former First Lady also went viral. Jessica Curry, Parker's mother, wrote an op-ed, "Looking Up to Mrs. Obama," for the *New York Times* about the original photo and what, for her, it symbolizes:

It shows a little girl looking up and seeing a dynamic woman who, coincidentally, is brown just like her. Maybe color, gender, and race will be insignificant when Parker is an adult—we'll just be individuals. This dream lives on and seems closer to realization in every generation. Regardless of whether you marvel at or dislike the Obamas, it's hard to deny that they changed the fabric of American history, and thanks to them, children like my daughter can dream bigger than they ever imagined.[4]

Curry's words speak eloquently—and her daughter's photo speaks metaphorically—to the recurrent themes expressed (and lived and breathed) by Michelle Obama before, during, and after her years in the White House. In her final speech as First Lady, she addressed a group of educators who had gathered at the White House to honor school counselors. With her eyes welling up and her voice cracking with emotion, she said to them, "Being your First Lady has been the greatest honor of my life. I hope I've made you proud."

Then the woman who called herself the "mom-in-chief" turned her attention to her real focus all this time, the next generation. "For all the young people in this room, and those who are watching, know that this country belongs to you   to all of you, from every background and walk of life," she said. "I want our young people to know that they matter. That they belong.

"So don't be afraid. You hear me, young people? Don't be afraid. Be focused. Be determined. Be hopeful. Be empowered. Empower yourselves with a good education. Then get out there, and use that education to build a country worthy of your boundless promise. Lead by example with hope. Never fear. And know that I will be with you, rooting for you and working to support you, for the rest of my life."[5]

After eight years in the White House and presumably for many years to come, Michelle Obama, the mom-in-chief, remains our First Lady of hope.

Introduction

Michelle Obama

Imagining Anything for Ourselves

In February 2008, as the race for the Democratic presidential nomination heated up, Larry King interviewed would-be First Lady Michelle Obama on CNN's *Larry King Live*. Michelle spoke about her husband, the unique attributes that she believed would make him the best president, and the issues that mattered to her as an American woman, working mother, and—potentially—the first black First Lady.

"I think, wow, what an opportunity!" she said, responding to a question about what her husband's election would mean for her personally. "What a platform I'll have, potentially, to talk about a whole range of issues that affect the country. What a privilege it will be to have the opportunity to speak to peoples' hearts, to be a part of moving this country in a different direction."[1]

Wearing a sleeveless black top that accentuated her toned arms, with a triple strand of pearls draped around her neck and a perfectly coiffed bob framing her youthful face, Michelle's appearance that night and on several other occasions drew comparisons to another famously elegant—and young—First Lady, Jacqueline Kennedy. Michelle has appeared in the pages of *Vogue* and was placed by *Vanity Fair* on its International Best Dressed List. But it wasn't her physical appearance that night that had people talking. Rather, it was Michelle's intellect, verbal ability, and poise that left them breathless.

"What a home run!" Paul Begala, a CNN political analyst and then Hillary Clinton supporter, pronounced after the interview. "Somebody needs to make a button that says 'Vote for Michelle's Husband.' I support Hillary, but what a star! So poised."[2]

Jamal Simmons, a Democratic strategist and Obama supporter, was, unsurprisingly, equally enthusiastic. "I thought it was a great interview," he told Larry King. "She would make a great First Lady."[3]

Perhaps the highest praise came from less expected quarters. Michael Medved, a radio talk show host and backer of Republican candidate John McCain, called Michelle "terrific," even going so far as to say that she could be a "potential candidate herself years from now. I would love to see her debate Bill Clinton. How about a First Spouses' debate?"[4]

And former senator Tim Hutchinson, who was supporting Mike Huckabee (then still in the race), called Michelle a "tremendously impressive individual. Clearly when you hear her speak, not only is she articulate, you can imagine her in the White House."[5]

Comments posted online by viewers after the show aired were similarly enthusiastic. "I think that if Michelle would run for president in eight years after Barack finishes his two terms she would have a better chance in winning then [sic] Hillary does now," one viewer wrote.[6] Another said, "She will make a great First Lady. She is confident & strong. I truly do hope Barack wins because I don't believe Hillary's husband Bill will can [sic] ever be a first man!"[7]

It is hard to remember such widespread praise ever being heaped upon another would-be First Spouse, but the fact that the Obamas would be the first black couple to inhabit the White House makes their ascendancy—and the accompanying rhetoric—historic.

Likewise, the fact that Michelle was being touted, even if lightheartedly, as a potential presidential candidate herself when her husband's time is up—the second Hillary Clinton, as it were—says something about how far the United States has come, at least in the perception of who can or should fill the country's highest office. (Months later, she would elicit a similar response after her powerful speech at the Democratic National Convention.) The call for President Michelle Obama would resurface—loudly—in 2016 after the unexpected election of Donald J. Trump. (See chapter 14, "Michelle Obama's Legacy," for more detail.) But a mere week after the triumphant February 11 Larry King interview, the inevitable happened: The bloom came off the rose. At two rallies in Wisconsin before that state's primary, the Princeton- and Harvard Law School–educated Michelle Obama made her now-famous "For the first time in my adult lifetime, I am really proud of my country" statements. (What she actually said at one of the rallies was, "For the first time in my adult life, I am proud of my country, because it feels like hope is finally making a comeback." What she actually meant, according to the Obama campaign, was that she was proud to see so many people engaged in the voting process.)

Michelle also drew criticism for another comment she made in Wisconsin: "Life for regular folks has gotten worse over the course of my lifetime, through Republican and Democratic administrations." Although it's likely no one would have questioned the statements had she made them a few months later, after the economy took its terrifying nosedive, at the time people felt the words made her look bitter and ungrateful.

Opponents pounced. Almost instantaneously, Cindy McCain, wife of Republican nominee John McCain, met with reporters, pronouncing, "I have and always will be proud of my country." Conservative columnist Michelle Malkin called Michelle Obama her husband's "Bitter Half," while the conservative *National Review* ran an article about "Mrs. Grievance," accompanied by an image of Michelle with an "angry scowl" on her face.

People began to wonder where Michelle's statements came from. The woman who had seemed so poised—so Camelot-like—in the Larry King interview had another side. Were her comments born of the same sentiment she had expressed in the thesis she wrote in 1985 during her senior year at Princeton? In "Princeton-Educated Blacks and the Black Community," the sociology major wrote that her experiences at Princeton "have made me far more aware of my 'blackness' than ever before. I have found that at Princeton no matter how liberal and open-minded some of my White professors and classmates try to be towards me, I sometimes feel like a visitor on campus; as if I really don't belong. Regardless of the circumstances under which I interact with Whites at Princeton, it often seems as if, to them, I will always be Black first and a student second."[8]

After she made her "For the first time I am proud" statement, the questions became: Does Michelle Obama still feel she doesn't belong? And is she ungrateful for the opportunities she was given?

The issue was further compounded a few weeks later when controversial sermons by the Obamas' then pastor, the Reverend Jeremiah Wright, were made public, leading Barack Obama to deliver his "More Perfect Union" speech about race, inequality, and racial tensions in America. When the would-be president explained that he could no sooner divorce himself from the man who officiated at his wedding and baptized his daughters than he could from his beloved white grandmother who had, herself, made race-based comments that made him "cringe," Barack Obama was lauded as perhaps the one person capable of leading Americans across the racial divide.

Of course, in the end it wasn't that simple. Reverend Wright continued to make outrageous statements, fulminating publicly against the government and suggesting that it may have helped create the AIDS epidemic. When he brought his claims to the National Press Club in April, the Obamas decided enough was enough. They made the difficult decision to leave Trinity United Church of Christ, the church they had attended and supported financially for years. "Our relations with Trinity have been strained by the divisive statements of Reverend Wright, which strictly conflict with our own views," the Obamas wrote in a jointly signed letter to current Trinity pastor Reverend Otis Moss. "These controversies have served as an unfortunate distraction for other Trinity members who seek to worship in peace, and have placed you in an untenable position."[9]

The Obamas' move was met with satisfaction from many quarters, but all was not necessarily forgiven. And for whatever reason, Michelle seemed to receive much of the blame. In a piece he wrote for the online magazine *Slate*, journalist and author Christopher Hitchens seemed to suggest that Michelle was the reason her husband had stood by Reverend Wright, whom Hitchens called "a conceited old fanatic," a "crackpot mentor," and a "moral idiot" who has done "incredible damage" to the

Obama campaign. Indeed, he titled his piece "Are We Getting Two for One? Is Michelle Obama Responsible for the Jeremiah Wright Fiasco?"[10]

In May—as the seemingly endless race for the Democratic nomination appeared to be winding down, with Barack Obama the presumptive nominee—he famously told his opponents to "Lay off my wife." Obama's directive was sparked by a video being disseminated over the Internet by the Tennessee Republican Party during that state's primary. In the clip, footage of Michelle making her "first time in my life/proud of America" statement was interspersed with images of various Tennesseans talking about how proud they are and always have been of their country.[11]

In mid-June, with the Democratic nomination finally sealed in Obama's favor, the campaign made the decision to address rumors that had been circulating over the Internet head-on. Launching FightThe Smears.com, the campaign took on a slew of wild stories and innuendos, including a particularly pernicious one about Michelle. Spread via e-mail and then through blogs and commentaries, there was word that a videotape existed of Michelle railing against "whitey." The tape never surfaced, and FightTheSmears.com flatly denied its existence or that she had ever uttered the word.

The Obama campaign also announced in June that they were building a team around Michelle to help respond to any additional attacks presented by opponents, and the founders of the blog WhatAboutOur Daughters.com founded a separate website, MichelleObamaWatch.com. According to Salon.com, MichelleObamaWatch.com was set up to "track the most egregious examples of racism, sexism, and general WTF."[12]

In addition to a forceful show of support from her husband, his campaign, and WhatAboutOurDaughters.com, Michelle also garnered support from some unlikely quarters. During an interview with ABC News in Slovenia, where she was traveling with her husband, First Lady Laura Bush seemed to come to Michelle's defense, suggesting that Michelle probably didn't mean to say that she was proud of her country for the "first time" when she made her statements in Wisconsin. A seasoned First Lady, Laura Bush cautioned that someone in her position probably needs to "be really careful what you say," because everything is scrutinized and ultimately often "misconstrued."[13]

Obama's Republican opponent, John McCain, also seemed to warn the public to lay off the potential First Spouses. The day after FightThe Smears.com was launched, McCain said in an interview with CNN's Dana Bash that he thought that a candidate's wife "should be treated with respect, and if there's any disrespectful conduct on the part of anyone, those people should be rejected." McCain went on to say that he has "the greatest respect for both Senator and Michelle Obama," adding that he has never met Michelle but that "she's a talented and very effective person. And I admire both of them."[14]

Meanwhile, a slew of opinion columns and blog posts began to appear on behalf of Michelle and the Obama campaign, many of them decrying the "shameful sliming of Michelle Obama," as an opinion piece by Roland S. Martin was titled. "In case anyone has forgotten, when voters go to the polls in November, they will be voting for either Sen. John McCain or Sen. Barack Obama. Cindy McCain won't be on the ballot, and no one will be voting on the policies of Michelle Obama," Martin wrote.[15]

Whether the press and the public would, as Michelle's husband had requested, "lay off" the potential First Spouses remained to be seen. And whether they even should do so was another matter to be debated. Are spouses fair game, particularly when they are out there publicly stumping on behalf of the candidate to whom they are married? Does it perhaps say something about the candidate's judgment that he or she chose to marry a particular person? And should it matter that that person is most likely a very close confidante, the probable recipient and deliverer of pillow talk, at the very least?

Regardless of how America chose to answer those questions in this and future campaigns, what had begun to seem clear by the start of the summer of 2008 was that while much of the country appeared ready to accept Obama as the designated Democratic presidential candidate, there was another segment that was equally reluctant. And whether it was prompted by the pride comment or news about her Princeton thesis or rumors about any alleged videotapes or simply by the fact that she is the kind of smart, outspoken, accomplished woman who makes some people uncomfortable, Michelle seemed to be a focal point of much of that reluctance.

As the campaign wore on, Michelle did seem to rein in some of that characteristic candor, and her masterful speech at the Democratic Convention seemed to help erase some—though perhaps not all—of the earlier criticisms. Even right up to the election, you could still find articles, editorials, and blogs speaking about the "bitter" and "angry" Michelle Obama.

So what about Michelle? Given her own statements in her college thesis, would she always "feel like a visitor"? Even as a resident of the White House, would she feel as if she "doesn't really belong"? Could she fully embrace her role as First Lady, or was she still a black woman first? Would she be able to demonstrate that she is truly proud of her country?

And what about her country? Was America ready to embrace its first black First Couple? And what would it all mean, both inside the United States and beyond the country's borders, to have this first African-American First Family living in the White House?

Beyond the US borders the answer seemed relatively clear. In the days after Obama secured the Democratic nomination, media outlets the world over welcomed the news, recognizing the historic nature of his nomination.

"Obama . . . has rekindled America's faith in its prodigious powers of reinvention—and the world's admiration for America," a *Times* of London editorial said. "It has been a bruising journey. . . . But today at least the tide of history seems to be with him. Win or lose in November, he will have gone farther than anyone in history to bury the toxic enmity that fueled America's Civil War and has haunted it ever since. . . . This moment's significance is its resounding proof of the truism about America as a land of opportunity; Obama's opportunity to graduate from Harvard and take Washington by storm; the opportunity that the world's most responsive democratic system gives its voters to be inspired by an unknown; the opportunity that outsiders now have to reassess the superpower that too many of them love to hate."[16]

In *Haaretz* from Israel, Schmuel Rosner wrote, "Now is the time to take in Obama's astounding political victory, if one can still feel awe for anything in this day and age. Against all the odds, the campaign broke down the boundaries of bias and race, and brought out voters to cast their ballots."[17]

From Kenya, Barack Obama's father's homeland, Alphayo Otiento wrote in the *Daily Nation*, "A core element of that Obama message has always been hope and inspiration. This is the one political message that simultaneously persuades swing voters and motivates mobilizable voters who rarely go to the polls. . . . Now it will be up to every Democrat, every progressive, to take advantage of this historical opportunity to make Obama the American president who leads the world into a new progressive era of unprecedented possibilities."[18]

The widespread adoration Obama received during his summer 2008 trip to Europe and two war zones only cemented that impression abroad. Indeed, Frank Rich even wrote a column in the *New York Times* about Obama's overseas trip which bore the headline, "How Obama Became Acting President."[19]

What it all means for the United States we may not know for some time, but Michelle's life story might provide one answer. We know that Michelle LaVaughn Robinson Obama grew up in a working-class, largely African-American Chicago neighborhood, where her family of four lived in a rented one-bedroom apartment. We know that, supported by her hard-working parents, Marian and Fraser Robinson, she excelled in school and skipped second grade. We know that she was a gifted athlete but that she shied away from competitive sports because, according to her brother, Craig, she hated to lose.

We know that she followed Craig, who would become the head basketball coach at Oregon State University and later work for the New York Knicks, to Princeton, and that she then went on to Harvard Law School. We know that she left a high-paying job at a top-flight Chicago law firm (where she met her future husband) to go into public service, and that when Barack became a US senator she declined to move to Washington with him, opting to remain in Chicago where her job was and where their young daughters were settled comfortably—her husband could fly home on weekends to see the family. Not insignificantly, she would also remain near her by then widowed mother, who watched the girls when Michelle was working or on the campaign trail. (Unlike many other working political couples, the Obamas employed a housekeeper but not a nanny, preferring to have friends and family look after their children when they couldn't themselves. During the campaign, she often said one of her husband's priorities was to "make sure that women and families have the kind of back-up system that we have to sustain ourselves.")[20]

We know that as a wife and mother Michelle can be a tough taskmaster. In the lead-up to the election, she told us that Barack's to-do list includes making the bed and taking out the garbage when he is at home, and that he must join his family for important occasions, such as parent-teacher conferences, birthdays, and holidays. Likewise, her daughters are expected to help out with household chores. We know that, for her, family comes first, and that she seriously weighed her husband's plan to run for president and the impact it would have on their family life before giving it her stamp of approval. (Apparently Michelle struck a hard bargain: She would wholeheartedly support her husband's candidacy, including helping out on the campaign trail, provided he would give up smoking.)[21]

We know that Michelle is smart, attractive, and well educated. We know that she can appeal to people across the political spectrum—as she did when she appeared on *Larry King Live*—but that she needs to watch her tongue, something that is not always easy for a quick-witted, articulate lawyer who is accustomed to speaking her mind.

We also know that on January 20, 2009, when Barack Hussein Obama was sworn in as the forty-fourth president of the United States with Michelle LaVaughn Robinson Obama at his side, it was an epic moment in the United States' history. The country would see its first black president and its first black First Lady, marking a major milestone in the struggle for racial equality.

The history books have yet to be fully written, but a story Michelle Obama told on the campaign trail about a young girl in a South Carolina beauty parlor during the campaign just might provide the best explanation about what it all really means, both for her personally and for the entire country. The ten-year-old girl told Michelle that if her husband is elected president, "it means I can imagine anything for myself."

Michelle has said that that story mirrors her own. "She could have been me, because the truth is, I'm not supposed to be . . . standing here," she said. "I'm a statistical oddity. Black girl, brought up on the South

Side of Chicago. Was I supposed to go to Princeton? . . . They said maybe Harvard Law was too much for me to reach for. But I went. I did fine. And I'm certainly not supposed to be standing here."[22]

But there she was, against all odds. In the end, Michelle Obama, First Lady, is a quintessentially American story. Indeed, taken in its broadest context, the mere existence of a President and Mrs. Obama, the forty-fourth president and First Lady of the United States, means that the ten-year-old girl in the beauty shop just may speak for all of us. The Obama story is a promise: As Americans, *any of us* can imagine *anything* for ourselves.

CHAPTER 1

Taking Her Seat at the Table

Michelle Obama's Formative Years

DURING THE ALL-IMPORTANT PENNSYLVANIA DEMOCRATIC PRIMARY in April 2008, Michelle Obama was a guest on Comedy Central's *The Colbert Report*. Her appearance came just days after the so-called Bittergate incident, which, in case it needs repeating, refers to Barack Obama's comment that he understood how economic circumstances in rural America—and the government's failure to respond—may have made some Americans bitter, leading them to cling to guns, religion, and antipathy toward those who are different.

His remarks, which were made at a private San Francisco fundraiser, were met with accusations of elitism, and they almost certainly cost him critical votes from working-class Pennsylvanians, delivering the Obama campaign a major defeat in that key state, though not quite the double-digit margin that the Clinton regime had predicted. From then on in the race for the Democratic nomination, white working-class voters remained a major chink in Obama's armor. (At least until he invited Sen. Joe Biden of Delaware to join the ticket as his running mate and until, a few short weeks before the election, the economy went into a tailspin and Obama suddenly looked like the better candidate to handle the economic crisis.)

Stephen Colbert, broadcasting his show that week from Philadelphia, jumped right into the swirling Bittergate controversy. "Everybody knows you and your husband are elitists," he said as Michelle, wearing an elegant bright-blue, sleeveless cocktail dress and looking every bit the long-limbed, high-society "It Girl" she had recently been dubbed by *Vogue*, settled in for her interview. "Tell me about your elite upbringing on the South Side of Chicago. How many silver spoons in your mouth?"[1]

Without skipping a beat, Michelle responded, "We had four spoons. And then my father got a raise at the plant and we had five spoons."

"That sounds posh," Colbert said.[2]

While the exchange reveals much about Michelle's wit, quickness on her feet, and willingness to crack a spontaneous joke, it also says something about who she was at birth and who she later became. And if there is anything posh about the story, like the apocryphal fifth silver spoon to her parents, it only came about through hard work, determination, and undying support from her family.

Although it's a good bet that Marian and Fraser Robinson had more than four spoons in their silverware drawer when their daughter Michelle LaVaughn Robinson was born on January 17, 1964, things certainly weren't cushy for the family of four in their one-bedroom apartment on the city's South Side.

Fraser Robinson worked the swing shift in the boiler room at the city's water purification plant, while Marian stayed home to take care of Michelle and her brother, Craig, sixteen months Michelle's senior. Michelle's father went off to work uncomplainingly each day, even after he was diagnosed with multiple sclerosis at the age of thirty, and though his health began a steady decline, he would send not just one but two children to college. And not to just any college—to Princeton, among the most difficult schools to gain admission to in the country, if not the world. Michelle's mother returned to work when her daughter was grown, leaving her latest job at a bank so she could be with her granddaughters, Malia and Natasha, nicknamed Sasha, whenever their mother can't.

"I was raised in a working-class family on the South Side of Chicago," Michelle told an audience at the University of South Carolina in January 2008. "My mother came home and took care of us through high school, my father was a city shift worker who took care of us all his life. The only amazing thing about my life is that a man like my father could raise a family of four on a single city worker's salary."[3]

Michelle's childhood was shaped by the realities of growing up African-American in one of the country's largest cities and in a section of the city that boasts one of the largest—if not the largest—single groupings of African Americans in the entire country.[4] The Chicago Michelle was born into was a relatively segregated city, a place where black workers still had fewer career opportunities. In *The Audacity of Hope*, Obama writes about how black parents had to put in extra effort to make up for their lower incomes, the more violent neighborhoods they tended to live in, and the limited resources for their children.[5]

All families have stories about what life was like for their forebears. In the Robinson household, one of the oft-told tales was about Michelle's grandfather. A carpenter by trade, her maternal grandfather was not allowed to join the union because of the color of his skin. As a result, he was denied access to the city's top construction jobs.[6]

During Michelle's childhood, the world her parents knew would slowly begin to change. The civil rights movement of the '60s would usher in the Civil Rights Act of 1964 and the Voting Rights Act of 1965 as well as prominent African-American leaders such as Reverend Dr. Martin Luther King Jr. and Malcolm X.

In the Robinsons' own city, a place long dominated by white politicians by the name of Daley, another family would rise to prominence. Like Michelle's, this family was African-American, and its nominal leader—the Reverend Jesse Jackson—would be the first black man to run for president.

In fact, Michelle grew up alongside the Jacksons. Jesse Jackson's daughter, Santita, was one of her closest friends in high school. A professional singer, Santita sang at the Obamas' wedding, and she is the godmother of the Obamas' oldest daughter, Malia. Jesse Jackson Jr. was the national cochair of Obama's campaign. Jesse Jackson Sr. had his moment in the spotlight during the 2008 presidential campaign—more on that later.

Still, during Michelle's childhood, the South Side was a largely black, urban environment with its own set of urban problems, and it was in that environment that the Robinsons taught their children to work hard, reach high, and never give up.

"When you grow up as a black kid in a white world, so many times people are telling you, sometimes not maliciously, sometimes maliciously, you're not good enough," Craig Robinson, at the time head basketball coach at Oregon State, told the *Washington Post*. "To have a family, which we did, who constantly reminded you how smart you were, how good you were, how pleasant it was to be around you, how successful you could be, it's hard to combat. Our parents gave us a little head start by making us feel confident."[7]

The family digs were modest at best. While she was growing up, Michelle, her parents, and brother rented a one-bedroom apartment in a classic brick bungalow belonging to Michelle's great aunt, who lived downstairs. While her parents enjoyed the sole bedroom, the living room was partitioned with wood paneling into three spaces to accommodate one bedroom for Craig, another for Michelle, and a third space for studying. Marian, now a widow, continued to live in the same apartment, behind a burglar-proof wrought-iron door until she moved into the White House with her daughter, son-in-law, and grandchildren after the election.[8]

"If I had to describe it to a real estate agent, it would be 1BR, 1BA," Craig told the *Washington Post*. "If you said it was 1,100 square feet, I'd call you a liar."[9]

Given those dimensions, it's not hard to imagine how cramped things must have been for this growing family of four (particularly when you take into account how large some of them grew: at five feet, eleven inches, Michelle is one very tall woman; Craig, the former basketball star turned investment banker turned basketball coach, is six feet, six inches). And yet, the layout of the modest apartment speaks volumes about this particular family's values.

By sacrificing their living room—the quintessential entertainment and relaxation space for many an American household—the Robinsons were able to give each of their two children a small space to call their own. The fact that they also carved out a room specially designated for studying shows how much emphasis they placed on education. Indeed, unlike many other children growing up in the '60s and '70s, Michelle and Craig were allowed to watch only one hour of television per night. Rather than waste their time on such trivial pursuits, they were expected to engage in mind- and body-stretching activities such as reading and playing chess and participating in sports.[10]

(The Obamas chose to follow a similar routine with their children, limiting the amount of television the girls watch and encouraging things like games and physical activities. This is a subject both Obamas brought up during the campaign—the notion of parental responsibility.)

Although neither Marian nor Fraser attended college themselves, they were both keenly aware of the value of a good education. Under their tutelage, both Michelle and Craig would learn to read by the age of four, and both children later skipped second grade. Interestingly, Marian and Fraser also each skipped a grade, so the Robinson children's academic successes must have had as much to do with natural intelligence as with a strong work ethic and fierce parental support.[11]

Despite all of this emphasis on education, even more important than learning to read and write was knowing how to think and ask questions, Marian told the *New Yorker*. "We told them, 'Make sure you respect your teachers, but don't hesitate to question them,'" she said. "Don't even allow us to just say anything to you. Ask us why.'"[12] Those same values can be seen today in the frank and honest discourse Michelle exhibits whenever she speaks. Never the silent Stepford wife–type of political spouse, Michelle always seems ready to speak her mind, as, in fact, do her children.

While in many ways Michelle was a typical young girl, reportedly enjoying playing with Barbies and her Easy-Bake Oven, there were early signs that she was unique, and not just because of her academic abilities. Michelle's great-aunt was her piano teacher, and Michelle was a relentless music student. "She would practice piano for so long you'd have to tell her to stop," Marian said.[13]

She brought the same intensity to other pursuits, and though she was a gifted athlete, Craig says she eventually shied away from competitive sports because she always wanted to win.

"My sister is a poor sport—she didn't like to lose," Craig told the *Chicago Sun-Times*,[14] recalling how he used to let her win at Monopoly just often enough so she wouldn't stop playing with him altogether. But Craig is also the first to admit that that spirit of competition does have its upside. Michelle "really does hate to lose, and that's why she's been so successful," Craig said.[15]

Michelle also apparently had a bit of a temper, which similarly might have served to motivate her. Verna Williams, a Harvard Law School friend, told the *New York Times* that she remembers Michelle "telling me about a teacher complaining about her temper in elementary school. She said her mom told the teacher, 'Yeah, she's got a temper. But we decided to keep her anyway.'" (I guess we also know where Michelle got her legendary sense of humor, which she sometimes directs—lovingly but not without an occasional bite—at her nearest and dearest.)[16]

Starting in sixth grade, Michelle joined a class for gifted children at what is now Bouchet Elementary School. There, she would study French and take a special biology class at Kennedy King College. Students in the class studied photosynthesis, did work in a lab, and dissected rodents, studying their musculature. "This is not what normal seventh-graders were getting," her childhood friend Chiaka Davis Patterson told the *Chicago Sun-Times*.[17] When she graduated from middle school, Michelle was class salutatorian.

From there, she went on to the Whitney M. Young Magnet School in Chicago's West Loop, a public high school for the best and the brightest that routinely sends students to top universities, including Craig's and Michelle's alma mater, Princeton. Founded in 1975 by the Chicago Board of Education, Whitney M. Young Magnet High School is known nationally as a premier college preparatory high school, and in addition to myriad athletic championships, its students have dominated the state Academic Decathlon over the course of the last two and a half decades. Whitney Young also has a long tradition of ethnic and cultural diversity, with a student body that, at the time of the election, was 31 percent African-American, almost 21 percent Latino, more than 17 percent Asian, and 30 percent Caucasian.[18]

When Michelle entered Whitney Young, it was still a relatively new school. "Our first full graduating class was in '78"—Michelle graduated in 1981—"so it was pretty experimental to come here," Michelle's teacher Bernadette McHale told the *New Yorker*. "She made a decision to choose an integrated environment that had more diversity in both curriculum and population."[19]

Chiaka Patterson said Whitney Young was "the school to go to. It was considered state of the art."[20] By 2008, a typical Whitney Young graduating class had "more than 95 percent of students admitted to four-year institutions," including such schools as Harvard, Yale, MIT, Stanford, Duke, and Howard.[21]

Michelle's 1981 Whitney Young yearbook shows a photo of a "serious" girl in a yellow silk shirt. Although athletic, she did not play varsity sports. Apparently this wasn't simply because she disliked competition. As her brother Craig told the *New Yorker*, "That's the best way to get her not to do something. She didn't want to play just because she was tall and black and athletic."[22] Michelle did, however, excel academically. She made the honor roll all four years, was in advanced-placement classes, and was a member of the National Honor Society. She was also elected treasurer of the student council.[23]

In 2005, Michelle Obama served as honorary chairperson and mistress of ceremonies for the Thirtieth Anniversary Gala Dinner Dance at her high school alma mater. Her cochairs for the event included mayor Richard M. Daley; Arne Duncan, the CEO of Chicago Public Schools who would later become President Obama's secretary of education; and Michael W. Scott, president of the Chicago Public School Board. Dr. Kenner said at the time that the event's theme—A Bridge to the World: Celebrating Thirty Years of Academic Excellence—reflected "the fact that Whitney Young graduates are prepared to compete in an increasingly globalized economy and their options are virtually without limit."[24] Certainly Michelle Obama, Class of 1981, fits that bill.

When it came time for college, the spirit of competition that kept Michelle from engaging in competitive sports, the spirit of competition that compelled her to strive for success in the arenas in which she did engage, also propelled her to apply to Princeton. As Michelle recalls, when her brother applied to colleges, he was a shoo-in at Ivy League schools, both because of his academics and his athletics. "A black kid from the South Side of Chicago that plays basketball and is smart," she told *Newsweek*. "He was getting in everywhere. But I *knew* him and I was like, 'I can do that, too.'"[25]

In fact, Craig was such a strong student and athlete that he was offered full-ride scholarships at several schools, but his father told him to think about where he would get the best education. Even though he had won only a partial scholarship to Princeton, his father insisted that he go there. "Dad said it didn't matter about the cost—it was the education that was important," Craig told author David Mendell.[26]

While still in high school, Michelle visited her older brother at Princeton. Some of her high school teachers warned her against applying there herself because of her test scores. But Michelle, competitive younger sister that she was, chose not to heed their warnings and, of course, we know the result. Not just Princeton—*cum laude*—but also Harvard Law School.

Likewise, as Marian Robinson told *Newsweek*, her daughter "was disappointed in herself" because of her test scores. "She used to have a little bit of trouble with tests, so she did whatever she had to make up for that. I'm sure it was psychological, because she was hard working and she had a brother who could pass a test just by carrying a book under his arm. When you are around someone like that, even if you are OK, you want to be as good or better."[27]

But was it just sibling rivalry that propelled Michelle to defy her teachers and reach so high? Or was it something more deep-seated, something related to her awareness that she could and should make something of herself? Something connected to her position as a high-achieving African-American girl in a predominantly white world? Something akin to Hillary Clinton's determination to see a woman in an office held heretofore by men, to shatter that glass ceiling now sporting eighteen million cracks?

In a January 2008 speech at Benedict College in Columbia, South Carolina, Michelle urged her largely black audience to take chances and to aim high, even in the face of opposition:

> *We are confronted with doubters. People who tell us what we can't do. You're not ready. You're not good enough. You're not smart enough.*

You're too tall. Each and every one of you here has heard and felt those ceilings, somebody pushing you down, defining your limitations, who are you? You know damn well what you are capable of doing. . . . This election is just as much about that as it is about change because the truth is there are millions of shining lights just like me all over the country. Kids living in shadows, being told by their own communities what they can and cannot do. This is an opportunity for all of us to send a different message to those shining lights.

You know, every time somebody told me, "No, you can't do that," I pushed past their doubts and I took my seat at the table.[28]

Michelle credits her parents with being her biggest advocates, the people who would do their utmost to ensure that her particular light could shine its brightest, that she would, indeed, pull up her chair and sit down at that table. "My parents told us time and again, 'Don't tell us what you can't do. And don't worry about what can go wrong,'" she says.[29]

These are words Michelle has no doubt called upon, if only in her mind, many times during her life. When she decided to apply to Princeton against the advice of teachers, and later as she applied to Harvard Law School. When she chose to leave her high-paying job at a law firm and become a civil servant. When she and Barack made the decision that he would run for office, first for the State Senate, later Congress, then the US Senate, and ultimately the presidency. During the interminable Democratic primary and in the months leading up to the election. And undoubtedly those words would continue to echo in her head in the ensuing years, as this girl from the South Side of Chicago became the First Lady of the United States.

Michelle's parents also showed her, by their own dogged example, how to work hard, ignore obstacles, and never give up. Along the campaign trail, Michelle would often tell the story of her father and how he refused to let multiple sclerosis affect the way he lived his life. Once a standout swimmer and boxer who had also served in the military, Fraser eventually limped so badly that he could hardly cross the street—and then only with the aid of two canes—but he still went off to work each day, never complaining, never giving in. When Michelle was twenty-five, her father died after a kidney operation, but he remains very much with her to this day.

"I am constantly trying to make sure that I am making him proud," Michelle said in a campaign speech. "What would my father think of the choices that I've made, how I've lived my life, what careers I chose, what man I married? That's the voice in my head that keeps me whole and keeps me grounded and keeps me the girl from the South Side of Chicago, no matter how many cameras are in the room, how many autographs people want, how big we get."[30]

It was from her parents that Michelle also had her first lessons about giving back. Even as her father battled his illness and worked day in and day out for the city, he also volunteered as a Democratic precinct captain in Mayor Daley's Chicago. Her mother, meanwhile, volunteered at her children's schools, helping to ensure that they were as good as they could be, not just for her own children but for the others for whom education could be the stepping-stone to a better future.

Michelle followed suit. After working for the corporate law firm where she would meet her husband, she left that high-paying job for one in the public sector, a position in Mayor Richard M. Daley's office that would pay a fraction of the salary she had been earning at Sidley & Austin. She later moved on to a series of other positions in the nonprofit world, including a stint as executive director for Public Allies Chicago, a program that helps engage young people in public service, a job for which she was uniquely suited. Before resigning to take up her nonpaying role as First Lady, she served as vice president of community and external affairs for the University of Chicago Hospitals. In that position she served as a bridge between the academic university hospital and the South Side neighborhood where she grew up, another role which spoke to her unique experience.

She also sat on a number of boards, including the Chicago Council on Global Affairs and the University of Chicago Laboratory School, where, like her mother before her, she was able to ensure that her children's school was the best it could be, not just for her daughters but for the many other children who hope to use education as a springboard to a brighter future.

The final critical lesson that Michelle learned from her parents was about the irreplaceable importance of parents in a child's life. Although some have questioned her decision to remain in Chicago with Malia and Sasha after her husband was elected to the Senate—and to refrain from campaigning full-time during his run for the presidency— Michelle has said time and again that her children are her priority. And when she is First Lady, her First Job, she said at the time, will be to take good care of her children.[31]

This was the example she grew up with. When they were young, Michelle and Craig were expected to join their parents every night for a family dinner—none of those throw-it-in-the-microwave, gulp-down-your-food-whenever-it's-convenient experiences for the Robinsons. Dinnertime was a touchpoint at the end of every day, one of those daily acts that helped keep the parents in tune with the children and children attuned to their parents. (Perhaps it was at the dinner table that Michelle honed her undeniable talent for discussing, debating, and ultimately persuading others to move to her side during an argument. It is that powerful skill that led her husband to nickname her "The Closer" on the campaign trail, where she proved uniquely capable of attracting as-of-yet uncommitted donors, not an insignificant asset for a political spouse.)

The Robinsons were also close to members of their extended family, and there were frequent and spirited family gatherings. According to her husband, visiting the Robinson household after he met Michelle in the late 1980s was pretty much like "dropping in on the set of *Leave It to Beaver*." (No doubt it was very different from the households Barack Obama experienced as a child in Hawaii and Indonesia, without the presence of his own father or cousins, aunts, and uncles.) There was Michelle's cheerful father, Fraser, dedicated both to his job and his kids' activities; pretty mother Marian, making cakes and staying involved at the children's school; brother Craig, a funny and friendly investment banker who hoped to coach basketball. And extended family often stopped by to add to the mix, joking, eating, and listening to music for hours on end. It was the quintessential family scene, minus a dog. As her husband writes in *The Audacity of Hope*, Michelle's mother didn't like the notion of a dog messing up the house.[32]

Barack Obama is keenly aware of the power of the parent-child relationship Michelle knew growing up, and he has written wistfully about how his own choices have made it difficult to replicate that relationship, particularly the father-daughter dynamic. He writes that when Michelle talks about her father, he senses such love and respect, feelings that came about not through any large actions but through small everyday actions, by simply being present. He writes that he often wonders if his daughters will one day talk of him with that same sense of love and respect.[33] (One thing his daughters will be able to lay claim to—something that their mother never had in her youth—is the dog. As Michelle said in an interview before the election with CNN's Suzanne Malveaux, "Win or lose, they get a dog. They didn't choose this. They have been uncomplaining individuals.")[34]

Although the Robinson household may have felt like the set of a TV show, Barack also wrote that he eventually became aware of the underbelly of that vision of bliss—the fact that for twenty-five years Fraser had had to struggle with his debilitating illness. As he grew closer to Michelle, Barack began to understand the ways her father's illness had affected the family: her mother's weighty burden, the precisely orchestrated efforts to maintain a normal life, the underlying sense of the randomness of life no matter how happy they appeared to be.[35] Perhaps it was that sense of the randomness of life—that things could change very quickly—that fuels Michelle's fierce desire to keep her girls close.

Both Michelle and Barack have admitted that it has sometimes been difficult to reconcile their expectations about balancing the demands of work and family, particularly given their radically different upbringings.

"I came into our marriage with a more traditional notion of what a family is," Michelle told *Vanity Fair*.[36] "It was what I knew growing up—the mother at home, the father works, you have dinner around the table. I had a very stable, conventional upbringing, and that felt very safe to me. And then I married a man who came from a very different kind of upbringing. He didn't grow up with his father; his mother traveled the world. So we both came to this marriage with very different notions about what children need, and what does a couple need to be happy."

However—and somewhat ironically—there may have been something attractive about the prospect of taking on that less-familiar tradition. For a man who had barely known his father, whose life had been fairly nomadic, the Robinson home "stirred a longing for stability and a sense of place that I had not realized was there." The exact opposite may have been true for his wife. If Barack found comfort in stability and a sense of place, Michelle may have seen in him "a life of adventure, risk, travel to exotic lands—a wider horizon than she had previously allowed herself," he said.[37]

From her working-class beginning on the South Side of Chicago, Michelle LaVaughn Robinson Obama's horizon was now very wide, indeed. Yet even as she prepared to take on the role of First Lady, a position that would bring more adventure, risk, and travel to exotic lands than most people will ever experience, her feet remained firmly planted on the ground, albeit no longer in the Chicago of her childhood. How many silver spoons when she was growing up on the South Side of Chicago? Who knows? Who really cares? And does it even matter?

After chuckling at Michelle's four and then five silver spoons response, Stephen Colbert moved on from the Bittergate/elitism question. He called her a "very good-looking lady," compared her to Jacqueline Kennedy Onassis, and even crooned "L is for the way you look at me" to make her husband a "little jealous," before asking why she thought American women should vote for Barack.

"Many women like myself who are independent, strong, focused, who care about family values, know that Barack is special, that he has something unique to offer the country, and that his perspective is really going to change the lives of working women," she responded. "He understands because he's living with me."

Mr. Colbert asked if she ever gets tired of the campaign and its slogans and if, when her husband comes home at night, "Do you ever say, you know, 'Right now you're my husband and I *hope* that you will *change* the cat litter?'" (Emphasis, of course, on the campaign slogans calling for change.)

In her deadpan way, coming right back at him with yet another slogan from the campaign, Michelle responded, "What I make sure Barack knows is that *Yes we can!*"[38]

Princeton- and Harvard-educated though she may be, eloquent and elegant enough to grace the cover of any number of fashion magazines, you don't get much more down to earth than that.

CHAPTER 2

The Ivy Years

Discovering That She Can Be "Both Brilliant and Black"

WHEN MICHELLE ARRIVED AT PRINCETON IN THE FALL OF 1981, SHE found herself in a very different world than the one she had known growing up. Princeton had only gone coed in the last dozen years, and it was just within the last twenty years that black students had been admitted in any significant number.[1] As Katie McCormick Lelyveld, Michelle's director of communications, said, for an African-American woman in the 1980s, Princeton was a "new frontier."[2]

In 1981, Michelle was one of 94 black students out of a total of 1,141 in the freshman class.[3] For the first time in her life, she was truly in the minority, at least compared to the environment she had known on Chicago's South Side, or even at Whitney M. Young, which prides itself on its diversity.

In recent years Princeton has made great strides to open its doors to students from all walks of life through innovative need-blind admission policies. In 2006 it announced a new Center for African American Studies "to serve as a model for teaching and research on race in America."[4] But when Michelle arrived, she was still a relatively unique phenomenon as an African-American woman on the storied Ivy League campus.

Unlike some of the other schools in the Ivy League, Princeton did not have any African-American undergraduates who went on to earn degrees until World War II, when the university opened a V-12 training program for the US Navy and four young black men "seized the opportunity." One of those four students, John Lee Howard, a biology major who later attended medical school and became an orthopedic surgeon, made history when he received his diploma in 1947. Two others received their degrees the following year; the fourth did not graduate. (Three black men had reportedly studied at the university in the eighteenth century, although none earned degrees; two African-American men earned master of arts degrees from Princeton, one in 1895 and one in 1906.)[5] By contrast, Harvard awarded a degree to its first black undergraduate in 1870,[6] while Yale conferred a degree on its first African-American undergraduate in 1874.[7]

Founded in 1764 and the fourth-oldest college in the country, Princeton was steeped in tradition. The school was even historic architecturally—in 1783, its Nassau Hall was the temporary capitol of the United States. With its Gothic stone arches and manicured lawns, it was the embodiment of the East Coast academic elite, with perhaps a hint of Southern gentry mixed in. An inscription over the entryway of a building that houses one of the school's wood-paneled lecture halls proclaims that sense of rarified history: "Here we were taught by men and Gothic towers and faith and righteousness the love of unseen things that do not die." In terms of physical environment, Princeton could hardly have been more different from the rows of brick bungalows in the South Side neighborhoods that Michelle called home as a child.

Of all of the Ivy League schools, Princeton in the 1980s was considered the most "preppy," at least according to that popular 1980 tome *The Official Preppy Handbook*. In addition to giving SAT stats (verbal 636; math 672), *The Official Preppy Handbook* said that 40 percent of Princeton's 1980 student body had graduated from a prep school (in other words, an expensive, often prestigious private high school to which a student must gain admission), "but by graduation it feels more like 100 percent." Princeton, the handbook said, is the "most Southern in spirit and accent of the Ivies. Lots of legacies, clubs, and house parties." No other Ivy League school made the list of the Top Ten Preppy Colleges (Princeton was number seven). In fact, Columbia—Barack's alma mater—was number one on the *least* preppy list.[8]

This was the world immortalized by writer and former Princeton student F. Scott Fitzgerald in his first novel, *This Side of Paradise*, which, though published in 1920, portrayed a climate not all that different from the one described in *The Official Preppy Handbook*. Indeed, Fitzgerald's protagonist Amory Blaine must have felt somewhat the way Michelle Obama did when he left home for Princeton, a Catholic Midwesterner eager to soak up life at the school he had heard so much about, with a reputation as the "pleasantest country club in America."[9]

When Amory arrives at Princeton, he finds a social system that excludes him, a place where boys from certain prep schools stick together, keeping a line of less popular social climbers around them to distance themselves from "the friendly, rather puzzled high school element."[10] Not that Michelle was after any country club–type atmosphere, but she had no doubt heard a thing or two about the benefits conveyed by a diploma bearing the name Princeton, and that must have had an allure all its own. Like Amory Blaine, what she found was perhaps different from what she expected, but with her characteristic determination to "take her place at the table," she made her way.

"Being one of the school's few African-American students at the time, I found there weren't many opportunities for minorities," Michelle told Sarah Brown in a 2005 interview with the student newspaper, the *Daily Princetonian*. "So we created a community within a community and got involved at places like the Third World Center," now known as the Carl A. Fields Center for Equality and Understanding.[11] Michelle eventually became a member of the center's governance board, and she also coordinated a literacy program that helped children from local neighborhoods, an appropriate work-study undertaking for a young woman for whom education was considered all-important. Other opportunities for black students came through the Black Thoughts Table, a discussion group about race and current events, as well as the Organization of Black Unity, a group that arranged speakers and organized programs for black students.[12]

Angela Acree, one of Michelle's Princeton roommates who remains a close friend, told the *New Yorker* that Princeton at the time was a "very sexist, segregated place," so she and her friends spent most of their free time together at the Third World Center.[13]

By contrast, the social lives of many of their classmates revolved around Princeton's fabled eating clubs. Lisa Robinson, an old friend of mine whom I rediscovered after noticing that she was the Robinson appearing just above Michelle Robinson in the 1985 Princeton yearbook, described a place where female students would don dresses and stockings and men would wear jackets and ties on Fridays and Saturdays to drink and dance the night away.[14] This world of moneyed and carefree students was, understandably, foreign to Michelle. "I remember being shocked by college students who drove BMWs," she told the British newspaper the *Telegraph*. "I didn't even know parents who drove BMWs."[15]

But a roaring social life wasn't Michelle's purpose for being at Princeton. She was there to focus on academics, and despite the clubby, preppy reputation, Princeton was as rigorous an academic school as any. As ever, Michelle was conscious of wanting to make her parents—who had not had the opportunity to go to college themselves—proud. "Michelle and Craig spoke a lot about their parents," Michelle's friend, Hilary Beard, told the *Boston Globe*. "She was going to succeed as much for them as for herself."[16]

Angela Acree described Michelle's work ethic: "She was very organized. We got up very early in the morning, studied before breakfast. We went early. Breakfast started at 7 a.m., and we were usually the only people in the dining hall."[17] (Apparently old habits die hard—until things got too demanding during the campaign, Michelle's custom was to wake up every morning at 4:30 a.m. for an intensive workout. During the campaign the regime changed to three ninety-minute workouts per week, whenever they could be squeezed in.)

Besides finding herself a true minority for the first time, residing in a dorm in suburban New Jersey also marked the first time Michelle had lived away from her parents, although she was fortunate to have her big brother on campus and he was, in fact, a very big man on campus. While at Princeton, Craig was twice named Ivy League Player of the Year, and, as of the presidential campaign, was the fourth leading scorer in Princeton basketball history.

For his part, Craig reportedly watched out for his little sister, although as one of Craig's classmates told Sarah Brown of the *Princetonian*, "To Craig, Michelle was his baby sister, but it was clear the first time I met Michelle that she was nobody's baby."[18]

As always, Michelle was outspoken, even in this new, unfamiliar environment. Michelle's mother likes to share a story about her daughter. "Michelle's always been very vocal about everything," Marian Robinson told the *New Yorker*.[19] "If it's not right, she's going to say so. When she was at Princeton, her brother called me and said, 'Mom, Michelle's here telling people they're not teaching French right.'"

Apparently Michelle thought the teaching style wasn't "conversational enough." Her mother's response? "I told him, 'Just pretend you don't know her.'"[20] (Marian's teasing but full-of-adoration answer sounds like some of the comments Michelle has thrown her husband's way— comments about his failure to pick up his socks, for instance, or the notion that he can, indeed, change the cat litter.)

That assertion that Michelle was "nobody's baby" and the family anecdote about Michelle challenging her French instruction show some of the lingering confidence—or was it a determination to make her mark, to take her seat at the table?—that Michelle brought with her to college, but the reality is that not everything was easy in her new world.

As Angela Acree recalled, black and Hispanic students were invited to school a few weeks before the rest of the freshman class, presumably so they could acclimatize to their new surroundings. For Acree, who had attended an East Coast prep school before Princeton, it was hard to understand why. "We weren't sure whether they thought we needed an extra start or they just said, 'Let's bring all the black kids together,'" Acree told *Newsweek*.[21] No doubt the decision to invite minority students early was made with the best of intentions, but when the white students joined the students of color on campus a few weeks later, the two groups never totally melded.

Michelle's experience with one of her freshmen roommates only underscored some of those divisions. In an interview with the *Atlanta Journal-Constitution*, Catherine Donnelly, Princeton '85, recalled how, upon moving into her dorm room in the fall of her freshman year, she discovered that one of her roommates was black. When she reported that fact to her mother—who had driven Catherine up to New Jersey from their home in New Orleans—her mother went "storming" into the campus housing office and asked that her daughter be moved to another room.[22]

"I told them we weren't used to living with black people—Catherine is from the South," Alice Brown, Catherine's mother, told the newspaper. "They probably thought I was crazy."[23]

Some twenty-seven years later, Catherine, now a lawyer, and her mother, a retired teacher, said they regret that response. Times have changed and they have, too. Around the time of the first campaign Catherine rediscovered her old roommate, whom she never saw much of after freshman year and about whom she had largely forgotten, when she began to read about her and her politician husband in newspapers and magazines and to see her image on TV.[24]

In 2008, Catherine and her mother said they were delighted that Michelle—with whom Catherine lived until the second semester of freshman year when another room opened up—was now poised to become the First Lady. (Catherine did not think Michelle ever knew about her mother's request, and said the room change was not because of her mother's reaction but because it made sense to move to more spacious quarters.)[25]

But Catherine also said she has another regret: She is sorry that she and Michelle never became closer. She recalls how friendly Michelle was, and how she liked her "from the moment we met." Still, it became clear almost immediately that the two wouldn't spend much time together as they solidified their separate groups of friends. "I don't think I ever set foot in the Third World Center—it's like this mystical place," Catherine recalled to the *Journal-Constitution*.[26]

For her part, Michelle told the *Boston Globe* that she had only learned about Catherine's mother's request during the campaign, but she does wonder if it might have affected their relationship. "We were never close," she wrote to the *Globe* in an e-mail, "but sometimes that's the thing you sense, that there's something that's there, but it's unspoken."[27]

She also sees some hope in the story. As she wrote in an e-mail to the *Globe*'s Sally Jacobs, "What it demonstrated was the growth this parent had. What that told me is that, yes, the problems we face in this nation around race are real . . . but we also have to remember that people change and grow."[28]

After she moved out of the room, Catherine doesn't remember having had many more interactions with Michelle, although it is interesting to note that she wrote her junior-year psychology paper on affirmative action. Her paper's conclusion? That "covert, deep-rooted prejudice" endures.[29]

Affirmative action was apparently much on the minds of many Princeton students in the 1980s. Although like other schools, the university tried to break down barriers—with affirmative action being one of the means at its disposal—there apparently was a perception among white students that that very policy may have paved the way to Princeton for some students who weren't entirely deserving.[30]

Michelle looks at her personal situation a little differently. A campaign spokeswoman told *Newsweek* that Michelle believes she was given an edge in the admissions process not because of affirmative action, but because she had an older brother who was already enrolled at Princeton.[31] This made her a "legacy" admit, like many of her more privileged white classmates for whom Princeton had long been a family tradition, some since long before the days of F. Scott Fitzgerald.

Still, given this atmosphere and the contrast with the inner-city environment she grew up in, it is perhaps not surprising that Michelle wrote her senior sociology thesis on what it is like to be a black student at Princeton and how the Princeton experience shaped the futures of black alumni. She dedicated her thesis, "Princeton-Educated Blacks and the Black Community," to her family and friends. To "Mom, Dad, Craig and all of my special friends. Thank-you for loving me and always making me feel good about myself," she wrote. By contrast, she found there was a lack of "adequate support groups which provide some form of guidance and counsel for Black students having difficulty making the transition from their home environments to Princeton's environment."[32]

The Obama campaign was initially reluctant to make Michelle's Princeton thesis public, requesting that it be embargoed until the presidential election. But in February, sensitive to the charges that the campaign has always claimed it stood for transparency, the document was released to Politico.com.[33]

For the project, Michelle surveyed four hundred African-American alumni, many of whom would have attended Princeton during the 1970s, "when affirmative action which provided numerous opportunities for Blacks economically, educationally, and occupationally was put into effect," Michelle wrote. From the responses of the one hundred or so who answered the survey, Michelle found that as students graduated and moved upward educationally and socioeconomically, they stopped identifying fully with the black community.[34]

Michelle seemed surprised to see that same pattern begin to emerge in her own life. "Earlier in my college career, there was no doubt that as a member of the Black community, I was somehow obligated to this community and would utilize all of my present and future resources to benefit this community first and foremost," she wrote. However, as she approached graduation, "it is conceivable that my four years of exposure has instilled within me certain conservative values," she wrote. "For example, as I enter my final year at Princeton, I find myself striving for many of the same goals as my White classmates—acceptance to a prestigious graduate or professional school or a high paying position in a successful corporation. Thus, my goals after Princeton are not as clear as before."[35] (Michelle's career path—a journey from the corporate world through the public sector and on to nonprofits—would reflect this dilemma.)

It was also in this paper that Michelle revealed how she really felt as a black woman in a largely white environment. Her experiences at Princeton have made her "far more aware of my 'blackness' than ever before," she wrote, and she sometimes feels like a "visitor" on campus, as though she doesn't "really belong," regardless of how "open-minded some of my White professors and classmates try to be towards me." She wondered if, in the eyes of her white classmates, she would "always be Black first and a student second." And would she always "remain on the periphery of society: never becoming a full participant"?[36]

Much has been made of this Princeton thesis, written when Michelle was barely out of her teens. Undoubtedly, both Princeton and Michelle have changed more than a little in the intervening years, and yet the thesis may still be enlightening. Ben Macintyre, a close friend who served as US editor for the *Times* of London during the second Bill Clinton election and who wrote several articles about Michelle Obama during the first campaign, told me, "While I think it is slightly unfair to analyze [the thesis] because it was written such a long time ago, there is a tone to it that I think is instructive. . . . It's not that it is a ranting piece at all—it's more that it's anxious and it's pained, and it's alienated, and it's tremendously articulate, when you think of the age of the person who wrote it. I think it's reasonable to analyze it, because it's part memoir. It's about Michelle Obama."[37]

The observations Michelle made in her thesis are supported by conversations I had with a handful of white students who attended Princeton at the same time. Interestingly, not one of the four white Princeton 1985 graduates I spoke to recalled Michelle Obama, although with her height she must have been hard to miss.

The reason, according to Lisa Robinson, Princeton '85, is that the two worlds really were separate. (Lisa is the high school friend I rediscovered after another Princeton alum e-mailed me a scan of Michelle's yearbook page and I saw my old classmate's face staring out at me, the Robinson who was, alphabetically, just above Michelle in the order.) Like Michelle, Lisa wasn't interested in participating in the eating-club scene, so she spent most of her free time in her residential hall. Michelle did the same in the largely African-American Stevenson Hall.[38]

Lisa said she hadn't heard about Michelle's thesis, but when told about it, she thought its main argument was spot on. "That whole point is really true—that blacks really were segregated," she said. As an African-American woman at Princeton, Michelle "would have been black first and she would have been an outsider," Lisa said.[39]

She was excited about the prospect of Michelle Obama, her former classmate, as First Lady. "How wonderful to have a First Lady who actually has something to say," she said.[40]

Louise Ambler Osborn, the Princeton classmate who sent me the yearbook page, had essentially the same observations. Like Lisa, who followed her uncle to Princeton, Louise followed her father. "It was the natural thing for me to do," she said.[41]

As for Michelle, "she was coming into a situation that was a whole new world," Louise said. "It didn't occur to me to connect with people for whom it wasn't the most natural thing in the world." Nor, she added, were there "many people who were trying to make it any less hard to adjust to."

Louise said she had read a newspaper article about Michelle's thesis. She thought the topic was both "fascinating" and "really intellectually honest," because Michelle had chosen a subject "that was relevant and interesting to write about and is still relevant today, whereas if someone looked at mine, they'd fall asleep." (Louise was a comparative literature major; her thesis was about Baudelaire and Poe.)

Louise said she does not go back to Princeton often, but said she went to the Princeton Alumni Association of New England annual meeting not long ago. Michelle's brother, Craig, spoke, and he was "funny and really good." During the event, a race relations award was given to people who are working on interracial and intercultural efforts. "That's something the alumni association here does every year," she said. "I think it's a pretty great thing that people are stepping up and saying we want to make a statement about that."[42]

Princeton's director of communications during the presidential campaign, Lauren Robinson-Brown, was also an African-American member of the class of 1985, and as the former Lauren Danielle Robinson, she shared a spot on that same yearbook page. (She is directly above my friend, Lisa Robinson. When the yearbook page was e-mailed to me, I was intrigued because of a poem about being black that she included with her photo. It was only after researching current-day Princeton, however, that I discovered that Lauren Robinson-Brown, director of communications, and Lauren Danielle Robinson were one and the same.)

In a telephone conversation, Robinson-Brown told me that the university has made great strides in becoming a more diverse and inclusive school. "There's no time in Princeton's history when it has been more diverse in all senses of the word—socioeconomically, geographically, racially, ethnically, and in terms of gender," she said during an interview in July 2008. "It's also a great time of . . . opportunity for the university, a time of growth," she said.[43]

Robinson-Brown, an English major who earned a certificate in African-American studies, lived in the same dorm as Michelle—Stevenson Hall—and often joined her for dinner.[44] They both also spent much of their free time at the same organizations (in the 1985 Princeton yearbook, Robinson-Brown identifies herself as "upper-class rep" for the Organization of Black Unity and cochair of the Black Thoughts Table).

Robinson-Brown, who received a master's degree in journalism from Columbia University and went on to become an award-winning journalist for newspapers including the *Newark Star-Ledger*, the *Dallas Times-Herald*, and the *Boston Globe*, declined to talk about her personal experience or the experience her classmate Michelle Robinson Obama had as African-American women at Princeton in the 1980s, preferring to focus on the Princeton of today. She did say that "the black students who went to Princeton [in the 1980s] were pursuing the American dream."[45] Judging by the career trajectories of both Michelle and Lauren Robinson, Princeton '85, that pursuit was pretty successful.

For those who say Michelle Obama's thesis reflects a "bitter" person who, as a black student, kept herself largely separate from her white peers, it might be illuminating to read excerpts from the short poem Robinson-Brown included along with her yearbook picture. The poem talks about leading "my people to greatness." It says: "I will not be ignored"; "I have strength, beauty, wisdom"; "I am Black and I am Proud." It ends with the words, "And the I—is We."[46]

In the year 2008—with the United States having elected its first black president—the poem's final line seems prophetic. Robinson-Brown was not the spokeswoman for the black population of Princeton; she was a spokeswoman for the entire population of Princeton. Barack and Michelle Obama were not the president and First Lady of Black America; they were president and First Lady of all of America.

Almost a quarter-century after Lauren Danielle Robinson chose to include those words on her yearbook page, the "I" has truly become a "We." Robinson-Brown was quick to point out that times have, indeed, changed, both at Princeton and in the world at large. "It's a different world today—students of all races and backgrounds are much more accustomed to interacting with each other and our campus is representative of that," Robinson-Brown said.

She also emphasized the importance of diversity to the Princeton experience. "Our presidents, going back many presidents, have acknowledged that diversity is fundamental to the academic experience," she said. "Our students learn and grow when they are engaged in dialogue with people from divergent backgrounds and perspectives."[47]

A January 21, 2008, article in the *Daily Princetonian* focused on Princeton faculty members and who they were supporting for US president, based on federal records of donations to presidential campaigns. Senator Obama was the "runaway favorite."

Robinson-Brown was one of the Princeton employees interviewed. Asked why she had chosen to support Senator Obama over the other candidates, Robinson-Brown told authors Michael Juel-Larsen and Josh Oppenheimer that it was not because of her old classmate, whom she said she knew "very well." Instead it was because of what Obama could mean for the future.

"I do believe that he is a candidate of hope and vision, and I love that he's inspiring young people to engage in the political process," she said.[48]

During a visit to the Princeton campus in July 2008, it was pretty clear that the environment Michelle had described twenty-three years before had, indeed, changed, at least in terms of the university's focus. In addition to the traditional viewbook every college makes available, Princeton's admissions material included a forty-eight-page four-color book called *Princeton: Defining Diversity*. The publication, which focused on fifteen students who hailed from a variety of different backgrounds, included this quote from Princeton's dean of admission, Janet Lavin Rapelye: "We want to reach out to students from every background. What we value are their personal qualities, achievements, and intellectual successes."[49]

It also included a quote from Janet Smith Dickerson, vice president for campus life, which talks about getting students to break out of their comfort zones, interact with new people from diverse perspectives, and thereby make meaningful discoveries: "I hope that you will find your niche, then leave it. Leave it to explore, make new connections, face challenges, and make exciting discoveries along the way."[50]

During an admissions information session, an admissions officer spoke about how Princeton has changed in recent years. "We really have made a commitment to offering financial aid and to being an interesting leader in financial aid policy," she said. "We've really broken some ground and it's changed the university for the better, opening doors to all kinds of families."[51]

In 2007, the incoming freshman class (the class of 2011) comprised 1,245 students, of whom 9 percent identified themselves as African-American, 15 percent Asian-American, 8 percent Hispanic, less than 1 percent Native American, and 6 percent multiracial. More than half of the student body receives financial aid. The admissions system is need-blind, meaning students are accepted first, without the university ever being aware of their ability to afford tuition.[52]

The school's Center for African American Studies underscores the emphasis the university places on questions of race and ethnicity. In a 2006 press release announcing the new center, Princeton president Shirley M. Tilghman said, "Of all the challenges that confront America, none is more profound than the struggle to achieve racial equality and understand the impact of race on the life and institutions of the United States."[53]

One of Michelle's observations in her thesis was that "predominantly white universities" like Princeton "are socially and academically designed" to cater to the needs of the students who comprise "the bulk of their enrollments." For instance, she pointed out, in 1985 there were only five black tenured professors on the faculty "and the program of Afro-American studies is one of the smallest and most understaffed departments in the university." She also pointed out there was only one major university-recognized campus organization "designed specifically for the intellectual and social interests of Blacks and other Third World students."[54]

In the 2006 press release about the new African American Studies center, Princeton announced that recruitment efforts would double the number of "current, full-time equivalent faculty positions allocated to African-American studies—from five to eleven." This meant that, including joint and sole appointment possibilities, "the center will have the potential for eleven to twenty-two faculty working to support more course offerings."[55]

Among the faculty listed as associated with the Center for African American Studies was the Class of 1943 University Professor of Religion Cornel West, the well-known writer and scholar who is a leading voice in the discussion on issues of race. Celebrated African-American writer Toni Morrison was the Robert F. Goheen Professor, *Emerita*.

Princeton: Defining Diversity lists the various campus centers that feature social, cultural, and academic programs. These include: the Frist Campus Center, the Davis International Center, the Carl A. Fields Center, the Center for Jewish Life, and the Lesbian, Gay, Bisexual, and Transgender Center. By 2008, Princeton clearly had many campus centers where students could "take an active role in organizing programs, whether for the overall student body or for more targeted identity groups," as the diversity book pointed out.[56]

During the information session, the admissions officer told us that the eating-club environment has changed, as well. Although many students do still join these clubs after their sophomore year—giving them, essentially, a place to eat their meals outside of dormitories—"the eating clubs of today are very different from ten, twenty" or more years ago. They are "not fraternities and sororities," and all are coeducational, she said. Social events do take place at the eating clubs, but many are open to the entire student body. In school literature, it says that some of the eating clubs are open by lottery, while others are open by a membership selection process.

It is interesting to note that Michelle Obama and her thesis—though some have deemed it critical of Princeton and others have dismissed it as the product of a whiner who was "ungrateful" for the benefits she was given—are prominently displayed in 2008 Princeton materials. The viewbook included a spotlight on senior theses. Among those on the list are: actress Brooke Shields '87—"The Initiation: From Innocence to Experience: The Pre-Adolescent/Adolescent Journey in the Films of Louis Malle, *Pretty Baby* and *Lacombe Lucien*"; Queen Noor of Jordan

'74—"96th Street and 7th Avenue"; Supreme Court justice Samuel Alito '72—"An Introduction to the Italian Constitutional Court"; former US senator Bill Bradley '65—"On That Record I Stand—Harry S. Truman's Fight for the Senatorship in 1940"; and former vice president, University of Chicago Hospitals, Michelle Obama '85—"Princeton-Educated Blacks and the Black Community." Michelle and her thesis were also represented in the Sociology Department's list of alumni and their work on the school website.

Michelle's thesis was much more than a meditation on her own experience. As she wrote in the introduction, examining various attitudes by black alumni as they have changed over time is important because "as more Blacks begin attending predominantly White universities it will be helpful to know how their experiences in these universities affect their future attitudes."[57] In the conclusion, Michelle suggests that a further study should be undertaken to determine if the attitudes reflected in her study are common for college-educated blacks in general. "Such a study could prove to be invaluable to bettering the educational environments for Blacks who are able to attend college, thereby improving the overall quality of a college education for Blacks."[58]

At the age of twenty-one, Michelle was clearly thinking in a global way about a subject that would affect more and more people over time. Although it is unlikely that her thesis itself directly sparked any of the changes that later took place at Princeton regarding issues of race and social justice or the university's commitment to be a leader in the struggle to confront those challenges, it did focus in on a problem and enlarge it for anyone who read her work to see. Just as she had done at various points during the campaign, rather than shy away from the problem, as someone with less of a stomach for conflict might, she pointed a spotlight right at it, adding her voice to a conversation, exposing that elephant in the room.

As Michelle's classmate Louise Ambler Osborn said, "The fact that she took on a topic that was uncomfortable for a lot of us on campus says a lot about her. What struck me when I was reading that article was that she was bringing up race and making a big deal about it because it *was* a big deal."[59]

On her yearbook page, Michelle listed her many activities (Third World Center, coordinator of its after-school program, Organization of Black Unity, etc.). She also chose to include two more personal messages. The first reads: "There is nothing in the world more valuable than friendships. Without them you have nothing." The second says: "Thank-you Mom, Dad, and Craig. You all are the most important things in my life."

In the accompanying yearbook photo, Michelle is smiling. Her hair is shorter and "bigger" in the way that 1980s hair was bigger. She is wearing a simple collared dark blouse, with a double strand of pearls around her neck, perhaps prefiguring the gumball-sized beads she became famous for during the presidential campaign.

She looks pretty and put together, every bit a young woman ready to take on her next challenges—Harvard Law School, followed by a first job at a prominent law firm. With her confident smile and direct gaze, one would be hard-pressed to find traces of a young woman who wondered whether she would "remain on the periphery of society" and never become "a full participant."

In fact, her forthright, self-assured expression and bright eyes seem to augur something else altogether. In the photo, Michelle looks ready to open her mouth. You can imagine her saying something unexpected, to initiate a *real* conversation. If Michelle Robinson was ever really unsure of herself and how she fit in at Princeton, you get the sense that by the time she left—and perhaps because she had wrestled with the issues so thoroughly—the questions had all but evaporated.

Prominent journalist and author Charlayne Hunter-Gault called Barack Obama's *Dreams from My Father* "one of the most powerful books of self-discovery I've ever read."[60] As a sociology thesis with all of its sociology lingo, Michelle's "Princeton-Educated Blacks and the Black Community" may not be as moving a piece of prose, but it is every bit the journey of self-discovery that her husband's bestselling memoir is.

When, a few months after her Princeton graduation, she arrived on the campus of Harvard Law School, it was clear that Michelle had fully come to terms with some of the questions that had plagued her during her undergraduate years. As her law school adviser Charles J. Ogletree said, Princeton was a "real crossroads of identity for Michelle,"[61] a place where she wrestled with notions about race and identity and whether—in this largely white world—she could maintain the legacy provided by her ancestors.

"The question was whether I retain my identity given by my African-American parents, or whether the education from an elite university has transformed me into something different than what they made me," Ogletree, working on the Obama campaign, told the *Boston Globe*. By the time she became his student, she had already wrestled with and resolved that dilemma; as her adviser said, Michelle had discovered that "she could be both brilliant and black."[62]

Being confident and comfortable—whether you are black or white—in an atmosphere as austere and heady as Harvard Law School is no mean feat. When Michelle first arrived in Cambridge, on the law school's fabled and ivied campus she found some of the same racial divides that had existed at Princeton. Once again, there seemed to be a perception that the black students at the law school were charity cases, said Verna Williams, Michelle's friend from law school who is now a law professor in Cincinnati.

This time, though, Michelle appeared to be undaunted. She "realized that she had been privileged by affirmative action and she was very comfortable with that," Williams told *Newsweek*.[63]

In all the movies we see that are set at Harvard Law School—*Love Story*, *The Firm*, *The Paper Chase*, *Legally Blonde*—it is a cutthroat, intense place, where students pull all-nighters and jockey for professors' attention and the top grades. The atmosphere seemed to suit Michelle just fine. As Verna Williams said, Michelle was an extraordinarily intelligent and able law student, so much so that she asked her to be her partner on a mock trial case. Even back then, "she had this incredible presence," Williams said. "She could very easily be the Senator Obama that people are talking about. She's very, very smart, very charismatic, very well-spoken—all the things that Barack is."[64]

Michelle made a similar impression on her law school professors, making her mark as a firm and compelling advocate for her own positions (early signs that she would make an unparalleled "closer" on a campaign trail someday).

One of her professors, David B. Wilkins, recalled that Michelle was unusually outspoken and clear about her own opinions—again, not one to shy away from a difficult conversation. "Michelle was a student in my legal profession class, in which I ask students how they would react to difficult ethical and professional challenges," he said. "Not surprisingly, many students shy away from putting themselves on the line this way, preferring to hedge their bets on deeply technical arguments that seem to absolve them from the responsibilities of decision making. Michelle had no time for such fig leaves. She always stated her position clearly and decisively."[65]

Randall Kennedy, another one of Michelle's professors for whom she served as research assistant, called Michelle "quiet and determined." She was "very well organized," but even he had "no idea that she would develop the poise" that she exhibited during the grueling campaign season.[66]

If you'll pardon this analogy, the image of the outspoken, forthright Michelle calls to mind Reese Witherspoon's fictional Elle Woods of *Legally Blonde* fame. A California sorority girl who wears only pink and even takes her lecture notes using her pink feather-topped pen, Elle arrives in Cambridge and is totally out of her element. She is completely different from her more traditional classmates, and yet she manages to take that stuffy, sexist, snooty world by storm.

Like Michelle, Elle has no use for fig leaves; she states her position clearly and decisively—if with a Valley Girl accent—and in the end, wins everyone over through a combination of brains, decency, and convincing oratory. As an African-American woman at the law school, Michelle wouldn't have been quite the fish out of water that the pink-clad, manicured and pedicured Elle Woods was, but she was still a minority entering a pretty traditional, tradition-filled world. Like Elle, she won the crowd over.

In addition to excelling at her studies, Michelle also found a way to address some of the concerns expressed in her Princeton thesis. Rather than spending her out-of-class time working for the law review or another traditional part of law school life, as her future husband would when he became the first African-American president of the *Harvard Law Review* a few years later, Michelle spent her extra hours benefiting the black community from which she came: She worked with the law school to help attract more students of color to the school and also participated in demonstrations seeking more minority students and professors at Harvard.[67]

She did all of this and performed so well academically that by the time she was ready to graduate in 1988 she had a prestigious job waiting for her in her hometown. She would indeed take on the "high paying position in a successful corporation" that she'd talked about in her thesis, at least for the time being.

How did she feel returning to Chicago, no longer the young girl who had had to confront doubters and forcibly take her seat at the table, but an accomplished woman with degrees from two of the top universities in the country and a job most law school graduates would kill for? As her friend and mentor Valerie Jarrett said, "She takes a great deal of pride in saying, 'I've done better than maybe people thought I would have done.'"[68]

Or, to quote her law school adviser once more, she had proved—to everyone who crossed her path, and to herself—that she was, indeed, "both brilliant and black."

CHAPTER 3

Working Toward a World as It Should Be

The Journey from the Corporate World to Public Service

SPEAK TO ANYONE WHO HAS EVER WORKED WITH MICHELLE OBAMA, and there seems to be a common refrain: She is a dynamo, she is always prepared, she makes things happen.

Perhaps this should come as no surprise when you figure that this was the little girl who had to be told to stop practicing her piano—enough was enough; the college student who got up early to study and then was first to the dining hall each morning so she could get back to her studies; the woman who, friends say, works out "like a gladiator" even when she's balancing the responsibilities that come along with being a wife, mother, hospital executive, and partner on the presidential campaign trail. Whatever she does, Michelle Obama seems to do it to the nth degree.

"Michelle works harder than anyone I know," big brother Craig said. As a child, "I'd come home from basketball practice, and she'd be working. I'd sit down on the sofa and watch TV; she'd keep working. When I turned off the TV, she'd still be working."[1]

Which is why, when she graduated from Harvard Law School and landed her job at the top-flight firm Sidley & Austin (which later became Sidley Austin), Michelle immediately became a valuable part of the team. At Sidley, she specialized in marketing and intellectual property, meaning she handled transactional and anti-trust issues, among other matters. In one of her assignments, she worked on a team that represented AT&T in its takeover bid for NCR, and Union Carbide in its fight to complete the sale of a chemical business unit to Arco over FTC opposition.[2]

In the Arco deal, she apparently impressed the counsel for Union Carbide. Nate Eimer, a former Sidley partner, told the *National Law Journal* that Michelle "stood out from the average associate. She reserved her comment before she was sure of what she wanted to say. Her analysis was clear and precise."[3]

After just one year at the firm, she was also apparently respected enough that she was assigned to mentor an especially promising young summer associate. For Sidley, for Michelle, and for that summer associate, the assignment couldn't have been more fateful.

The associate, of course, was Barack Obama, who would become Michelle's boyfriend and later her husband. His rhetoric about—and commitment to—being of service to his community and the larger world would eventually help lure Michelle from a promising career in corporate America to an equally accomplished career in public service.

Michelle has spoken about how the job at Sidley & Austin helped her pay off some of her student loan debt but didn't speak to that other part of her, the part that was interested in making the world a better place.[4] During the summer of 1989, she got a real taste of that other side when she went with her new friend—not yet her boyfriend—to hear him speak at Altgeld Gardens, an underprivileged area on the South Side where he had served as a community organizer before attending law school.

She watched, spellbound, as Barack talked to the largely poor, largely African-American audience about committing to make a difference, even when things didn't seem fair and it seemed like the cards were stacked against you. He spoke about imagining a "world as it could be" rather than settling for a "world as it is."

"What I saw in him on that day was authenticity and truth and principle," Michelle said. "That's who I fell in love with."[5]

Michelle was in her mid-twenties, finding tremendous success as she climbed the corporate ladder at Sidley & Austin, propelled, perhaps, by those "conservative values," that urge to strive "for many of the same goals as my White classmates," as she had written in her Princeton thesis. And yet she wasn't sure she was content.

As she would say later in an interview with the British newspaper the *Telegraph*, "The thing about these wonderful schools is they can be surprisingly narrowing to your perspective. You can be a lawyer or you can work on Wall Street; those are the conventional options. They are easy, socially acceptable, and financially rewarding. Why wouldn't you do it?"[6] The summer Michelle met Barack, she was beginning to think about why, perhaps, she no longer wanted to be part of that world.

A few months after she met the man who would become her husband, two life-altering events occurred, one after another. Michelle's beloved father died unexpectedly after surgery, followed very quickly by the loss of a dear friend, Suzanne Alele, to cancer at the impossibly young age of twenty-five. Suzanne had been one of Michelle's Princeton roommates and also one of her closest friends. Michelle's father, we know, was both a source of strength and inspiration to his daughter. The dual loss caused Michelle to really take stock of her life.

"I was confronted for the first time in my life with the fact that nothing was really guaranteed," Michelle told an audience before the Iowa caucus. "One of the things I remembered about Suzanne is she always made decisions that would make her happy and create a level of fulfillment. She was less concerned with pleasing other people, and thank God. Was I waking up every morning feeling excited about work and the work I was doing? I needed to figure out what I really loved."[7]

And so, as she contemplated what she should do with her life, Barack's words from that meeting in Altgeld Gardens began to replay in her mind. How could she make a difference? And where?

It was the same conundrum she had described a few years earlier in her thesis, a conundrum expressed by many of the Princeton alumni she had surveyed. As she wrote in the thesis, "In an individual's lifetime, it is necessary that the individual focus his/her interests on benefiting a limited number of things at a time because it is impossible to help everyone and everything equally at the same time." An individual, she wrote, must create a "motivational hierarchy from which the individual can determine which social groups are most important to benefit." The groups an individual might select for this motivational hierarchy include: themselves or their families, their occupational fields, God, and/or "the U.S. society, the non-White races of the world or the human species as a whole."[8] What would Michelle's motivational hierarchy be?

In a July 2008 interview with Rebecca Johnson of the *Telegraph*, Michelle describes how she came to a decision. In her usual fashion, it had to do with first asking questions of herself and later posing them to others.[9]

The loss of her father and her friend "made me realize that I could die tomorrow," she told Johnson. "I had to ask myself, 'Is this how I want to spend my time?' I knew I would never feel a sense of passion or joy about the law. I was on a conveyor belt. Law school had just been the next step."[10]

So she began to articulate her questions. "Rebellion for me is articulating my views, trying to be honest about what I see," she said. "I don't think a lot of people in the public arena do that, because why are people so amazed when I do?"[11]

As her questions all came to a head in 1991, she met with friends and discussed the notion of jumping ship and entering the public sector. One of her friends put her in touch with Valerie Jarrett, who was then Mayor Daley's chief of staff and who would become a longtime friend and mentor.

When Michelle went to see Jarrett in her office at City Hall in 1991, she explained the situation in which she found herself: She had a dream job at a top law firm, she was making a large salary, and yet she wasn't happy. When she told people that she was fantasizing about trading in her position at a top law firm for a low-paying job in public service, most people told her she was nuts.

Not Jarrett. A graduate of Stanford University and then University of Michigan Law School, she had made a similar decision a few years earlier.

"We hit it off," Michelle told Don Terry of the *Chicago Tribune*. "She understood how I felt. It was difficult to find people who understood my decision to leave a high-paying corporate job. She went through the same kind of feelings, wanting to do more for the community, wanting to have a civic life."[12]

Recognizing a kindred spirit—and a very qualified job candidate—Jarrett offered her a position on the spot, but before signing on, Michelle said she wanted her fiancé's input. (By then, she and Barack were engaged.) Jarrett agreed to meet with both Michelle and Barack over dinner a few days later. Like the assignment to mentor a particular summer associate, it was a fateful meal.

Over dinner, everyone seemed to like what the others had to say. Michelle signed on for the City Hall job working for Daley, the son of one of Chicago's longtime bosses, the first Mayor Daley—the man for whom her father had volunteered as Democratic precinct captain. The evening also marked the beginning of a friendship with Jarrett that would help propel Michelle to a series of increasingly high-profile service jobs and her husband to a quest for the highest office in the land.[13]

"There's a cadre of people like me who have worked for [Valerie Jarrett] who are like family," Michelle told Terry. "Valerie at some level has advised me and Barack. She's always one of the people that he and I talk to when we're about to make a move." (Moves like deciding to run for president.)[14]

When Michelle announced her plan to leave Sidley & Austin, her departure was mourned. "She would have been a superstar," said Sidley senior counsel Newton Minnow.[15] "We were all crazy about her."

Although the new job came with a huge pay cut, Michelle believed the field would come with a greater degree of satisfaction, and she was more than adequately prepared to make a major difference in the world of public service. "What she learned at Harvard Law School and Sidley & Austin has served her well in all of the judgments she has had to make as an administrator and a manager," said her Harvard Law professor Charles Ogletree.[16]

Not insignificantly, she also was taking her first step on the path that, years later, she and her husband would urge others to follow. On July 2, 2008, Senator Obama unveiled a plan for national service that he believes could help solve some of the country's most challenging problems. It will not just be a "call issued in one speech or one program," but a "central cause of my presidency," he said.

"We will ask Americans to serve," he said in a speech delivered at the University of Colorado in Colorado Springs. "We will create new opportunities for Americans to serve. And we will direct that service to our most pressing national challenges."[17]

Among other measures, the plan called for expanding the Ameri-Corps program and doubling the size of the Peace Corps; enabling more citizens to serve in the armed forces; integrating service learning into schools; providing additional volunteer opportunities for retirees and working adults; and expanding service opportunities that "engage disadvantaged young people and advance their education."[18]

Senator Obama also pointed out that service is not a one-way street. When he worked as a community organizer or helped register 150,000 new African-American voters in Chicago through Project Vote, "I wasn't just helping other people. Through service, I found a community that embraced me, citizenship that was meaningful, the direction I'd been seeking. Through service, I discovered how my own improbable story fit into the larger story of America."[19] Clearly, these are sentiments shared by his wife.

At times it appeared those sentiments were lost on Senator Obama's opponents, however. One of the more unattractive moments of the campaign came during the Republican National Convention when former New York mayor and Republican presidential contender Rudy Giuliani mocked Senator Obama for his years as a community organizer. Governor Sarah Palin echoed the sentiment in her own speech, saying, "I guess a small-town mayor is sort of like a community organizer, except you have actual responsibilities." Her voice hit a high-pitched note when she got to the words "sort of" and "actual," apparently underscoring what she saw as a major difference between her experience as mayor of Wasilla, Alaska, population 9,780, and Obama's experience as a community organizer in one of the nation's largest cities.

Although many in the audience roared with laughter, a coalition of faith-based groups complained that political leaders should be thanking community organizers for their efforts, not insulting them.

Jerry Kellman, the person who hired Barack Obama back in 1985 to work at the Developing Communities Project for a salary of $10,000 a year, said Obama's responsibilities back then included determining what people's needs were—from job training to asbestos removal—and helping them work to realize those needs. Kellman told *USA Today* that Obama learned to listen to people and to work alongside them in pursuit of a mission, helping to "bring out their gifts."[20]

In the hours following Palin and Giuliani's sneering statements, the Obama campaign began to rake in donations, courtesy, it would seem, of the GOP jokes.

"They insulted the very idea that ordinary people have a role to play in our political process," Obama campaign manager David Plouffe wrote in an e-mail. "Let's clarify something for them right now. Community organizing is how ordinary people respond to out-of-touch politicians and their failed policies."

But back to Senator Obama and his call for a community service plan. The proposal he annunciated during the campaign was not the first time Obama has called for a national service plan. In an item called "Experts Praise Barack Obama's National Service Plan" dated December 5, 2007, on the Barack Obama website, experts hail his calls for national service.[21]

"Barack Obama points the way to a quantum leap in citizen service, at home and abroad, for Americans of all ages, from all walks of life," said Senator Harris Wofford, former associate director of the Peace Corps, former special assistant to President Kennedy on civil rights, and former CEO of the Corporation for National and Community Service. "He has picked up the torch that John Kennedy lit—and once again turned 'Ask' into a strong, challenging verb. Through this plan, we can again show the world—and show to ourselves—the best of America."[22]

Alan Khazei, cofounder of City Year and CEO of Be the Change at the time, said: "Americans are looking for new and innovative ways to serve in their communities, and to help change our country. The number of young people participating in national service is on the rise, and has the potential to grow significantly in the years to come. By targeting service into proven, innovative programs that are achieving real results, we can tackle some of our country's greatest challenges. . . . It is vital that presidential candidates call on all Americans to serve and provide meaningful opportunities to do so. Senator Obama's national service proposal is a strong step forward."[23]

Alan D. Solomont, who was appointed to the board of the Corporation for National and Community Service by presidents Bill Clinton and George W. Bush, said: "Both Barack and Michelle Obama understand from their own lives the transformative impact of service. They also know the difference that citizens can make tackling difficult challenges in their own communities. Obama's plan for universal voluntary citizen service takes an idea that has earned bipartisan support and grows it to a new level so that citizens, both at home and abroad, will be the new hallmark of American democracy."[24]

In a November 2007 interview with Peter Slevin of the *Washington Post*, Michelle spoke about that powerful call to service that she and her husband experienced as young adults. She described the dilemma they faced as educated, talented Americans who were at once attractive to the corporate world and yet interested in working for the world at large. It is an issue she brought up many times on the campaign trail, when she urged students to contemplate a career in public service rather than automatically following the expected path into corporate America.

"Barack and I had both struggled with the question: When you know you've been blessed and know you have a set of gifts, how do you maximize those gifts so you're impacting the greatest number of people?" Michelle said. "And what do you do? Is it community organizing? Is it politics? Is it as a parent? Our answer at some level is it can be all of that."[25]

For Michelle, the job in the mayor's office was only the first in a series of jobs in the public sector and eventually the nonprofit sector. She had been in City Hall for a short period of time when Jarrett moved on to chair the Chicago Transit Authority, and Michelle opted to follow her there, offering to lead the citizens' advisory board.

Jarrett has said that her protégée is an invaluable resource in a work situation, particularly when the situation involves group dynamics. Of course, Michelle is diligent and always prepared, but her true value added, as always, is her willingness to confront an issue head-on.

"I've been in so many settings or meetings with Michelle where people are talking all around an issue, and she has a way of succinctly getting to the issue and putting it on the table," she told the *Chicago Sun-Times*. "She's willing to say what other people dance around."[26]

In 1993, Michelle took on another job close to her heart: heading the Chicago chapter of Public Allies, a program that trains young people about the world of public service through internships at nonprofits. The program was a spin-off of President Clinton's AmeriCorps effort, and it meant that she could actively assist other "bright shining lights" as they worked to shape a "world as it should be," rather than simply work within the confines of the "world as it is."

This was a particularly good role for Michelle, because she is also "really good at taking nothing and creating something," said Jarrett, who lured her three years later to the University of Chicago. (At the time of the election, and before assuming the role of President Obama's senior adviser, Jarrett was serving as vice-chair of the university's board of trustees.)[27]

Before she left Public Allies for the University of Chicago, Michelle certainly worked her magic. In her role as the Chicago director, Michelle pulled together a powerful board of directors and raised enough money so that when she left in 1996, the Chicago office of Public Allies had "about one-year reserve, which none of our sites since have had," said Paul Schmitz, national CEO for Public Allies. "She built it to last."[28]

Michelle's new University of Chicago position was built on the same ideals that drew her to Public Allies. Serving as associate dean of students and director of the University Community Service Center, Michelle helped coordinate volunteer work by students, allowing her to assist other young people as they developed their "motivational hierarchies."

During this time, Michelle became a mother—first to Malia, who was born in 1998, then to Sasha, born in 2001. Meanwhile, her husband had embarked on a career in politics, and when he was on the campaign trail or traveling for his political work, she often found herself without the support of a husband, especially in parenting their young children. This dynamic gave her a whole new perspective on what it means to be a working woman. Again, she was forced to take a look at her own motivational hierarchies.

A few years into her job at the university—and one year into her life as the mother of two—Michelle's reputation attracted the attention of the University of Chicago Hospitals' president, Michael Riordan. In 2002, he invited Michelle in for an interview, which he describes as "probably the most unique interview I've ever had."[29]

Michelle may have felt it necessary to include her fiancé in her discussions with Jarrett before she jumped ship from the corporate world to the public sector; for her interview with the hospital president, she brought along another family member, infant Sasha in her "little car-seat carrier."[30]

Explaining the situation years later, Michelle said she had had some child-care issues—something most working moms know a thing or two about—so she figured she'd just bring her baby along. The fact that she went to an interview accompanied by her newest family member apparently didn't dissuade her would-be employer. Michelle was hired as the hospital's executive director of community affairs, a position in which she served as a link between the hospital and its surrounding neighborhood.

Of course, this was again the South Side of Chicago, where Michelle spent her entire childhood. But it was also the University of Chicago, an open-minded, socially conscious, uber-intellectual academic institution, another environment where Michelle felt right at home.

"The truth is that having lived and experienced both sides of the situation, I know the community does not trust and understand the university and the university does not trust and understand the community," she told Slevin of the *Washington Post*. "And until you can bridge those gaps and hear out both sides and understand why they are afraid, you can't really have a conversation."[31]

That was where Michelle came in. She was both the link between the two worlds and the person capable of putting the issues on the table, getting the conversation started. Among other goals, the hospital hoped to open a series of health clinics on the South Side, near where she grew up and where she first heard her husband give a speech in that church basement all those years ago.

In 2005, Michelle was promoted to vice president of external affairs, a position that carried a salary of close to $275,000, according to 2006 tax returns. Some have claimed that Michelle has benefited from her husband's prominence in the political world. (Her promotion came shortly after her husband became the new US senator from Illinois.) But her boss, Michael Riordan, says Michelle earned the promotion all on her own. "Michelle is the real deal," he told the *Chicago Sun-Times*, explaining that he wanted to "send a strong message to our community that I was committed to it, so I wanted to make this a vice presidential position."[32]

Riordan is not the only one singing her praises.

"In community affairs, you're dealing with a range of people, from presidents of hospitals to community leaders to people who are poor . . . and she just has a way about her, a real kindness," said Susan Sher, the hospital's general counsel.[33]

In a press release announcing her promotion, Riordan said, "We have been impressed with the care, imagination, and energy that Michelle has brought to every project she has worked on since coming to the Hospitals. We are excited to have her join the ranks of senior management. She brings to our team a new level of compassion, commitment, and close connections to the community."[34]

For her part, Michelle said her goal in the position "is to continue to broaden the Hospitals' relationship with our neighborhood and our city. . . . We have an obligation to ensure that we use our resources on behalf of our neighborhood and our city. In this new role, my goal is to better integrate community involvement into the culture of this institution and to expand our partnerships with local organizations and institutions."[35]

Michelle continued to work hard at her position, even after her husband moved to Washington to take up his new job in the Senate and she became a single mother much of the time. She continued to work as he explored the notion of a run for president. She continued to work after he announced his candidacy and began to campaign.

"She never takes the easy way out," Jarrett said, noting that Michelle continued to work just as hard as she always had. "You never would have known what was going on in her life."[36]

Eventually, Michelle cut back her hours at the hospital so she could both help out her husband on the campaign and also be there for her children. As the campaign really heated up, she eventually took a leave from the hospital.

On top of her professional duties, Michelle has also served on a number of boards, including her children's school, the Chicago Lab School; the board of the Otho S.A. Sprague Memorial Institute; Facing History and Ourselves; the Muntu Dance Company; the Chicago Council on Global Affairs; and TreeHouse Foods.

Michelle took a little heat when she accepted the position at Tree-House Foods, a Wal-Mart vendor, a role she assumed around the time her husband became a US senator. She later resigned after her husband said he would not shop at the anti-union store, although TreeHouse said the resignation was due to Michelle's "increased demands." For her part, Michelle said: "As my campaign commitments continue to ramp up, it is becoming more difficult for me to provide the type of focus I would like on my professional responsibilities." She said it was in the "best interest of my family and the company" that she quit. Her tax returns show that Michelle Obama earned $51,200 from Tree-House in 2006.[37]

Before taking on the role of First Lady, Michelle declined to talk about what her agenda would be, saying she needed to make sure that her two young daughters were well taken care of. (As she told *Ebony* magazine, "My first job in all honesty is going to continue to be 'Mom-in-chief,' making sure that this transition, which will be even more of a transition for the girls . . . that they are settled and that they know they will continue to be the center of our universe.")[38] She did, however, discuss the three main areas that interest her, and all reflect her career choices as well as the reality of her life as a working mother.

"I ran a national service program, so I care very deeply about national service," she said in an interview with Katie Couric of CBS News. "I work for an academic medical center, so I know the challenges in health care. I am a mother and a professional and a wife. And I know the struggles of trying to balance work/life/family."[39]

It is the latter that really seems to get her going.

Trying to balance work, life, and family is "something that every woman I know is struggling with," she says. Likewise, every American family is "impacted by the challenges that we face when we try to do it all without resources and support."[40]

Michelle has said that the only way she manages is because of her mother, her friends, and—before she took her leave to focus her energies on the campaign—a job in which she is allowed to be flexible "because I'm a vice president and I can set my hours when I need to." These "informal support structures" have worked for her, but "How on earth are single-parent mothers doing it, nurses and teachers and folks who are on shifts?" she asks.[41]

"The truth of the matter is that we are only as strong in this society . . . as the health of our families and the people who head them," she said. "But we haven't talked enough about that in just real practical ways. I mean, up to this point, as a woman, I've been told, 'You can have it all, and you should be able to manage it all.' And I've been losing my mind trying to live up to that. And it's impossible. It's impossible. We're putting women and families in a no-win situation."[42]

As she spoke to women across the country during the campaign, this was the issue that surfaced again and again. Speaking to a gathering of "Women for Obama" in Chicago at the end of July, she pointed out how important the voices of women would be in the presidential election. In 2004, 54 percent of the electorate was made up of female voters, she said, adding, "We're going to decide the outcome of this race."[43]

Transforming a country's policies so that they support families won't be an easy task, but Michelle said she was convinced that if any political leader can do it, it is her husband. Primarily because he understands the struggle.

For one thing, his own mother was "very young and very single when she had him." And then he "sees me, his wife, who struggles every day with the guilt that we all hold deep in our hearts as women—that guilt that you don't have the choice to stay home, and even if you do you feel guilty," she said.[44]

"He has seen me struggle with this my entire life," she said. "Trust me, Barack understands the struggles of women."[45]

So what would her husband do to address those struggles? Speaking to women in Michigan on the campaign trail, she talked about improving access to good health care, wage discrepancies between men and women, and the difficult choices women must make because of the woeful state of the economy.

"People make decisions about whether to put gas in the car to get to work or buy groceries," she said, "and that needs to change."[46]

At the "Women for Obama" event in Chicago on July 28, 2008, guests were given a blue booklet outlining her husband's plan to help women and families strengthen economic security, strike a good work/family balance, and ensure a healthy family. The book outlined a series of proposals, from making the federal government a model employer in terms of adopting flexible work schedules to doubling funding for federal cancer research efforts. Other measures included mandating seven paid sick days per year, expanding the earned income tax credit, increasing the minimum wage, and expanding the Family and Medical Leave Act.

In a personal message in the front of the booklet, then-Senator Obama credited three women with being his inspiration: his mother, his grandmother, and his wife. "We have a chance to move America in a fundamentally different direction, and that starts with empowering women and strengthening families," he wrote in the preface called "A Message from Barack." "This belief is at my core because I wouldn't be running for president today without the strong, capable, loving and brilliant women in my life."[47]

He also mentioned two others who help motivate him in this quest to support women and strengthen families: his daughters, Malia and Sasha. "Now Michelle and I want our daughters to grow up in an America where they have the freedom and opportunity to live their dreams and raise their own families," he said. "I want Sasha and Malia and your daughters and sons to grow up in an America where both work and family are a part of the American Dream, and where the Dream is available to all."

You can feel Michelle's influence, both in the proposals and in the sentiment behind them. Indeed, Michelle had her own "Message from

Michelle" in the blue book, which is titled "Barack Obama's Plan to Support Working Women and Families." "This booklet is about helping women reclaim their dreams for themselves and their families," Michelle's message said. "It's about giving them a helping hand, not a handout. The subjects here are near to my heart, and they're at the center of this campaign. But the policies will only succeed if they address your needs. So please let us know what you think."

Although she had talked about these same issues for months on the campaign trail—and, one imagines, for years inside her own home—Michelle admitted it may take a while before the country sees any improvement on these fronts. (After all, by his own admission, it took her own husband some time to realize the stress she was under as she tried to be the quintessential working mom, doing it all.)

"Even when Barack is president of the United States, it's going to take some time and investment before we see the results of a different strategy," Michelle said—but she was convinced the time will come.[48]

"When we start seeing more people with access to health care, and when we see results of an investment in new kinds of economies, and we see the results of higher investments in public education, that's when I think we'll start getting excited," she said.[49]

During stops along the campaign trail, Michelle also got excited about her interactions with children. "You're very delicious," she told a baby at a cafe in Manchester, New Hampshire, in October 2007. She went on to describe what her daily life was like at home with her two young daughters—getting them ready and off to school, then going to work, trying to figure out how they will get to their after-school programs, then returning home in time to help them with homework, make dinner, put them to bed. "I know everyone is very busy, because I know what life is like," she said.[50]

When Michelle Obama says these things, you know that she really has been there—she is a sort of an everywoman, the quintessential working girl. You also get the sense that, as she has done all her working life, she will pour her heart and soul into whatever job comes next, doing all in her power to help bring about a "world as it should be."

CHAPTER 4

You and I (We Can Conquer the World)

Becoming Mrs. Obama

BARACK'S ROCK. THE CLOSER ON THE CAMPAIGN TRAIL. JACKIE TO Barack's JFK. Barack's Better Half (or "Bitter Half," if you're the conservative columnist Michelle Malkin). The Love of Barack's Life. The Funniest Person in the House. The One Who Keeps Him Real.

Each of these terms has been used to describe Michelle Obama during her journey alongside her husband on the campaign trail. But how did this African-American working-class girl from Chicago's South Side come to be a presidential contender's "rock," the closer, Jackie to his Jack, or even the "bitter half"? Every relationship has a starting point. Where did the Obamas' begin? And what is the spark that keeps it going despite the pressures of two demanding careers (one of them arguably among the most demanding in the world), parenthood, and life in the unblinking public eye?

As marriages sometimes do, particularly, it seems, in the world of politics, the Michelle Robinson/Barack Obama relationship began with an imbalance of power. But this time the scenario was flipped on its head: At least notionally, when Barack met his future wife, she was his boss.

Although nearly three years her husband's junior, Michelle got a jump on graduate school when, after graduating from Princeton, she went directly to Harvard Law School. So she was already a practicing lawyer at the white-shoe Chicago law firm Sidley & Austin when Barack arrived there in the summer of 1989 to work as a summer associate.

Barack, by contrast, had just completed his first year at Harvard Law School, where he had enrolled after three years as a community organizer in Michelle's hometown.

Although he enjoyed his studies, he wrote that he privately worried that the choice to go into law "represented abandonment of my youthful ideals, a concession to the hard realities of money and power—the world as it is rather than the world as it should be,"[1] so he arrived at Sidley & Austin with no small amount of ambivalence. (Sounds reminiscent of the fears Michelle expressed in her Princeton thesis—that by striving for many of the same goals as her white classmates, such as acceptance to a prestigious graduate school and/or a high-paying position in corporate America, she would be selling out to a more conservative agenda.)

Michelle had been told by her firm that a Harvard Law student would be spending a few months as a summer associate, and that she would be assigned to mentor him, to show him the ropes, and make him feel comfortable. The word from the secretaries who had already met him was that he was "cute"; that, like Michelle, he was African-American (there were only a handful of black lawyers at the firm at the time); and that he had the rather unusual name of "Barack." Associates were talking about how well this newcomer had performed at Harvard during his first year of law school, while partners extolled the "brilliance" of his introductory memo.[2]

Despite the accolades, Michelle had low expectations. "He sounded too good to be true," Michelle told David Mendell, the author of *Obama: From Promise to Power*, in a 2004 interview. To friends she reportedly said, "I'm sure this guy is weird."[3] In *The Audacity of Hope*, Barack wrote that Michelle later confessed as much to him, telling him that the drug-store photo he had mailed for the Sidley & Austin directory made his nose look big. Apparently she also doubted the secretaries who'd met him and who said he was cute. She assumed they were impressed by an employed black man wearing a suit.[4]

But regardless of whether the newcomer's reputation was overblown or not, whether he was weird or not, large-nosed or not, it was Michelle's job to welcome him to the firm, and so she invited Barack to lunch that first day. Over their meal, they discussed things like billable hours and other issues related to work at Sidley & Austin, and they found that the conversation flowed easily. As she told Katie Couric during an interview with CBS News in February 2008, she pretty quickly set aside the notion that the new summer associate was weird. "Immediately I liked him because he didn't take himself too seriously but he was very bright, had an interesting background, just a good guy to talk to," she said.[5]

Barack's first impression of Michelle? He doesn't remember much about their actual conversation, but he does remember that his mentor was as welcoming as she was tall and attractive in her attorney attire. For his part, Barack recalled that he was dressed—courtesy of his community-organizer-turned-student budget—in one of three newly purchased but bargain-basement suits and a pair of too-small shoes.[6]

Michelle apparently didn't notice the attire any more than she noticed the nose. She found it easy to laugh with Barack, though she also made it clear over lunch that she didn't have room in her life for disruptions such as boyfriends, Barack recalled. Still, the conversation flowed and she didn't seem to be in any rush to finish their lunch meeting.[7]

Barack also noticed, behind that all-business facade, "a glimmer that danced across her round, dark eyes whenever I looked at her, the slightest hint of uncertainty, as if, deep inside, she knew how fragile things really were and that if she ever let go, even for a moment, all her plans might quickly unravel." Barack was touched, admitting that he "wanted to know that part of her."[8]

So he asked her on a date, but Michelle immediately shot him down, believing it would be improper for a firm mentor to date a mentee. "I thought, well, my advisee. Hmm, I don't think that looks right," she said.[9] So she tried to set him up with some of her friends instead.

It didn't take. Apparently Barack wasn't interested in anyone else, and he worked hard to wear Michelle down, arguing that just one date could hardly be considered a serious violation of the rules of the firm.[10]

One night Barack invited Michelle to accompany him to one of the churches on the city's South Side where he had worked during his community-organizing days. The church was also located close to where Michelle had grown up, and because this wasn't really a date, she agreed to come along.

When they arrived in the church basement where the meeting was to be held, they found a crowd that was made up mostly of single mothers, most of them African-American. Barack was there to do a training course based on the concept of "the world as it is and the world as it should be," and how ordinary people can organize and work together to "narrow . . . the gap between those two ideas," Michelle recalled.[11]

What Michelle saw as she watched Barack speak to this audience moved her profoundly. "To see him transform himself from the guy who was a summer associate in a law firm with a suit and then to come into this church basement with folks who were like me, who grew up like me, who were challenged and struggling in ways that I never would, and to be able to take off that suit and tie and become a whole other person and connect with people in the same way he had connected with folks in that firm, you don't see someone who can make that transition and do it comfortably in his own skin and to touch people's hearts in the way that he did."[12]

She said she "knew then and there there's something different about this guy. Barack lived comfortably in those two worlds. And it was impressive. And his message was moving. I mean, it touched me."[13]

Katie Couric put it this way: "And you were smitten after that." Michelle's response: "I thought . . . I could hang out with this guy. I was impressed. I really was."[14]

But before Michelle would agree to seriously date her summer colleague, Barack had to pass another test, this one involving her family. In an interview with Slate.com's Melinda Henneberger, Michelle's big brother, Craig, recalled that when Michelle brought a work colleague around to the family home that summer, the family thought that he was just "another one who wasn't going to make it." Apparently she had had a handful of previous suitors who simply didn't measure up.[15]

"Not that she had a lot of boyfriends, because she didn't; it was hard to pass muster with my sister," Craig said. Like the others before him, this new guy "had a gauntlet to go through," he said, and Craig himself had a lot to do with the particular gauntlet Michelle chose. Call it the Craig Robinson "court"ship test.[16]

Michelle asked Craig—one of Princeton's all-time leading scorers, the two-time Ivy League Basketball Player of the Year who was working as an investment banker but dreaming of becoming a college basketball coach—to challenge her new friend on the basketball court. (The six-foot, one-inch Barack had played in high school at Punahou in Hawaii; he has continued to play pickup ever since, but that hardly prepared him to take on the six-foot, six-inch basketball star who had actually been drafted—though later cut—by the NBA's Philadelphia 76ers.)[17]

As Craig explained it, he and their father had always told Michelle that you could learn a lot about a person's character on a basketball court. "So, when she got serious, she said, 'Take this guy and go play.'"[18]

Would Barack be selfish or was he a team player? Was he a wimp or would he take the shot? Would he accept defeat or was he a sore loser? Likewise, would he win with grace or would he taunt his opponent and gloat? Would he be intimidated by someone with more size and experience?

The answer, according to Craig: Barack may not have been good enough to play Division I, "but like every pickup ballplayer in the world, he could play with 80 percent of the players of the world. . . . He wasn't selfish. He was team-oriented, and the game is self-policing when you don't have refs."[19]

Most of all, Barack was definitely not a pushover. "He wasn't like a soft guy," Craig said. "He was aggressive without being a jerk, and I was able to report back to my sister that this guy is first-rate."[20]

Pretty high praise from a man who would ultimately follow his dream and become a college coach, first at Northwestern, later Brown, and then at Oregon State (and who would then join the New York Knicks as vice president of player and organizational development). For Michelle, the assessment was absolutely essential. "We're a sports-playing family at heart," Michelle said. "We grew up in gymnasiums and baseball fields, generally watching Craig play. Craig has always said you measure character by what kind of sportsman they are, and it was good to hear directly from my brother that he was solid and he was real and he was confident, confident but not arrogant, and a team player. Something that you could sense on the court."[21] Talk about jumping through hoops.

Many years later, Craig would use a basketball analogy to weigh in on whether he thought his brother-in-law should run for president. In 2004, when, in his first appearance on the national stage, Barack delivered his now-famous speech at the Democratic National Convention, Craig Robinson said he was sweating so much he could hardly stand it. But when he spoke to his sister about the notion of whether Barack should contemplate a presidential run, his opinion was pretty clear.

"Craig said to me that [Barack is] the guy with the skills, that he has to take the shot," Michelle said. "You go to the guy with the hot hand, and there's no way he could pass up this opportunity. The country is hungry for that kind of leadership, and don't pass that up. Craig was able to tune into that before even I recognized that we had to do this."[22]

Michelle and Barack's first actual date was to see the movie *Do the Right Thing*. Directed by Spike Lee and focusing on bigotry and racial conflict in Brooklyn's Bedford-Stuyvesant neighborhood, the film had just been released. They also visited Chicago's Art Institute and strolled around the city. According to Michelle, the evening was a success, and from then on there was no looking back.

"It was fantastic," Michelle recalled of that first date.[23] "He was definitely putting on the charm. . . . It worked. He swept me off my feet."

Years later, Barack met Spike Lee in Martha's Vineyard. He reportedly thanked the director, because it was while he and Michelle sat in the movie theater watching *Do the Right Thing* that Michelle allowed her suitor to touch her knee.[24]

When the summer ended, Barack returned to Harvard, while Michelle remained in Chicago at Sidley & Austin. Despite the demands of school for Barack and work for Michelle, they continued their relationship long-distance.

Tragically, some six months after they met, Barack was back in Chicago at Michelle's side. Her father, Fraser, had died suddenly following kidney surgery, and Barack flew to Chicago for the funeral. In *The Audacity of Hope*, Barack recalls how being with Michelle at such a time only seemed to cement their relationship. During the funeral, Barack silently promised Fraser Robinson that he would take care of his daughter.[25]

As we have seen, Michelle's father's death and the almost simultaneous loss of her dear friend Suzanne Alele to cancer seemed to mark a turning point for Michelle. As she told Katie Couric, "It made me think differently about what I am doing with my life, and how am I adding to the notion of getting us to the world as it should be? Am I doing it in my law firm?"[26]

Meanwhile, the long-distance relationship persisted through Barack's second and third years of law school, as Michelle earned a stellar reputation at the law firm in spite of her doubts and he gained notoriety (and a book contract that led to *Dreams from My Father*) as the first black president of the *Harvard Law Review*.

For Barack, the length and depth of this relationship was a first. Although he had had other girlfriends, this thing with Michelle was different. He admitted that he had been too immature in the past, but something appeared to change as he entered his thirties, and he began to think about the value of a solid relationship and, ultimately, marriage and family.[27] Not that he was too quick to bite the bullet, however.

When Barack graduated in 1991, he headed back to Chicago, where, rather than joining a corporate firm like Sidley, he chose to join a small public-interest firm. That was the year, bolstered by Barack's presence and his commitment to "the world as it should be" rather than "the world as it is," that Michelle would also jump ship from the corporate world to take up a job in public service, initially in Mayor Daley's office.

Against that backdrop, the romantic relationship continued and flourished, but it didn't seem to be going anywhere concrete. This caused no small amount of tension: Michelle, from the more traditional background, was all in favor of marriage, and sooner rather than later. Barack, the product of less-traditional parents, continued to debate whether marriage really meant anything as an institution.[28]

"We would have this running debate throughout our relationship about whether marriage was necessary," Michelle said in an interview with the *New Yorker*.[29] "It was sort of a bone of contention, because I was, like, 'Look, buddy, I'm not one of these who'll just hang out forever.' You know, that's just not who I am."

Her boyfriend, meanwhile, said "'Marriage, it doesn't mean anything, it's really how you feel,'" she recalled.[30]

And then one day, as the two dined at Gordon's, a fancy restaurant on Chicago's Clark Street, Michelle told her boyfriend that he needed to get serious in their relationship. Barack seemed nonplussed. Eventually dessert arrived, and on the plate was a box. Michelle picked it up, lifted the lid, and, to her utter surprise, found an engagement ring inside. "He said, 'That kind of shuts you up, doesn't it?'" Michelle recalled.[31]

Years later, asked what the dessert was next to the ring, Michelle said she had no idea. "I don't even remember," she said. "I don't even think I ate it. I was so shocked and sort of a little embarrassed because he did sort of shut me up."[32]

The two were married on October 3, 1992. The bride and groom danced their first dance to "Unforgettable," the song made popular by Nat King Cole and later his daughter, Natalie, as well. They also featured Stevie Wonder's "You and I (We Can Conquer the World)," a song whose title and lyrics seem strangely prophetic today.[33] Santita Jackson sang during their wedding, while Reverend Jeremiah Wright performed the service in Trinity United Church of Christ.[34]

We pretty much know the rest of the story. Michelle took on a series of jobs in the public sector, while Barack wrote his memoir about growing up as the son of an African father and a white American mother, worked at a public-interest law firm, taught constitutional law, and then dipped his toe into politics. Soon he would jump in headlong, a move that came with Michelle's blessing but that would also have enormous consequences for the kind of life they would lead.

Six years into the marriage, they became parents. In an interview with *US Weekly*, friends said Michelle had longed for children ever since she was a little girl, and becoming a mother wasn't necessarily as easy as she might have liked. "It was hard for her to get pregnant," said Michelle's close friend of twenty years Yvonne Davila, a public relations executive. "In fact, I got pregnant first and didn't want to tell her. When she knocked on my door one day and said, 'I'm pregnant!' I cried."[35]

Malia Ann was first—a patriotic baby, as her parents like to say, born on July 4, 1998. Natasha, known as Sasha, came next, on June 7, 2001.

Meanwhile, Barack was elected to the Illinois State Senate and began serving in 1997. In 2000 he made his unsuccessful bid for the US House of Representatives, and in 2004 became a US senator. That same year he delivered the keynote address at the Democratic National Convention, the single event that would catapult him into the national spotlight, leading, in effect, to the position in which he found himself at the end of 2008—the next president of the United States. Talk about fitting a lot into a decade.

As this powerful couple—whom Michelle described to a campaign audience as "Power Parents"—continued to live their day-to-day lives, both privately and in the unrelenting glare of the public eye, they juggled work and family responsibilities—and like the rest of us, it was not always without tension. Michelle wasn't sure she liked the political life, which she said could be "mean." As a working mother, she also didn't have much time for the events and rallies political wives were expected to attend.

In *The Audacity of Hope*, Barack wrote candidly about the arguments he and his wife often had about balancing work and family in a way that was fair to each of them and also took into account the children's best interests.[36] Things got particularly tense after Sasha was born, and Michelle began to feel that Barack was too focused on himself. As he says she often said, she didn't get married to raise children alone.[37]

Years later, after the girls had started school, Barack began to appreciate what his wife had been going through. He realized that even though he fully believed that he and Michelle were equals and her goals and career just as important as his, once they became parents it was his wife who was making all the adjustments.[38]

Michelle put it another way. In a 2004 interview with the *Chicago Tribune*, Michelle said, "What I notice about men, all men, is their order is me, my family, God is in there somewhere, but 'me' is first. And for women, 'me' is fourth, and that's not healthy."[39]

Like many a married couple, the Obamas also had tensions over financial issues. For many years, both Michelle and Barack were heavily in debt with student loans, and their mutual decisions to leave the corporate world and go into public service didn't help that situation much.

Although Michelle's most recent job at University of Chicago Hospitals would eventually earn her a high salary, it was the royalties from her husband's two books—*Dreams from My Father* and *The Audacity of Hope*—that truly enabled them to pay off those student loans.[40]

In *Obama: Promise to Power*, David Mendell writes about a moment in 2000—before the ship (or books) came in—when the family's economic situation really hit home. With his credit card maxed out, in part due to campaign debt after his unsuccessful congressional race, and with student loans still looming, Barack had purchased a cheap ticket to Los Angeles so he could attend the Democratic National Convention. But when he arrived at the Los Angeles airport, his credit card was rejected by the car rental agency. "I was broke," Obama told Mendell. "And not only that, but my wife was mad at me because we had a baby and I had made this run for Congress. . . . It wasn't a high point in my life."[41]

By this time, Michelle's initial thoughts about politics had given way to something more skeptical. When Barack first told her he wanted to try his hand at politics, she encouraged him, confident that he had all the qualities people look for in their elected officials. Later, with the financial issues and other concerns mounting, though, she wasn't so sure.[42]

When Barack told her about his US Senate plan, she was much less enthusiastic. Financially, she said, his career choice was "killing us. My thing was, this is ridiculous, even if you do win, how are you going to afford this wonderful next step in your life? And he said, 'Well, then, I'm going to write a book, a good book.' And I'm thinking, 'Snake eyes there, buddy. Just write a book, yeah, that's right. Yep, yep, yep. And you'll climb the beanstalk and come back down with the golden egg, Jack.'"[43]

Of course we know what happened. Her husband did write the book, delivering the proverbial golden egg, and he also won the election.

In addition to helping to pay off student loans, funds from Barack's best-selling books also helped the Obamas purchase their six-bedroom house in Chicago's Hyde Park, a racially diverse, largely academic neighborhood near the University of Chicago. The Obamas purchased the brick Georgian revival for $1.65 million in 2005.[44]

In an article in the August 4, 2008, *People* magazine, Sandra Sobieraj Westfall writes that the house feels like a typical American household—

until, that is, Sasha skips out to the front porch, where a waiting Secret Service agent speaks quietly into his sleeve. "Front porch," he says.[45]

The Obama house is comfortable, with a piano for the girls, lots of books in the den, and Asian and African artwork from their travels on the walls. A family portrait by Annie Leibovitz lies on its side. The Obamas haven't had too much time to fuss about interior decoration, and Michelle apologizes for a mismatched light fixture as her visitor enters the dining room. "I know it's wrong," she says. "I've been meaning to change it for two years now." I guess that's what happens when you work, have young children, and help your partner run for president.[46]

In October 2008, almost one month to the day before the general election, Michelle and Barack celebrated their sixteenth wedding anniversary. The marriage was going strong. There's all the talk about the "love of my life," "My Rock," and "The Closer" on the campaign trail. There is the footage of the radiant, embracing couple. There's the lengthy paean to his wife that Barack wrote in *The Audacity of Hope*—a sort of ode to Michelle in which he says that when people meet the mother of his children, they are completely bowled over. They hear Michelle speak, and they tell him he's good, but his wife is something else altogether. In perhaps the highest compliment this would-be president could pay, he says that if Michelle were ever to run against him for public office, he would be in trouble. Fortunately, as Michelle's husband says, she is not interested in politics. She tells him she's not patient enough. "As is always the case," Barack writes, "she is telling the truth."[47]

So what are the Obamas' secrets? How do they make it work?

Without a doubt, one secret is humor.

As Michelle told Rachael Ray during the race for the Democratic nomination when she appeared on Ray's television show, laughter helps them get through the toughest day. "I'm the funniest person in the household," Michelle said. "I can always crack him up."[48]

When asked by a reporter during the Senate campaign what it was like being a political wife, Michelle admitted that it was hard work. Then she added wryly, "And that's why Barack is such a grateful man."[49]

There are plenty of examples of her humor on the presidential campaign trail. Joking about the couple's finances and how long it took them to pay off their student loans, Michelle said during a campaign stop in South Carolina, "I'm still waiting for Barack's trust fund. Then I heard Dick Cheney was supposed to be a relative! Thought we might be in for something there!"[50]

During an appearance at an Indianapolis middle school, she said that Americans are "decent people" who are willing to toil and sacrifice, so long as the bar isn't constantly being raised too high. "Barack and I know this all too well, with our elite selves," she said, emphasis on "elite," as she referred to the Bittergate controversy and elitism charges sparked by Barack's religion and guns statement.[51]

In a 2006 interview with *Ebony* magazine, Michelle cracked an irreverent joke about how she had responded to her husband when he told her he wanted to run for the US Senate. "I said, I married you because you're cute and you're smart, but this is the dumbest thing you could have ever asked me to do," she said.[52]

The humor goes both ways. In another *Ebony* article, Barack made a joke about his own inadequacies as a husband. "It is important when I'm home to make sure that I'm present and I still forget stuff," he lamented to Lynn Norment. "As Michelle likes to say, 'You are a good man, but you are still a *man*.' I leave my socks around. I'll hang my pants on the door. I leave newspapers laying around. But she lets me know when I'm not acting right. After fourteen years, she's trained me reasonably well."[53]

Related to humor is candor, or honesty, and that's something Michelle, in particular, is famous for. Or, to quote her husband's frequent refrain once again, "As is always the case, she is telling the truth."

In a reader Q&A piece accompanying an interview in *Glamour* by Tonya Lewis Lee, author and wife of director Spike Lee (he of the Obamas' first date), a reader asked Michelle why she thinks she was criticized for comments she made about how her husband forgets to pick up his socks.[54] (After the *Glamour* article ran, Michelle also faced criticism for telling Ms. Lee that her husband can be "stinky" and "snorey" in the morning.)[55]

"I think [most] people saw the humor of that," Michelle responded. "People understood this is how we *all* live in our marriages. And Barack is very much human. So let's not deify him, because what we do is we deify, and then we're ready to chop it down. People have notions of what a wife's role should be in this process, and it's been a traditional one of blind adoration. My model is a little different—I think most real marriages are."

There was more of that theme in the CBS News interview when Katie Couric pointed out that some people have called Barack "messianic." Michelle's response: We are *all* human. "That's one of the reasons why we try to laugh at ourselves to sort of keep all this excitement to a reasonable level," Michelle said. "That's why I teased Barack about putting up the socks and, you know. Making sure he's putting up the butter. It's not that, you know, I'm trying to . . ."

"Emasculate him?" Couric asked.

"Exactly," Michelle responded. "The point is that Barack, like any leader, is human. And, you know, our challenge in this country isn't finding the next person who's gonna deliver us from our own evil. Because our challenges are us. The challenges [*sic*] that this country faces is how are we as individuals in this society gonna change?"[56]

As Michelle's spokeswoman Katie McCormick Lelyveld says, when Michelle teases her husband, "there is a method to her madness." She shows that "he is a real person, he is reachable, he is human, he is just one man."[57]

Not everyone appreciates the Obama humor and candor, and some feel it may not be the best political move in the long run. "I wince a bit when Michelle Obama chides her husband as a mere mortal—a comic routine that rests on the presumption that we see him as a god," *New York Times* columnist Maureen Dowd wrote. "But it may not be smart politics to mock him in a way that turns him from the glam JFK into the mundane Gerald Ford, toasting his own English muffins. If all Senator Obama is peddling is the Camelot mystique, why debunk this mystique?"[58]

My friend Ben Macintyre, the British journalist, as intrigued as he is by Michelle, Barack, and Michelle-and-Barack, also said, "There is the danger that if you think you can rag on him, others will do the same."

"When she says he's got bad breath in the morning, we all know those are the true things about life, but actually that's being a real hostage to fortune," he said. "That becomes, 'Oh, she's so disrespectful,' 'She doesn't understand the game,' 'She's over-naive,' and 'She's overcritical.'" However, he added, it is absolutely honest. "I think it's a fascinating dynamic," he said. "We're actually seeing an honest relationship take place."[59]

Another secret to their marriage may be the Obamas' determination to carve out family time, regardless of what else is going on in their busy lives.

"Barack and I don't have interesting lives, never did," Michelle told the *Chicago Sun-Times.* "We're basically family people. When we go on a date, it's either dinner or a movie because we can't stay awake for both."[60]

Of course, dates began to include the Secret Service, but even that hasn't altered the way the Obamas live very much. "They give us our space," Michelle says.[61] And Malia and Sasha appear to be fine with the notion that they must share their lives with Secret Service agents. "They're very comfortable with the Secret Service." Michelle has said. "They call them the Secret People."[62]

During the campaign, under the heading "Activities" on her Facebook page, Michelle listed the following: "Hanging out with my husband, Barack, and our daughters. . . . Hitting the campaign trail. Working out." Under "Interests," she wrote: "Being a mom, Sudoku." For "Favorite Movie," she said: "I've only gotten to see kids' movies recently—saw *Enchanted* not too long ago." And "Favorite Books"? "We read a lot of kids' books at our house. Recently, Harry Potter."

In other words, this Princeton- and Harvard-educated lawyer and her Columbia- and Harvard-educated husband who happened to be running for president of the United States chose to spend their time just the way most parents of young children do: watching kid movies, reading kid books, hanging out as a family. It may not be glamorous, but it works for them.

At the end of June 2008, some four weeks after the nomination had been sealed, Barack and Michelle were caught in a private moment by a press pool photographer as they relaxed at one of their daughters' soccer games. (As two Bloomberg reporters, Kim Chipman and Kristin Jensen, said in a July 5, 2008, article, the pool is called Obama's media "Body Watch," and its job is to record every little movement, from workout sessions to haircuts.) As he did whenever he could, Barack had flown home for a break with his family, and Michelle and Barack, dressed casually, were just like every other parent at the soccer field that day. Except, of course, every move was watched by the pool reporters, not to mention Secret Service agents.

They unfolded their matching Sports Authority chairs and plopped down to watch the game, jumping up periodically—like all the other parents—to applaud a great move or shout out some instruction about technique. At one point, Michelle seemed to tell her husband to shut off his BlackBerry. Another time, the camera caught Barack leaning in toward his wife, a big grin on his face as he whispered something to her. Whatever it was, it must have been slightly mischievous, because he was laughing as Michelle playfully swatted him away. The pool photographer recorded the action on the written log that accompanied the video. "8:30—MO and BO flirt," the log said.[63]

Which gets us to what may be the next secret of the marriage: that indefinable connection or spark which, in the Obamas' case, seems to be both real and very apparent to those around them. Even the pool reporter couldn't help but notice—and record—the physical connection between the Obamas.

In "Why Barack Loves Her," the *US Weekly* cover story about the Obama marriage, Kevin O'Leary writes about the contrast between the rally in Minnesota on June 3 after Barack captured the Democratic nomination and an intimate, private moment four days later.

On June 3, the candidate and his bride, radiant in her purple dress, took to the stage before 18,000 ebullient people in St. Paul. To the beat of U2's "Beautiful Day" and thunderous applause, they greeted their supporters and then proffered their own small public display of affection, their now infamous fist bump, before Obama headed to the microphone to deliver his acceptance speech.

During a birthday dinner on June 7 for their youngest daughter, Sasha, who was turning seven, a small crowd of family and friends gathered near their home in Chicago to help celebrate. One of the guests was the Obamas' close friend, Yvonne Davila, who described a private but intense moment at the birthday celebration.

"We sang 'Happy Birthday,'" she told *US Weekly*'s O'Leary. "I caught him looking at his wife, then just sort of smiling. He didn't realize what he was doing, but I saw it, and it was so touching."[64]

In 2007, *Ebony* magazine named Barack and Michelle to its Ten Hottest Couples list. Accompanying the candidate and his wife were such notable partners as Beyoncé and Jay-Z.[65]

My friend Ben was also struck by what he saw as a palpable connection between Barack Obama and his wife. Describing their interactions as "incredibly natural," he said they have true "chemistry as a couple." "There seems to be an awful lot of hugging," he said, adding, "Maybe I'm just a sucker for it. They have a kind of tactile relationship which is extraordinary. . . . Maybe that's just their style. It looks very natural. It doesn't look calculated."[66]

Another marriage secret may be belief, or faith, in each other—and also in the future.

Although initially reluctant to give her blessing to Barack's run for president, Michelle has said she couldn't stop herself when she thought about what his candidacy could mean for her children and the future.

"We need a unifier, you know?" she said in the Katie Couric interview. "We need someone who can bring this country together. . . . You know, Barack is demonstrating an ability to reach across party lines and change blue and red states to purple in ways that potentially will help us build a working majority in Congress where we can get some of this stuff done."[67]

To Tonya Lewis Lee at *Glamour*, she said, "I feel so much passion for this candidacy. When we made the decision to get in this race, there was a side of me that said, 'Oh no. This is going to be so personally disruptive—why put yourself through that?' But then I let myself dream about what his presidency would mean and I get goose bumps."[68]

As for Barack, his ode to his wife in *The Audacity of Hope* or the way he introduced her on the campaign trail—the "Closer," the "Love of My Life," "My Rock"—pretty much says it all.

That belief in each other extends to the notion of fidelity. Although we have seen many a political marriage face challenges over the years, Michelle refuses to worry about things like infidelity. "I never worry about things I can't affect and with fidelity . . . that is between Barack and me, and if somebody can come between us, we didn't have much to begin with," she said.[69]

Which is not to say the issue hasn't at least been discussed in the media. In the wake of New York governor Eliot Spitzer's prostitution ring/sex scandal, *Vanity Fair* ran an article called "It's the Adultery, Stupid." While most of the presidential candidates and other high-profile politicians came in for some sharp scrutiny, the Obamas seemed to come off clean.

"There is next to no speculation about Barack Obama's sexual secrets," author Michael Wolff wrote. "This is a seismic shift in racial subtext. The white men are the sexual reprobates and loose cannons (while Mitt [Romney] and Hillary [Clinton] are just strange birds) and the black man the figure of robust middle-class family warmth."[70]

Wolff goes on to quote a friend, "a middle-aged white doctor and an active Obama supporter" who "curiously dropped into something like street talk to say Obama would never have the sex problems of middle-aged politicians, 'because Michelle would whip his skinny ass.' A good man, in other words, is a controlled man." Wolff describes Obama as "the only one in the entire field who doesn't suggest sexual desperation. He represents our idea of what a good liberal's sex life ought to be."[71]

The subject was also brought up in *Obama: Promise to Passion*, Mendell's biography. As many male politicians have throughout history, Obama suddenly found himself a magnet for female attention. Dan Shomon, Obama's former campaign adviser, told Mendell that you wouldn't want any woman you were interested in to meet Obama, because all the women fall for him.[72]

Meanwhile, a friend told Michelle that she had overheard women in a health club talking about her husband, saying they wanted to go watch Barack work out.[73] Valerie Jarrett said Michelle refuses to worry about her husband's chick-magnet effect because she knows he knows what she would do if he fooled around. As Jarrett said with a chuckle, "she'll kill him first—and then she'll leave him."[74]

Another subject Michelle said she refuses to worry about is what might or might not happen, either during the campaign or afterwards. In the interview with Larry King on February 11, Michelle said, "I don't think about what might go wrong. I've never spent my life sort-of thinking what could go wrong or else I wouldn't be here."[75]

Likewise, when King said that "we all know that Alma Powell discouraged Colin Powell from running for president because of fear something would happen to him" as the first black president, Michelle had a one-word response: "Right."

After deflecting the question, she spoke about how—as a black man—her husband had won the varied states of Utah, South Carolina, Louisiana, Maine, and Illinois. "I mean, you know, he's touched on every element of this country—every race, every political party—Republicans, Independents. And I think, you know, he is uniting people not around race, but around hope."

To a largely black audience in Atlanta in January, Michelle "obliquely addressed fears that her husband's presidential run might put him in danger," Shaila Dewan wrote in the *New York Times*. "There are still voices, even within our own community, that focus on what might go wrong," Michelle said, adding that a history of racism should not keep her husband and others like him from running for office.[76] Rather than focusing on the fears, Michelle repeatedly chooses to focus on the campaign's central theme: Hope.

Another element that may contribute to the state of their marriage is the Obamas' desire to serve as role models for their children as well as others and to support each other in that quest.

When Barack told Michelle that he wanted to run for president, she had a couple of questions and one condition. The questions were related to things like how they could afford a campaign and what it might mean for their family life. The condition was that he quit smoking.

For Michelle, the issue was personal, because both her parents smoked, and as children, she and Craig would pull tobacco out of their cigarettes and drown them with hot sauce. It was also important for their family, particularly for Malia, who has asthma, although Michelle said her husband never smoked in front of their daughters. Most of all, though, it had to do with setting a good example. "To me it's a role model thing," she told the *Chicago Tribune*.[77] "You can smoke, or you can be president." (Barack has said his attempt to quit smoking has been successful, in part because of Nicorette gum. "I've been chewing on this Nicorette, which tastes like you're chewing on ground pepper, but it does help," he said on *The Ellen DeGeneres Show*.[78] He also credited Michelle with forcing the issue: "That's an example of my wife making me a better man once again," he told DeGeneres.)

For his part, Barack has spoken passionately about the importance of fathers being role models for their children, a message that is perhaps particularly poignant coming from a man who was effectively abandoned by his own father at the age of two. As he has said many times himself and written about in both *Dreams from My Father* and *The Audacity of Hope*, Barack himself has felt the painful reality of growing up without a father.[79] Indeed, *Dreams from My Father* was all about his quest to forge an identity despite that absence in his life.

In his now-famous 2005 Father's Day message delivered to a largely black audience in a Chicago church, Barack called on fathers in the African-American community to set an example for their children, to take responsibility for their actions, to behave like "full-grown men."

"There are a lot of folks, a lot of brothers, walking around, and they look like men," he said in the half-hour sermon delivered at Christ Universal Temple in Chicago on June 19, 2005. "And they're tall and they've got whiskers—they might even have sired a child. But it's not clear to me that they're full-grown men."

Too many fathers "engage in childish things," are "more concerned about what they want than what's good for other people," he continued, exhorting men to reach higher. "If we are going to pass on high expectations to our children, we've got to have high expectations for ourselves," he said.[80]

Obama delivered a similar Father's Day sermon during the presidential election, calling on worshippers in another traditionally African-American church on Chicago's South Side to take responsibility for their lives and their children. Acknowledging that more jobs and opportunities are needed, he said, "We also need families to raise our children. We need fathers to realize that responsibility does not end at conception. We need them to realize that what makes you a man is not the ability to have a child. It's the courage to raise one."[81]

In the sermon delivered at the Apostolic Church of God on June 15, 2008, he spoke about the importance of family, something Obama has learned about, both as a son and as a parent himself. "Of all the rocks upon which we build our lives, we are reminded today that family is the most important," he said. "And we are called to recognize and honor how critical every father is to that foundation."

For her part, Michelle has also been concerned about being a strong female role model for her daughters. Although her husband's political life has meant that she has had to curtail her own professional aspirations at least for the time being, she believes it is critical that she continue to have a viable career. (When she was needed more on the campaign trail, she reduced her hours at the hospital to 20 percent so she could help out on the campaign and also spend quality time with her children, the one use of her time on which she refuses to compromise. And when the campaign's demands became too great, she took a leave of absence from work.)

In an interview with David Mendell, she said she worries that if something were to happen to her husband, she would need to be the sole source of emotional and financial support for their daughters. Michelle is nothing if not a pragmatist who believes in those lessons learned at her father's knee, lessons about perseverance, responsibility, and self-reliance. And so she knows that while she would receive sympathy and support if something happened, she also recognizes that maintaining her professional life is crucial, not just because she enjoys it, but because it is a way to be able to continue to look out for her children.[82]

Which gets us to the final—and perhaps most important—ingredient of the Obama marriage: the children.

For both Barack and Michelle, Malia and Sasha are the tie that binds, the glue that keeps them grounded, the answer to some of life's most difficult questions. In *The Audacity of Hope*, Barack writes about one evening in Chicago when he climbed the stairs to tuck his little girls into bed. He was back at home after delivering a speech earlier that day in Birmingham, Alabama, right across the street from the church where, in 1963, four young girls lost their lives when a bomb planted by white supremacists exploded. He was thinking about those four girls and also about his mother, whom he had recently lost to cancer, when his thoughts turned to a conversation he'd once had with his youngest daughter. Sasha had told him that she didn't want to die, to which her father responded that it would be many, many years before she had to worry about such a thing.

But that night he also wondered to himself whether he should have "told her the truth, that I wasn't sure what happens when we die, any more than I was sure of where the soul resides or what existed before the Big Bang." As he climbed the stairs, he thought about what he hoped for: "That my mother was together in some way with those four little girls, capable in some fashion of embracing them, of finding joy in their spirits."

What he knew without a doubt, Barack wrote, was that "tucking in my daughters that night, I grasped a little bit of heaven."[83]

On a more mundane level, Malia and Sasha help their parents define who they are.

During a campaign stop in central Ohio, the Obamas spoke to fifty seniors in Columbus, where Governor Ted Strickland introduced them as a power couple. Michelle deflected Governor Strickland's title, saying that she and her husband really see themselves as power parents.[84]

The girls also serve as a check for how crazy things can get on the campaign trail. Asked how they generate a positive atmosphere at home while Barack the candidate (and Michelle the candidate's wife) were constantly being scrutinized, sometimes torn apart, in the media, Michelle responded that they are always watching Malia and Sasha for their responses. "My girls prefer SpongeBob to CNN, so keeping the energy positive is easy. But Barack and I are always checking: Are they still OK? Every week there's a gut check."[85]

The girls help them keep their priorities in line. When Barack moved to Washington to take up his role as a US senator, Michelle and the girls chose to remain behind in Chicago. Despite the sacrifices this would entail, it was a decision both parents felt comfortable with because of what it would mean for their children. "We made a good decision to stay in Chicago, to remain based in Chicago, so that has kept our family stable," Michelle said in 2005. "There has been very little transition for me and the girls. Now he's commuting a lot, but he's the grown-up. He's the senator. He can handle it. That's really helped in keeping us grounded."[86]

Although Malia and Sasha joined their parents from time to time for campaign appearances, one notable television interview, and during the convention speeches, for the most part they maintained their ordinary schedules back in Chicago during the long and grueling race for the presidency. Initially Michelle would spend a day or two on the trail, but as the campaign heated up and her presence became more and more essential, she spent more time away. Even so, she tried to fly home most nights to be with the girls, and Barack was with them as much as possible as well, joining them on some weekends and for special occasions such as parent-teacher conferences, Valentine's Day, Mother's Day, Father's Day, and birthdays.

Ironically, although Barack's decision to run for office often took him away from his own children, at least on a day-to-day basis, Michelle and Barack have said that it is Malia and Sasha—and all the other "bright shining lights," to steal a phrase from Michelle as she talked about her own childhood—who inspired them to forge ahead in the exhausting quest for the White House.

Malia's tenth birthday was on the Fourth of July, 2008. The entire family, including Barack's half-sister Maya Soetoro-Ng and other relatives, congregated in Butte, Montana, for an Independence Day parade, picnic, and joint political rally/birthday celebration. At the microphone to introduce her husband during the picnic, Michelle first led the crowd in a rendition of "Happy Birthday" (which she admitted probably thoroughly embarrassed the birthday girl). She then looked around at the assembled crowd and said it was the children, "those little people and all the beautiful kids all over this park," who are inspiring her husband to run for president, despite the difficulties his candidacy has brought upon the Obama family.[87]

"The reason why I am standing here today is that if he cares half as much about this country as he does about his own children, we're going to be just fine," she said.[88]

Michelle delivered a similar message in her convention speech when she said, "I come here as a mom whose girls are at the heart and the center of my world—they're the first thing I think about when I wake up in the morning and the last thing I think about when I go to bed at night. Their future—and all our children's future—is my stake in this election."[89]

Back in Montana, on July 4, Malia and Sasha spent the day playing, laughing, and having fun. (They also, as we later learned, joined their parents for an interview with *Access Hollywood*. More on that in the next chapter.) Cheers and spontaneous renditions of "Happy Birthday" greeted them everywhere they went. A smile on his face, Barack cautioned that Malia shouldn't get too caught up in the party atmosphere.[90]

"All the fireworks and stuff are not just for her," the father of the birthday girl, the presidential candidate, joked, as his audience burst into laughter.[91]

This whole scenario—the candid, humorous, down-to-earth speak; the playful husband and wife/mom and dad team; the adored, adorable, game-playing, easy-to-embarrass, happy, normal children—was pretty new for the United States. Not only had it been years since the country had seen a president with such a young family, but the Obamas were turning some of the behaviors we expect to see from a First Family right on their head.

For the most part, the First Family model we have seen in recent years—if not forever—has been pretty traditional: There is the President/husband, and then there is the First Lady/wife, supportive, adoring, always standing—both metaphorically and literally—by her man. There is the fixed grin of a Laura Bush; the adoring gaze of a Nancy Reagan; the bemused smile and solid stance of a Barbara Bush; the firm, steadfast, unflinching support of a Hillary Clinton (even though she insists she isn't some Tammy Wynette just standing by her man).[92]

As for the First Children, we almost never saw the Bush twins, Barbara and Jenna, except to read about some of their early missteps or which schools they would be attending or, when the time came, to learn that they would be married and to whom. (Indeed, in an interview in 2008, Jenna said she never really lived in the White House, so she chose to have her wedding at her "real" home, the family ranch in Crawford, Texas. No Tricia Nixon White House festivities for her!)[93]

We saw Chelsea Clinton grow up more or less in front of our eyes, but the images we remember are of a quiet, curly-haired girl smiling shyly alongside her parents or—in perhaps the most indelible image of all—a teenage girl walking between her parents, each parent holding one of her hands, the link (or buffer?) between her mother and father during a very difficult moment in their marriage. Of course, we remember Caroline Kennedy playing under her father's desk, and sweet little John-John saluting at his father's funeral. We remember Amy Carter as she was when she entered the White House, a freckled strawberry blonde of nine. We saw her grow and play and then watched again years later as she found her own political voice.

The Obama model is altogether different. How many times have you heard a First Lady complain that her husband's breath can be smelly in the morning? That he forgets to pick up his socks? That he most certainly *can* change the cat litter? That he is welcome to run for president *if* he stops smoking?

How many times have you heard a would-be president laugh about those kinds of comments from his wife and, with his own self-deprecating humor, openly acknowledge his failings? To paraphrase Tammy Wynette again, how many times have you heard a male politician of any rank admit that, "After all, he's just a man"?

When was the last time we saw a First Couple—or potential First Couple—set up their folding chairs at a soccer match so they could watch their girls play and then playfully swat at each other with cameras running? Sing "Happy Birthday" to their daughter at a political rally and tell her, essentially, to not get a swelled head; the country is celebrating its birthday too?

Call it what you want; the Obama marriage is both very real and very modern. When Barack introduces Michelle, he calls her "My Rock," because, he says, she keeps him grounded.

For Michelle, Barack does seem to represent the opposite—with his global childhood and his willingness to jump into something so grandiose as a presidential election after just four years in national politics, he has indeed brought her a life of "adventure, risk, travel to exotic lands," the "wider horizons" he wrote about in *The Audacity of Hope*. Michelle Obama, First Lady, seems happy—if not bemused—to be going along for the ride.

In an interview, Michelle once said, "Barack didn't pledge riches, only a life that would be interesting. On that promise he's delivered."[94]

CHAPTER 5

This First Lady's First Job: Mom

Michelle Obama's First Spouse Platform

I know of no more worthy ambition for a father,
than for his sons to be the best of men.

—PLATO

THE OFT-QUOTED PHILOSOPHER APPARENTLY VOICED THAT SENTIMENT more than two thousand years ago, but a good idea seems to have staying power, even if these days we extend it to mothers and daughters as well. Asked what her agenda would be as First Lady, Michelle consistently answered that her first order of business would be to make sure that her girls, Malia and Sasha, are taken care of. Or, as she put it in February 2008, "To make sure my kids have their head on straight. We can talk about the high-falutin' notion of a First Spouse platform, but here I am, a woman professional who has to work on top of my first job as a mother."[1]

So how does a mom make sure her children have their heads on straight in this day and age of busy, distracted parents and boys and girls gone wild? By a combination of good old-fashioned discipline, setting limits, presence (not presents), and love, it would appear. As Michelle herself has said, she had a stellar example in her own parents.

"She's very straightforward, very disciplined," her brother Craig said. "Her kids are loveable, because she has raised them very similar to how my mom and dad raised us."[2]

For Malia and Sasha, this means a pretty firm set of expectations. Rule number one is "No whining, arguing, or annoying teasing," according to the family list of rules that appeared in *People* magazine during the summer of 2008 accompanied by an interview with, and some new photographs of, the ultra-photogenic would-be First Family at their Chicago home and on the road.[3]

Another rule is that the girls must make their beds every day—it does not have to be perfect, but they need to at least pull the sheet up over the bed. The girls also set their own alarm clocks and get themselves out of bed and dressed. If they do these things—and also set and clear the dinner table, manage their toys, and go to bed by their prescribed 8:30 bedtime—they each earn a dollar allowance per week. (However, their wage dispenser is often on the road, so the amount owed can sometimes add up. "I'm out of town for weeks at a time, so Malia will say, 'Hey, you owe me for ten weeks,'" Malia's father, the presidential candidate, said.)[4]

Malia and Sasha have also been taught about limits from their parents. For instance, Santa comes at Christmas, but their parents don't give the girls additional presents. This has had the added benefit of helping the girls "believe" a little longer. As Michelle told *People*, "Malia says, 'I know there is a Santa Claus because there's no way you'd buy me all that stuff.'" The girls also don't get birthday presents from their parents, who spend "hundreds" on birthday slumber parties. As their father says, they "want to teach some limits."[5]

Just as their mother and uncle were when they were growing up, Malia and Sasha have been encouraged to ask questions and speak their minds. "Our girls love to talk," Michelle told *People*. "They feel confident in their own opinions because we value them even if they're silly or wrong or a little off."[6] Remember the advice Michelle's mother used to give her and her big brother, Craig, when they were children? Things like, "Make sure you respect your teacher, but don't hesitate to ask questions."

The girls have also learned about physical discipline. During the presidential campaign, Malia danced, played soccer, and did drama, while Sasha did gymnastics and tap dancing. Both girls played piano and tennis. (Their parents model that active behavior; during the campaign Michelle tried to work out three to four times a week, doing a combination of cardio and weight activities. The candidate himself was frequently spotted heading to gyms to lift weights or shoot hoops, leading to all sorts of talk about his layup and three-point shot. You can even find speculation about his workout regime on various blogs. One called "Train Like a Warrior," which claims to feature the workouts of "athletes, soldiers, and celebrities," surmises that his workout program "consists of combinations of the following activities: lifting weights, playing basketball, running, swimming, smiling, waving.")[7]

Michelle genuinely seems to enjoy running her children to their various activities. In an interview with *USA Today*, she was asked how she relaxes. Her response? Taking her daughters to soccer, tennis, swimming, and play dates. "That tends to relax me," she said. "I'm usually doing it with other moms who have been friends, and we gossip and catch up and watch the kids play."[8]

By all accounts, Michelle has done a great job so far. "She is a wonderful mother and those kids are so grounded and so loved," said Yvonne Davila, her longtime friend whose children are great friends of the Obama girls, in a July 2008 interview with ABC News.[9] Yvonne is one of the moms with whom Michelle has sometimes swapped parenting responsibilities—a member of that informal network of support that Michelle has said makes her demanding schedule possible.

Michelle also gets high praise from her husband on the parenting front. "Michelle is an extraordinary mother to our two girls," Barack Obama told *US Weekly*.[10] "When we started out on this campaign, we wanted to make sure that life for our girls would remain as normal as possible, and it's because of Michelle that they are so grounded. Nothing is more important to Michelle than being a good mother, and she works every day to instill in our girls the same values we were raised with."

Certainly what we saw of the girls on the campaign corroborates the claim that their mom is doing a good job. For most of the campaign, Malia and Sasha remained primarily behind the scenes, but every now and then we would catch a glimpse of the two cute little girls who would wave and smile (and sometimes pout or yawn) from the stage during a rally or emerging from a vehicle en route to a rare campaign event they were attending. Like most children of recent would-be presidents, the girls' lives were kept quiet and separate from everything that was going on in front of the camera. So we pretty much had to take others at their word when they said that the Obama girls are absolutely grounded and down-to-earth, typical soccer- and piano-playing, Hannah Montana–and Jonas Brothers–loving little girls in every way.

And then came that day in July—July 4, to be exact, the birthday of the country and the birthday of the Obamas' oldest daughter—when, in the celebratory atmosphere, the girls had a sort of coming-out party.

It wasn't supposed to happen, according to both the Obama campaign and *Access Hollywood*, but happen it did, and the world had a real glimpse of the would-be First Family, which, in this day and age of round-the-clock information delivery, could be repeatedly viewed day and night on television and over the Internet.

The scheduled interview with *Access Hollywood* correspondent Maria Menounos was originally intended to feature the parents alone as the family celebrated the holiday in Butte, Montana. But Menounos and the girls had spent a little time together as they waited for the filming to begin, bonding over such shared interests as the Jonas Brothers (apparently Menounos had just interviewed them). When it was time for the interview to get underway, Malia and Sasha snuggled in next to their parents and producers quickly attached microphones.

"There was a very loose atmosphere," said Rob Silverstein, executive producer for *Access Hollywood*. "It was one of those things where it was like lightning in a bottle."[11]

What did we learn from the interview? That the girls are as articulate as they are adorable (and as telegenic as they are photogenic). That they appear to be every bit as grounded as others have claimed them to be. That the family dynamic is, likewise, natural, normal, and down-to-earth and that, as between husband and wife, there seems to be a palpable, affectionate connection between parent and child.

Despite Barack Obama's stated regret at having to miss out on time with his daughters because of his chosen vocation, he and his girls seem to have a pretty typical father-daughter relationship. Like most dads, he can sometimes be embarrassing.

During the interview, Malia recounted a time when one of her friends came over to play. As he does all the time for work, her father, the candidate, stuck out his hand for a shake. Malia said she felt compelled to instruct her father on kid etiquette. "You know, Daddy, you don't really shake kids' hands that much. You shake adults' hands. And he's like, 'Then what do you do?' You just wave or say 'hi,'" she said.[12]

Senator Obama had his own take on the situation. "She basically avoids me embarrassing her by giving me these tips," he said. "Especially when I'm around her friends."

Even though he was to be the country's next president, Malia and Sasha said their daddy sometimes does annoying things. Such as his habit of plopping his bag right down by the door, where his family can trip on it, when he walks into the house. "That's right, I'm putting it down because . . . I'm so glad to come home and see you guys," their dad, the intrepid campaigner, said. Still, he drops it right there by the door.

"On my shoes!" exclaimed little Sasha, who for the most part let Malia and her parents do the talking.

We also learned that their father does not have much of a sweet tooth. Although his daughters seem to find it baffling, this fact may help explain how he has maintained his trim physique when other candidates tend to pack on the pounds during a long and grueling campaign. (Then again, that disciplined workout ethic might have as much to do with it.)

We learned about Senator Obama's sweet tooth, or lack thereof, when, as seven-year-olds will, Sasha appeared to get bored sitting still and listening to a whole lot of talk during the interview. Out of the blue, with the camera rolling, she turned to her mother and said, "Mommy, when are we getting ice cream?"

To which Malia responded (instantaneously and with palpable glee, as any ten-year-old confronting the prospect of ice cream will), "We're getting ice cream? Ice cream is my favorite food. I could eat ice cream forever."

"Everybody should like ice cream," pronounced little Sasha. "Except Daddy. My dad doesn't like sweets."

The candidate then felt forced to confess. "I'm not a sweets guy," he said, although he and Malia pointed out that he does have a soft spot for pie, particularly pumpkin. (To anyone who followed the campaign, this probably didn't come as a tremendous surprise, given the earlier reports about the senator's "persnickety" dining habits. In what has been called the campaign's "Arugula Moment," Obama commented during a visit to a Whole Foods store in the early days of the campaign that he couldn't believe how much the price of arugula had increased. To some, Obama's familiarity with the finer points of arugula pricing made him a bit out of touch with the average Joe, sort of akin to the way George H. W. Bush was regarded when, in 1992, he seemed gobsmacked by the electronic scanners in a grocery store.)

Sasha also revealed that her father prefers minty gum to bubble gum, to which her dad felt compelled to make the further confession, "I'm a little conservative in my taste for gum."

Nor is he too fond of clothes shopping, apparently. The ladies of the household enjoyed poking a little fun at the man of the house, pointing out that his pants were "probably ten years old," and asking the camera crew to please not pan in on his shoes or his belt. (The fact that he really doesn't enjoy shopping may come as a surprise to the fashion world, which has hailed Obama's sense of style. *Esquire* magazine named him to the 2007 Best Dressed list and he appeared on the cover of *GQ*.)

In an introspective moment, the girls were asked what they do that their parents don't like, to which they responded, "Whining." After giving it a bit more thought, Malia added, "Arguing is the worst thing, because they sit us down and say, 'You know, you guys are the best thing that you have in your life.' We're never going to get something as good as each other."

(Remember rule number one?)

During the interview, there was also talk about how sometimes, when they accompany their parents on the campaign trail, Malia and Sasha will bring along toys such as water pistols for a little lighthearted play during the downtimes.

"It's a lot more fun than listening to Daddy talk," offered Michelle, in her characteristic teasing manner. To which little Sasha raised her hands and opened and closed her fingers, saying, "Blah, blah, blah."

"They basically cut out when I [start talking]," said Sasha's father, whose talent for oratory has been compared to John F. Kennedy and even Abraham Lincoln. Apparently the girls are impervious to that particular gift.

(In an April interview with Rachael Ray, Barack said Malia and Sasha are "not impressed" by their father's showing in the presidential race.

"When I call them and they say, 'Daddy, what did you do today?' I say, 'Well I spoke to 35,000 people.' It's like 'Boring.' It's not interesting," he said.)[13]

In the *Access Hollywood* interview, Malia admitted that it can be kind of cool to see her parents on the covers of magazines, but she let it be known that, in her mind, they are not true celebrities, not up there with the "real important" stars. Recalling her reaction to seeing her mother featured in a popular news weekly, Malia said, "I saw that magazine and I was like, 'Oh, Mommy, you're in this,' because I've never seen Mommy in that," Malia explained. "I usually see people like Angelina Jolie."

"Real important people," Michelle said.

"Real important people," Malia concurred, and then looked up at her mother and added with a smile, "No offense."

We learned what Malia found exciting about the prospect of living in the White House: "It would be very cool," she said. "My most exciting thing about it is that I get to redecorate my room."

Finally, we learned what it is like during those private moments, those times away from the cameras, when Barack and Michelle get to just be a husband and wife. How does it feel when the girls witness what others have described as the Obamas' "natural chemistry"? Do they like it when they see their parents hold hands or hug?

"Sometimes, when you get to be a teenager, sometimes people think it is embarrassing," the sanguine Malia said. "I like it though."

The focus then turned to the parents: With all the demands of the campaign trail, how do you still find time for romance?

"Barack is very romantic," Michelle said, turning to face her husband. "You brought me flowers the other day. . . . He always brings me flowers."

Michelle was asked what romantic thing she had done for her husband lately. She paused and thought a while, then said to her husband, "I take care of your children. That is love."

To which the presidential candidate responded, "That's very romantic." He appeared to mean it, absolutely.[14]

After the *Access Hollywood* interview began airing, both on the web and on television, it was all people could talk about. Mostly viewers marveled at how natural and normal the girls seemed, how articulate and thoughtful they were, particularly Malia, whom many said seemed far "older than her years."

As *Access Hollywood*'s Silverstein said, "The ten-year-old, Malia, is like something you've never seen before. She is a spitfire. She is way beyond her years. How fascinating it is to listen to these children talk. You can't imagine a ten-year-old so poised and smart and well-behaved."[15]

People remarked about the family dynamic, which was at once comfortable, affectionate, and light-hearted—the quintessential American family. My thoughts turned to Barack Obama's description of the Robinson household. Visiting Michelle's family, he wrote in *The Audacity of Hope*, was a bit like walking in on the set of *Leave It to Beaver*. Seeing the Obama family felt like watching a twenty-first-century version of the same thing.

Which was why it took some by surprise when Barack Obama told ABC's *Good Morning America* a few days after the filming that he and Michelle regretted having included the entire family in the interview. He said it gave him "a little bit of pause" as he watched some of the Q&A, adding, "I think we got carried away a little."[16]

It wasn't anything substantive that came out of the interview that bothered the candidate; rather it was the question of whether—by allowing the media a real look at the family for the first time—the Obamas had opened the door for more focus on their growing daughters. Prior to the *Access Hollywood* interview, the Obamas had made it clear that the girls should be more or less "hands off." Would the interview change anything?

Not if the Obamas can help it. "I don't think it's healthy and it's something we'll be avoiding in the future," he told *Good Morning America*.

It's worth noting that the Obamas extended that same sense of protection to the children of their political rivals as well. When newly selected vice presidential candidate Sarah Palin announced that her seventeen-year-old daughter was pregnant, the Obamas immediately declared that Governor Palin's children were off-limits. Barack Obama even went so far as to say that anyone in his campaign who brought the subject up for political gain would be fired.

"That's one of the reasons why I'm so proud of my husband and I love him—he's been very protective of our kids through this process.

"His view is that, 'What's good for my kids is good for everybody's kids,' and I completely agree with him," Michelle said. "I know that they [the Palins] care about their kids, and we should let them deal with this issue."[17]

The blogosphere wasn't so generous. E-mails circulated, blasting the hypocrisy of members of the Christian right, who for so long had preached the value of abstinence but now decided Bristol Palin's decision to keep her baby and marry the child's father was worthy of praise. What if it had been Michelle Obama's teenage daughter who had gotten pregnant, the bloggers asked. How would the conservative Christians have responded then?

If the Obamas do manage to keep their girls out of the media, they will be following the example set by their presidential predecessors. Both presidents Bush and Clinton had a hands-off policy about their daughters when they moved into the White House, and the media generally respected it. Others have had more of a struggle. The Kennedys—the political family the Obamas seem to be compared to most often—apparently had an internal dispute about what was the correct approach. Jackie Kennedy was reportedly very opposed to having her children photographed; memorable photographs of Caroline and John-John in the Oval Office were taken when their mother was not in town.[18]

As for Malia and Sasha, it seemed they were entirely nonplussed by the media attention during the campaign, even after the television interview. When their mother received some negative press at one point, and Malia happened to catch wind of it, she didn't seem to take it too seriously. "When some folks were attacking Michelle, Malia just asked, 'What was that all about?' And we talked it through," their father said. His daughter shrugged it off—"She's completely confident about her mommy's wonderfulness," he said.[19]

Joe Kelly, cofounder of Dads and Daughters, an organization that focuses on strengthening the father-daughter relationship, told the *Chicago Tribune* that he suspects the Obamas are learning about this whole process as they go along. "You learn as the kids grow and you learn about them as people and what's good for them and what's not good for them."[20]

Others were less forgiving about the Obamas' willingness to give the girls some media exposure.

In a piece titled "The Hubris of Obama?" Andrew Sullivan of the *Atlantic*, a self-proclaimed Obama supporter who is widely known as a conservative, blasted the would-be candidate and his wife for what he saw as their lack of judgment on this one. "One great aspect of the Obama marriage has been the way in which they appear to have brought up their daughters as very regular girls," Sullivan wrote in "The Daily Dish." "Displaying them this way was bad judgment and poor parenting."[21] Sullivan calls fame a "toxin," adding that children "deserve to be protected from it as much as they would from lead paint."[22]

No doubt, the last thing the Obamas intended to do was to expose their daughters to the "toxin" of fame. But as any parent knows, we are not infallible—we make mistakes, and we can learn from them.

As a parent, I can certainly appreciate how the Obamas must have felt on that special day, as they tried to give their oldest daughter a memorable and happy experience on her tenth birthday and yet also allow the public access to the candidate on the country's special day. It is that old work-family balance that Michelle has talked so much about and Barack has absorbed as a husband and father.

One of my favorite passages from *The Audacity of Hope* is when Barack comes to understand—as the children start to grow up and the "trials of those [early] years passed"—the tension Michelle had experienced as she tried to juggle family and career.

"I came to see that in her own mind, two versions of herself were at war with each other—the desire to be the woman her mother had been, solid, dependable, making a home and always there for her kids, and the desire to excel in her profession, to make her mark on the world and realize all those plans she'd had on the very first day we'd met," he wrote.[23]

I don't think it's too much of a stretch to say that Barack, the presidential candidate, had a real taste of that conflict himself on July 4—or perhaps the next day on July 5—when he realized the desire to "excel in his profession" may have collided with the desire to create a "solid, dependable" situation for his children.

I can also imagine getting caught up in the moment, getting caught up by my own children's splendor, by a desire to let others see these unique, special, marvelous people who are at the center of my universe. I can imagine making the same decision the Obamas made and also very likely regretting it later.

Every parent is proud of his or her children (and if they're not, it's usually very sad). Why do we get so many of those family photograph cards during the holidays, the ones showing the adorable children, arms around each other, posing on a mountaintop or sitting in the sand, smiling in the late afternoon sun, on the beach? Why do we receive so many of those long, typewritten letters that accompany the holiday cards? You know, the ones addressed "Dear Friends," that proceed to tell us how Susie's basketball team made it to the state semifinals and she got straight As in school and how Johnny was elected class president and is writing a novel even though he's still in sixth grade?

Why do we open up the school yearbook and see so many ads paid for by parents, tributes that proclaim things like, "Angela, You are the light of my life. The day you were born was a miracle. You never cease to amaze me"? And so on and so on and so on?

It is because we are proud of our children. We love them and we want the world to know how much. Inasmuch as a child can be a reflection of the parent, we want the world to witness our greatest accomplishment. Remember the Plato quote (with a few liberties taken here)? "I know of no more worthy ambition for a father [and mother] than for [their] sons [and daughters] to be the best of men [and women]."

That quote was actually brought to my attention by Bill Powers, the head of my children's school, in one of the last communiqués he sent to parents before summer vacation. My son had just graduated, and so I was particularly attuned to the notion of what a parent's greatest ambition is and how nothing matters more—not even the book I was writing and whose deadline was fast approaching—than that my sons and daughters become "the best of men and women."

I suspect it is exactly that ambition that drives the Obamas in the decisions they make for their own daughters. And it is presumably that ambition that would serve to guide President Obama's policies regarding the children of America.

For the moment, though, at least for Malia and Sasha, the focus was on the present, and in the Obama household, that meant thinking about a dog. As their parents said during the campaign, "win or lose," Sasha and

Malia get that dog. What remained to be seen was what kind, and even that was the object of much speculation.

Back in Iowa before the caucuses and primaries began, Senator Obama had said that Malia had investigated dog breeds and appeared to be settling on the hypoallergenic goldendoodle, a cross between a golden retriever and a poodle, because of allergies. His older daughter, "who seems to be driving this process," says the goldendoodle "is the optimal dog," her father said at the time.[24]

By the summer a small furor had arisen over the subject. The American Kennel Club apparently asked the country to vote on a list of five hypoallergenic breeds, while the Best Friends Animal Society urged the Obamas to adopt a dog from a shelter. Meanwhile, People for the Ethical Treatment of Animals (PETA) also shared a few thoughts with them. In a July 28, 2008, letter to the Obamas, Ingrid E. Newkirk, president of PETA, asked them to adopt a mutt.

"Dear Senator and Mrs. Obama," she wrote. "We hope you are well. We understand that greedy dog breeders are panting and drooling over the prospect that prominent figures may unwittingly promote their business and may try to 'sell' you on the idea of getting a purebred dog."

She goes on to say, "No one needs to tell you that this country is proud to be a melting pot, and there is something deeply wrong and elitist about wanting only a purebred dog. . . . Compassionate people nationwide are choosing to adopt a homeless pound puppy—a grateful refugee from a society that has not always treated the true 'underdog' kindly—rather than cater to special interests who do not have dogs' interests at heart. . . .

"Every animal purchased from a breeder or a pet shop takes away a home from a needy animal at an animal shelter, waiting and hoping for a chance at the American dream of life, liberty and the pursuit of happiness."[25]

Couldn't Malia and Sasha just get a dog?

CHAPTER 6

Skin as Tough as Rhinoceros Hide

On Being a Political Spouse (or Standing by Your Man)

THE UPROAR SURROUNDING MICHELLE OBAMA'S "PROUD OF AMERICA" statement, epitomized by the release of the Tennessee GOP online video and her husband's ensuing command that his opponents "Lay off my wife," illustrates just how difficult it is to be the spouse of a candidate running for president these days, particularly if you happen to be outspoken and accomplished yourself. Think: Hillary Rodham Clinton before she became a senator and then a presidential contender herself, back during her pre–First Lady and First Lady days.

When she burst onto the national scene alongside her husband way back in 1992, some sixteen years before her own presidential aspirations were dashed in the most competitive race for the Democratic nomination this country has ever seen (and then again eight years later in the bitter battle against Donald Trump), Hillary Clinton made an appearance on *Nightline*. Host Ted Koppel introduced the would-be First Lady this way: "Meet the new political wife. She has a career, she has opinions. A partner in every way. . . . And now she's become controversial."[1]

Here was this hugely brainy, tremendously accomplished woman—a woman who was twice ranked among the top one hundred lawyers in the country by the *National Law Journal*—who was nevertheless widely ridiculed for statements like "You know, I suppose I could have stayed home and baked cookies and had teas, but what I decided to do was to fulfill my profession, which I entered before my husband was in public life." Or "I'm not some Tammy Wynette standing by my man." There was all the chatter about her marriage, her changing hairstyles (check out HillarysHair.com), her laugh (check out "Hillary Clinton cackle"), and even various parts of her anatomy. (I won't go into any of that here, but it's all in an October 2007 *New York* magazine online article called "A Brief History of Hillary Clinton's Body Politic.")[2] Never mind the noise about the more substantive issues, such as the failed health care initiative and the notion that, with the Clintons, the country could get "two for one."

Despite her obvious talents, despite the many successes that came later as a senator from New York and then her two turns as a nearly unstoppable presidential contender, Hillary Clinton was viewed from the outset as a pariah by some members of the voting public. And although she gained a fiercely devoted following who very nearly made her the Democratic presidential nominee in 2008 (and president in 2016), she never fully recovered from the first impression she made when she was the controversial career woman, the partner, standing alongside her presidential candidate husband, voicing her own opinions.

The oft-cited parallels between Hillary Clinton and Michelle Obama are obvious. Just as Hillary was ranked as a top lawyer, Michelle Obama has received her own top billing. In 2006, *Essence* magazine listed Michelle as among Twenty-five of the World's Most Inspiring Women. A magazine about Harvard alumni called *02138* (02138 is the zip code in Cambridge, Massachusetts, Harvard's hometown) listed her fifty-eighth of "The Harvard 100," a listing of the university's most influential alumni for 2007. (Her husband was ranked number four.) Not that this has anything to do with any of her accomplishments or her ability to influence others—except perhaps in style fashion choices—but Michelle was also listed by *Vanity Fair* magazine as among the World's Best Dressed People in 2007 and 2008.

And yet, like Hillary, statements that she made early on in the campaign (and perhaps, in retrospect, wishes that she had expressed differently) refused to die. Some may have been taken out of context, and the public, in particular on the opposing side, simply refuses to forget.

Also like Hillary, Michelle has been picked apart piece by piece, from her facial expressions to her choice of clothing. Does she show too much leg? How come she doesn't wear pantyhose? What about that "angry scowl"? And what's the deal with those bare arms? (More on that later.)

Of course, Michelle and Hillary are hardly the only political wives who found themselves targeted by opponents, but there does seem to be a theme that those who speak up are the ones who get slammed. "A strong, outspoken wife is a way to make a candidate, especially a Democrat, look weak and unpatriotic," wrote Joan Vennochi, the *Boston Globe* columnist, in late June 2008.[3]

Teresa Heinz Kerry, the wife of Democratic nominee Senator John Kerry, found herself in the same boat during the 2004 presidential election. Google her name and you come up with a list of reported slips of the tongue, such as the time she talked about the prevalence of "scumbags everywhere." (This was in an interview with Pittsburgh's WTAE-TV in response to a question about whether the nobility has gone out of public service.)[4] And the time she was caught on tape telling a journalist to "shove it." (This occurred at the Massachusetts Statehouse when she was talking about growing incivility in politics and she felt a reporter had misquoted her. One of Mrs. Kerry's spokeswomen, Marla Romash, explained it this way: "This was sheer frustration aimed at a right-wing rag that has consistently and purposely misrepresented the facts in reporting on Mrs. Kerry and her family.")[5] Or the time she said she didn't know if Laura Bush had "ever had a real job," adding, "I mean, since she's been a grown-up." Mrs. Kerry later apologized, saying, "I had forgotten that Mrs. Bush had worked as a school teacher and a librarian, and there couldn't be a more important job than teaching our children."[6]

You wonder whether, if she had just stood alongside her husband smiling and never opening her mouth, things might have been different. Instead she spoke up, and all people could talk about were her malapropisms (or else her appearance, her extraordinary wealth, or the fact that, as a woman of Portuguese heritage, she was perhaps "too exotic" to make a proper First Lady).

Not even First Lady Betty Ford was immune. An outspoken supporter of the Equal Rights Amendment and a woman's right to choose, some blamed Mrs. Ford and her willingness to voice her views—on *60 Minutes*, no less—as contributing factors in her husband's eventual loss at the polls. In addition to speaking up about women's issues, Mrs. Ford will also be remembered for speaking candidly about other topics, including her own problems with substance abuse. Thanks to that willingness to share her story and courage with the world, the treatment center that bears her name came into existence, helping legions of others in their battle against addiction. Still, some wondered aloud if it was proper for a First Lady to air that kind of dirty laundry.

Of course, the grandmother of all of these outspoken, opinionated, controversial First Ladies was Eleanor Roosevelt, a woman who was at the forefront of much of the twentieth century's history and who, by the time she was through, influenced the world every bit as much as—or arguably even more than—her husband, President Franklin D. Roosevelt.

Like many of the First Ladies who followed her, Eleanor Roosevelt seemed to be a sort of Rorschach test: People either loved her or they hated her. To her fans, she was brilliant, brave, and passionate, a woman of action, always working to make the world a better place. To her detractors, she was a meddling nuisance, politically naive, and outrageously overreaching in her role as First Lady.

One thing is clear: Eleanor Roosevelt as First Lady was utterly groundbreaking. She wrote a syndicated column, she was a radio commentator, she held press conferences and spoke at political conventions. After her husband died, she continued to work in the public realm as US representative to the United Nations, where she helped win passage of the Universal Declaration of Human Rights.

Eleanor Roosevelt's outspoken candor and her willingness to serve the country alongside her husband, the elected leader, and then to continue serving even after he was gone left her open to criticism. Although painfully shy as a child, she did eventually learn how to deal with that criticism and life in the public eye: "Every woman in public life needs to develop skin as tough as rhinoceros hide," she once wrote.[7]

During the election of 2008 and the long primary season leading up to it, Michelle Obama was undoubtedly developing her own form of rhinoceros hide. In this new world of instantaneously delivered information, she was learning that it is important to watch what you say. And even when she did manage to do that, she was learning that words can be taken out of context or even entirely fabricated from the outset, and so you just have to be willing to take the hits.

No one had to teach that to Laura Bush—she had seen the perils of speaking up when her in-laws were in the White House (and no doubt learned more than a little about speaking before you think from her own husband), and she spent her eight years in the White House smiling politely, talking seldom, and writing only about uncontroversial subjects close to her heart. Toward the end of her husband's term, she appeared on television several times, but it was usually to speak about an entirely tame subject, such as her daughter's impending wedding or *Read All About It*, the children's book she coauthored with daughter Jenna.

So it was somewhat interesting when Mrs. Bush did speak up publicly during a trip to Slovenia with her husband in June 2008, just after the Democratic nomination appeared to be sealed. In what seemed like a show of solidarity with the wife of the presumptive Democratic presidential nominee, First Lady Laura Bush said she doubted Michelle meant to say she had never been proud of her country, adding "I think she probably meant I'm more proud." The current First Lady had some words of wisdom for the would-be First Lady: "You have to be really careful what you say, because everything you say is looked at and, in many cases, misconstrued."[8]

To recap, while appearing in Wisconsin, Michelle gave her husband's opponents the unforgettable sound bite: "For the first time in my adult lifetime, I am really proud of my country." By now we all know what she says she meant to say—that she was proud because so many people were engaging in the electoral process—but months afterwards the furor over that one sentence refused to die down. What about the fall of the Berlin Wall, people asked, or the time millions of Americans helped victims of the Southeast Asian tsunami in 2004?[9]

Just prior to the Tennessee primary, the Tennessee GOP posted a four-minute video on YouTube in which Michelle's remark is replayed six times, interspersed with clips of Tennessee residents proclaiming how proud they are to be Americans.

As we know, the video led Michelle's heretofore noncombative husband to come out strong against these negative attacks. "The GOP, should I be the nominee, can say whatever they want to say about me, my track record," Barack Obama told ABC's *Good Morning America*. "If they think that they're going to try to make Michelle an issue in this campaign, they should be careful, because that I find unacceptable, the notion that you start attacking my wife or my family."[10]

Perhaps the video shouldn't have come as a surprise to the Obama campaign. After all, this was the same state in which the Republican Party had produced a news release that called the candidate "Barack Hussein Obama" (pointedly focusing on his middle name, a traditional Muslim name) and also alleged that he consulted with anti-Semitic advisers.[11]

The Tennessee GOP press release also featured a photograph of Barack wearing what it claimed was "Muslim attire." In fact, it was the traditional outfit worn by Somalis—a white robe and headdress—a getup Barack donned during a visit to Wajir in remote northeastern Kenya in 2006. The release of the photo, which appeared on DrudgeReport.com, caused a stir in Kenya, where Kenyan elders threatened to impose a fine on the Clinton campaign, payable in livestock, unless they apologized. The Clinton campaign denied authorizing the release of the photo, but said that, with some seven hundred staffers, they couldn't be sure it had not been sent out without official approval.[12]

Among those critical of the press release at the time was Republican presidential nominee John McCain who called for "respectful debate" during the campaign. Much later he also called for the country to respect both potential First Spouses.

At the time of the Tennessee YouTube video controversy, however, Mr. McCain made no comment, and his wife was one of the first to pounce after Michelle made her initial offending statements. "I'm proud of my country," Cindy McCain said at a Wisconsin rally on February 19. "I don't know about you—if you heard those words earlier—I'm proud of my country." Months later, former secretary of state Lawrence Eagleburger used the phrase when he introduced Cindy at a fund-raiser in June, saying Mrs. McCain was someone who is "proud of her country, not just once but always."[13] In an interview on ABC's *Good Morning America* that aired on June 19, 2008, Cindy repeated the thrust of her earlier statements, saying, "Everyone has their own experience. I don't know why she said what she said. All I know is that I have always been proud of my country."[14] (Later she explained her comments as the product of a wife and mother of servicemen who feels "emotional" about military service.)

In his plea for respect for his spouse and family, Obama asked for the same on both sides of the political aisle, saying, "Whoever is in charge of the Tennessee GOP needs to think long and hard about the kind of campaign they want to run, and I think that's true for everybody, Democrat or Republican."[15]

Asking people to "Lay off my wife," Obama added, "[Michelle] loves this country. For them to try to distort or to play snippets of her remarks in ways that are unflattering to her is, I think, just low class. I think most of the American people would think that as well."[16]

As for Michelle, she told ABC that she thought people were ready to move on and focus on really important matters. "We are trusting that the American voters are ready to talk about issues and not talking about things that have nothing to do with making people's lives better."[17]

During an appearance as a guest host on ABC's *The View* in June, Michelle used the opportunity to publicly thank Mrs. Bush for her show of support from Slovenia. Saying she had been "touched" by Mrs. Bush's words, she announced that she had even gone so far as to write the First Lady a thank you note. "That's what I like about Laura Bush," she told her *View* cohosts, who included Barbara Walters and Whoopi Goldberg, among others. "You know, just calm, rational approach to these issues. And . . . I'm taking some cues. I mean, there's a balance. There's a reason why people like her. It's because she doesn't, sort of, you know, fuel the fire."[18]

Whether or not Michelle would be able to refrain from "fueling the fire" herself, the Tennessee video was just the tip of the iceberg. People continued to talk about things that had little—if anything—to do with making people's lives better. There were the rumors about an alleged videotape in which Michelle was supposed to have railed against "whitey." It never surfaced, but a reporter's question about it caused Barack Obama to display a rare show of annoyance, if not actual anger.

"Dirt and lies" are circulated in e-mail, "and they pump them out long enough until finally you, a mainstream reporter, asks me about them," Obama said to the reporter. "And then that gives legs to the story."[19]

"Simply because something appears in an e-mail, that should lend it no more credence than if you heard it on the corner," he continued. "And, presumably, the job of the press is not to go around and spread scurrilous rumors like this until there's actually anything, one iota of substance or evidence that would substantiate it."[20]

Margaret Talev, the reporter from the McClatchy Newspapers who had asked the question, later wrote in her blog that Obama "was visibly angry at being asked to dignify that rumor by denying it—and so was his staff."[21]

Not long after the "whitey" question had been posed to the candidate directly, the Obama campaign launched FightTheSmears.com. "Truth: No such tape exists," the website said. "Michelle Obama has not spoken from the pulpit at Trinity and has not used that word." It went on to state that others who proclaimed the tape's existence have failed to produce it and have now conceded that it "may be a hoax."[22]

The website also denied rumors that had been flying around for some time about the candidate himself: that he is a Muslim, that he was not born in the United States (it showed a copy of his birth certificate), that he would not say the Pledge of Allegiance, that he took the oath of office on a Koran, the holy book of Islam (the site showed a photograph of him taking his oath on the family Bible), and so forth.[23]

In a somewhat unique tactic, the website relied on a "viral" dissemination of information that worked much the way the original smears were spread. Readers were asked to sign up and send one of the smear-fighting e-mails to a friend or friends. Recipients were then able to send it along to other friends, until it had been distributed widely. Critics argued that the tactic could backfire. By spreading this smear-fighting information, they argued, the campaign could make untold numbers of people aware of the rumors, unfounded though they may have been.

Before the website's creation, some forty-plus articles and/or blogs about Michelle Obama, most focusing on whispers and unsubstantiated rumors, many focusing on the alleged "whitey" statement, were being snared through Google Alerts. A few days after the website was launched, each day brought only a handful of Michelle Obama Google

Alerts, with most of them dealing with things like the outfit she had worn that day or the campaign's attempts to "soften" her image.

Explaining the website, Obama spokesman Tommy Vietor said, "The Obama campaign isn't going to let dishonest smears spread across the Internet unanswered. Whenever challenged with these lies we will aggressively push back with the truth and help our supporters debunk the false rumors floating around the Internet."[24]

(Reading about this tactic in 2018, with the updating and reissuance of this book, it's too bad the smear-fighting, lie-answering tactics didn't continue past the campaign. We might be in a very different place now.)

For her part, Michelle told the *New York Times* she was "amazed sometimes at how deep the lies can be." "I mean 'whitey'?" she went on. "That's something George Jefferson [of the '70s and '80s television show *The Jeffersons*] would say. Anyone who says that doesn't know me. They don't know the life I've lived. They don't know anything about me."[25]

The "whitey" controversy was only a small part of it. There was the ridiculous and seemingly endless commentary about the "dap" or "fist bump" that Michelle and Barack Obama exchanged as a show of affection, congratulations, and good luck before Barack's speech the night he clinched the Democratic nomination. A gesture employed by every American Little Leaguer, their coaches, and even their parents when a child hits a home run or strikes out a batter or even when he just walks up to the plate (basically, one person makes a fist and bumps the fist of the other person; call it an athlete's handshake or a latter-day high-five), there is nothing remotely threatening—or even unusual—about it. (Believe me, I know. I have spent many a day and night in the stands at baseball fields all over the country; the fist bump is as commonplace as peanuts and Cracker Jack.)

Still, one British newspaper questioned whether the Obamas' gesture was a show of "black power," while a Fox News host, E. D. Hill, actually asked if it was a "terrorist fist jab." (She later apologized, and her 11:00 a.m. show was canceled, though Fox said the cancellation was not related to those comments.)[26] One wondered whether Hill has ever visited a ball field or turned on the television to see Manny Ramirez or

Derek Jeter cruise into home plate after a home run. Inevitably, there's that fist banging. Would she say that they, too, were exhibiting some secret terrorist sign language? Where has she been?

Compared to later accusations, the fist bump controversy seems almost laughable. With about a month to go in the election, Sarah Palin began railing about the Obamas' links to William Ayers, the Chicago education professor who was a founder of the Weather Underground in the 1960s.

"Our opponent . . . is someone who sees America, it seems, as being so imperfect, imperfect enough, that he's palling around with terrorists who would target their own country," Palin said to donors at an airport in Englewood, Colorado.[27] She later echoed the statement during two events in California.

While many felt the relationship was fair game, the dramatic responses to her comments did sound some alarm bells. "Terrorist!" "Off with his head!" "Kill him!" were some of the uglier epithets hurled during raucous GOP campaign events.

The attempt at a terrorist link also extended to Michelle. As the New York *Daily News* reported, "Michelle Obama has joined her husband on John McCain's too-tight-with-terrorists watch list."

Her crime? She worked at Sidley & Austin "at the same time as Bernardine Dohrn," the wife of Bill Ayers, the paper reported, adding: "So did 1,800 other people back in 1987." The claim about Ms. Dohrn was made during a McCain campaign conference call, the *Daily News* and other media outlets reported.

Compared to the rancor flying around in the weeks immediately prior to the election, the noise about the fist bump seems pretty tame, indeed.

A few weeks after the Obama fist bump fuss, President George Bush delivered a fist bump of his own and wouldn't you know it, there weren't any cries that he was exhibiting untoward behavior. The Bush fist bump came when the president was visiting in Arkansas with a twelve-year-old boy who was being honored for his volunteerism. The boy said the president had put his fist up, "And I knew what that meant . . ."[28] (Not a word about terrorist activity or black power. But then again, this was a president who had actually exchanged a belly bump with an Air

Force Academy graduate at the USAF graduation ceremony in Colorado Springs several weeks earlier without much of an uproar. Maybe that's what presidential candidates and their spouses will do when they clinch the nomination in the future—forget the fist bump!)[29]

In a television interview with NBC's Brian Williams, Barack Obama explained the fist bump he and his wife exchanged on the stage in St. Paul this way: "It captures what I love about my wife. That for all the hoopla, I'm her husband and sometimes we'll do silly things."[30] Silly or not, the Obamas were hardly trailblazers in the fist bump department. What was silly was all the commotion surrounding it.

Next came the "Baby Mama" incident, also courtesy of Fox News, in which a "chyron" (or type-based graphic) accompanying a news report identified Michelle as "Obama's Baby Mama." The way it came down was that then Fox anchor Megyn Kelly was interviewing conservative blogger Michelle Malkin about conservative attacks on Michelle Obama. While they were talking, a message was emblazoned across the screen. It read: "Outraged liberals: Stop Picking on Obama's Baby Mama!" "Baby mama" is urban slang for a woman who has fathered a child with someone out of wedlock.[31] You can imagine that there were a few outraged postings on websites and blogs after that one.

And then there were the pieces that were catalogued by Michelle ObamaWatch.com. Some were ridiculous, some were nutty, and some were downright heartbreaking because they so clearly crossed a line (and therefore won't be repeated here).

Given the relentlessness of some of these rumors, the Obama campaign decided to give Michelle a bit of extra help. In mid-June, the potential First Lady was given a high-profile new chief of staff: Stephanie Cutter, who had served as Sen. John Kerry's spokeswoman during his unsuccessful presidential bid. Presumably she had learned a thing or two about smears in 2004. Remember "Swiftboating"?

In case it needs repeating, Kerry's campaign received a damaging if not fatal blow when the so-called Swift Boat Veterans for Truth publicly questioned the legitimacy of Kerry's medals and service in Vietnam. Unlike the controversy surrounding Michelle Obama's "proud" statement or Hillary Clinton's Tammy Wynette quote, the Kerry swiftboat controversy had nothing to do with any action or statement generated by him or his campaign.

The term "swiftboating" has since become part of the lexicon of American politics, a fact made clear in a blog entry posted by the College of Communications at Pennsylvania State University. Appearing in a collection of case studies selected by public relations students, "The Downfall of John Kerry's 2004 Presidential Campaign" begins with a definition of swiftboating as a "highly evolved communication strategy involving enormous expenditures—by insulated front groups—on television ads containing audacious attacks sure to be covered by the news media." It goes on to perform a SWOT (strengths, weaknesses, opportunities, and threats) analysis regarding Kerry's ultimately failed campaign, and swiftboating is largely to blame.[32]

Although the term "swiftboating" may have been coined in response to Kerry's campaign, Senator Kerry was hardly the first candidate to suffer the effects of rumor and innuendo, and most likely Michelle and Barack Obama will not be the last.

A few other recent examples: During the 1988 presidential election, rumors and innuendo helped defeat the Democratic nominee, Massachusetts governor Michael Dukakis. The infamous "Willie Horton" ad depicting a black offender who committed rape and murder while out on furlough touched on all sorts of things—including race and fear, subliminal emotions that helped contribute to Dukakis's defeat.

Nor was the candidate's family immune from the rumor mill in that election. As he attempted to wrest the presidency away from the Republicans, Governor Dukakis's wife, Kitty, came under fire when a GOP senator from Idaho, Steve Symms, made a claim that she had burned an American flag to protest the Vietnam War.[33]

Of course, we all know that the campaign got uglier and uglier and in the end the Republicans were triumphant. What is perhaps worse, in the end Kitty Dukakis was also in trouble. A year after the election, she was hospitalized after drinking rubbing alcohol. In 1991 she frankly discussed her battle with alcoholism in her memoir *Now You Know*. In addition to discussing her addiction, she also wrote about the difficulties of being a political spouse.

(I have seen with my own eyes how personally cruel a campaign can be. In 1988 I was an intern with the Associated Press in Milwaukee, my first job upon graduating from journalism school. I remember being sent to an outlying suburb to cover a campaign rally for Dan Quayle, George H. W. Bush's running mate who was himself the victim of many cruel statements, most about his IQ. I will never forget the two young girls I saw at the rally. The girls were decked out in kilts and twin sets, a strand of pearls around their necks and matching hairbands in their hair, looking every bit the sweet sorority girl. Together they smiled and waved a handmade sign that read, "Let's Put Kitty in the Microwave!" A year later, when I read about Kitty being rushed to the hospital after swallowing rubbing alcohol, I couldn't help but think about those girls. I wonder if they felt any guilt or shame or even sadness.)

Cindy McCain, who tended to truly "stand by her man" without opening her mouth very often (a bit more the Laura Bush model), also had her share of bumps along the road. During the 2000 election, she was the victim of particularly nasty tricks in the South Carolina primary when opponents distributed leaflets featuring a photo of her husband with a dark-skinned baby. The leaflets claimed the baby was a child Senator McCain had fathered illegitimately. In fact, the photo was of the McCains' daughter, Bridget, whom they adopted from Bangladesh.[34]

In an interview with *Newsweek* magazine, Cindy had said she had hoped her daughter would never hear about the controversy. Not long ago, though, Bridget Googled her name and found the news articles. Sixteen at the time, she asked her mother why President Bush hates her. "I did the best to say it wasn't President Bush," Cindy told *Newsweek*. "But what she doesn't understand is . . . how could people say things like that."[35]

Understandably, the experience made Cindy McCain think twice before giving her husband the green light to move forward in the 2008 race. She admits that she still has a "grudge list" of people she believes have harmed her husband or her family.

"I think any mother would agree with me," Cindy told *Newsweek*. "You can go after me, but stay away from my children."[36] (Something tells me Michelle Obama might give Cindy McCain a high five—or a fist bump?—for that one.)

Cindy has also had to confront other, painful personal issues right in the glare of the public eye. When, in the early 1990s, she became addicted to prescription painkillers after back surgery (and began to steal pills from the medical charity she had founded), her battle was anything but private. Cindy has called this the "darkest period" in her life.[37]

After her addiction was discovered, Cindy paid restitution, attended counseling sessions, and performed community service. Knowing the news would eventually get out, she and her husband told her story to a group of reporters they trusted, so she was horrified to discover a cartoon in the *Arizona Republic* the next day showing a junkie—meant to be Cindy—"shaking down babies for pills."[38]

And then there was the incident that has been dubbed "Recipe-gate," in which a campaign intern apparently lifted recipes from the Food Network and presented them as some of Cindy McCain's "favorite" recipes. That made a few headlines.

In the early summer of 2008, Cindy came under scrutiny for being slow to release her tax returns. "This is a privacy issue—I am not the candidate," she said before eventually releasing the forms in June, explaining that she and her husband maintain separate finances. (Cindy is the heiress of a beer fortune estimated at more than $100 million.)[39]

It is true; Mrs. McCain was not the candidate. Nor was Mrs. Obama, Clinton, Kerry, Bush, or Ford. And yet, so much of what these women said, wore, ate, and did was scrutinized and placed in headlines on newspapers across the world. This was particularly true by the election of 2008, when the Internet, social media, and YouTube had made the dissemination of information so unbelievably quick (even things that had no relation to the truth).

Fortunately for the Obamas, by 2008 the Democrats seemed to have learned a thing or two since the Kerry swiftboating experience four years earlier. As David Axelrod, Obama's campaign manager, told *Newsweek* in April, Barack Obama is "not going to sit there and sing 'Kumbaya' as the missiles are raining in. I don't think people should mistake civility for a willingness to deal with the challenges to come."[40]

Presumably the campaigns decided they would be better off generating as much of the news themselves as they could, and given the ability of the Internet to spread rumor and innuendo like wildfire, they apparently also decided that a candidate's spouse needed almost as much marketing and packaging as the candidate him- or herself.

Which is why, by early summer, you could see signs of what appeared to be a heightened marketing campaign focusing on Michelle Obama. In an article called "Michelle Obama Looks for a New Introduction," the *New York Times* described what it saw as an effort to give the potential First Lady a "subtle makeover." Whereas her husband "often blurs identity lines" in a way that seems almost "post-racial," the newspaper wrote, "Mrs. Obama's identity is less mutable. She is a descendant of slaves and a product of Chicago's historically black South Side. She burns hot where he banks cool, and that too can make her an inviting proxy for attack."[41] The *Times* said the campaign would work to soften her image.

When a poll showed voters didn't seem to feel they knew Cindy McCain, the Republicans appeared to embark on a similar campaign. There was Mrs. McCain in a television interview filmed during a tour in Vietnam where she helped children with cleft palates. There she was posing for a *Vogue* photo shoot. And there she was a few days later alongside her husband in *People* magazine.

A race seemed to be underway to see how many "soft" articles could be written about the Obamas and/or the McCains, how many "soft" interviews could be aired on entertainment shows, all under the guise of "Getting to Know You" (but not because you open your mouth to say much).

John Quelch, a senior dean of business administration at Harvard University, said the unprecedented focus on the final two candidates' wives—and their respective campaigns' determination to present the wives in a favorable light—may have had something to do with the fact that Senator Hillary Clinton was no longer in the race.[42]

"What occurs to me is that there were three women running for president—and now there are two," he told the *San Francisco Chronicle*. "Such a large proportion of the U.S. population is interested in having a woman candidate, that the interest in the spouses is a knock-off effect following Sen. Clinton's withdrawal. There is still an absolute passion for the voice of women to be represented in the political dialogue in the highest office in the land," which might help explain Senator McCain's choice of a running mate over other, arguably more obvious choices.[43]

Others were less certain that there was a true passion for the *voice* of women to be represented in the political dialogue. In her column "Make Over Old Views, Not Political Wives," Joan Vennochi quoted her former colleague, journalist Eileen McNamara: "Reading about the lives of women . . . is so often like being trapped in a time warp, as if the last 30 years had never happened. Of course, we are curious about the spouses of our presidential candidates—we are a personality-obsessed culture—but don't we expect them to live on the same planet, in the same decade as we do?"[44]

The Clintons may have unwittingly contributed to this intense media focus in another way. The mere presence of a former president—Bill Clinton—as a potential First Gentleman "created an historic situation in which the media became focused on spouses in a way they never had before," said Phil Trounstine, a pollster and former communications director for former California governor Gray Davis.[45]

Which is, perhaps, why we were suddenly hearing so much about so many things, whether they had any relevance to the race or not. Take Michelle Obama's arms: Should they be bared so much of the time or should they be covered up? One interviewer said that, inspired by Michelle's beautiful biceps, which are on view each time she wears another sleeveless dress, she is now keeping five-pound weights on her desk next to her computer.[46]

Or Michelle's disdain for pantyhose: "I stopped wearing pantyhose a long time ago," she said on *The View*—too "painful." You might have thought that was the equivalent of bra burning, to hear some people cluck about the notion of walking about in public with bare legs. (As one comment posted on Lynn Sweet's *Chicago Sun-Times* blog read, "Bare legged First Lady representation of American female style can't be any more vulgar. Don't tell me it symbolizes a reduced carbon footprint either. If Cindy says yes to pantyhose [I'm sure she wears Wolford] then I'm voting for McCain and a First Lady who has a higher pain threshold and stylist expression!)[47]

Or why we know—courtesy of the "Pool Report"—that the wall across the street from the Obamas' redbrick Hyde Park house is covered in fire ants, that the Obama girls like to play in the sprinkler on the front lawn, and that Michelle looked "slammin'" in a black cocktail dress (yes, she was bare-armed, and the dress had a "severe slit" down the back), her hair up, as she and her husband headed out for a meal at Spiaggia, Chicago's "only four-star Italian restaurant," where meals start at $50. (The pool reporter couldn't tell us what the interior of the restaurant looked like—she wasn't allowed inside—but she graciously included the description from Spiaggia's website: "exquisite, tiered dining room, rich with soft neutrals and subtly contrasting textures. Towering 40-foot windows overlook the corner of Oak Street and Michigan.")[48]

Do we really need to know all of this? And what must life be like inside that fish bowl?

Given these conditions, you have to wonder why anyone would ever consider taking on the position of First Lady.

Reporter Emma Cowing ponders the prospects for the woman behind the American "throne." In an article published in the *Scotsman*, Cowing writes that the "role of First Lady is unpredictable. Despite the attempts of various former FLs, its exact position has never been clearly defined. There is no salary, she is not elected and has no official duties—yet having another job is so severely frowned upon that no First Lady has ever done it."[49]

Compare that to the United Kingdom, where, as Cowing points out, "the wife of the Prime Minister [or in the case of Margaret Thatcher, the husband of the Prime Minister] is free to work and has no governmental staff unless she [he] specifically chooses." In the United States, the First Lady "has her own office within the White House and a staff that includes a chief of staff, a press secretary, the White House social secretary, the White House executive chef and, of course, the chief floral designer." (Michelle has been many things in her relatively short life: a lawyer and a hospital executive, a public servant and a board member, a mother and a wife. However, nothing in her background thus far may have trained her as to how to handle a chief floral designer!)[50]

Cowing goes on to quote Melanne Verveer, Hillary Clinton's chief of staff when Hillary was First Lady, in Suzanne Goldenberg's book *Madam President: Is America Ready to Send Hillary Clinton to the White House?* As Verveer says, the role of First Lady is very particular. "You only have it by virtue of your marriage. You have not achieved it on your own."[51]

While it is true that none of the First Ladies in history have reached the office on their own, one would be hard-pressed in this day and age to say they haven't earned it. As difficult as it must be to live entirely in the public eye, it also cannot be easy to see your spouse torn to shreds. As Michelle said during the epic primary battle with Hillary Clinton, "We expected that Bill Clinton would tout his record from the '90s and talk about Hillary's role in his past success," she wrote in a note to supporters. "That's a fair approach and a challenge we are prepared to face.

"What we didn't expect, at least not from our fellow Democrats, are the win-at-all-costs tactics we've seen recently. We didn't expect misleading accusations that willfully distort Barack's records."[52]

Michelle was obviously referring to former president Bill Clinton's statements in which he accused Hillary's rival of distorting his record in Iraq and stirring racial conflict to win over voters.

Back in 2004, when the notion of a run for the White House was probably not the first thing on her to-do list, Michelle Obama was asked in an interview which First Lady she most admires. Her response at the time? Hillary Rodham Clinton. "She is smart and gracious and everything she appears to be in public—someone who's managed to raise what appears to be a solid, grounded child," Michelle said.[53]

Four years later, in a February interview with Katie Couric on *CBS Evening News*, she was asked whether she sees similarities between Hillary Clinton, her husband's erstwhile opponent, and herself. "I'm sure there are some [similarities], but I feel like I am uniquely me," Michelle responded. "You know, I think that every First Lady in the history of this nation has brought something uniquely different and has moved that role in a fundamentally different direction. I think it has been an evolution that has gotten us to this point where I can be here, potentially to become the next First Lady, with all of my outspokenness and my approach to life and the things that I say."[54]

Whether, after the bruising race for the Democratic nomination, Michelle would still cite Hillary Clinton as her favorite First Lady—or whether she can see the perceived similarities between Mrs. Clinton and herself—would Michelle ever follow Hillary's lead and run for office herself?

"No," Michelle said at the time. "Absolutely not."[55]

Thicker though it may be growing every minute, apparently Michelle Obama's skin isn't that thick yet.

CHAPTER 7

The Color Purple

The Role of Fashion and Image in the Race for the White House

*Should we be silent and not speak, our raiment
And state of bodies would bewray what life
We have led.*
—SHAKESPEARE'S *CORIOLANUS*, V, III

The apparel oft proclaims the man.
—*HAMLET*, I, III

JACQUELINE KENNEDY HAD HER PILLBOX HATS AND CHANEL-STYLE suits. For Nancy Reagan, it was shoulder pads and pouf dresses created by some of the world's top fashion designers. Barbara Bush had her trademark strand of fake pearls and handsome head of white hair. Hillary Clinton had her hair bands (at least in the early years) and pantsuits (later). For Laura Bush, it is hard to come up with one emblematic outfit. It just always seemed that whatever she wore, it was attractive but never flashy, sensible but well made, nice, understated, quiet—kind of like the person we imagine her to be.

And Michelle Obama? What is her trademark look? What do the outfits she chooses to wear say about who she is and what she stands for? To borrow a line from Shakespeare's *Hamlet*, how does Michelle's apparel "oft proclaim the [wo]man"? And does any of it have any bearing on anything at all?

Judging by the fashion sensation she stirred as the would-be First Lady, Michelle Obama's apparel proclaims a woman who is right out there in the forefront, turning heads, leading others to follow, introducing something altogether new. "People are watching Michelle Obama very closely—she's our 'Commander in Sheath,'" *Vanity Fair* special correspondent Amy Fine Collins told me. "She's got that physical stature that is always helpful in carrying off great clothes. She's got that height, that presence. She doesn't look like any First Lady we've ever had. She's not uptight. Not since Nancy Reagan has anyone close to the White House been watched this closely."[1]

I spoke to Amy Fine Collins in early August 2008, a few days after *Vanity Fair* magazine named Michelle Obama to its International Best Dressed List for the second year in a row. The list was full of the usual celebrities—actors, socialites, media figures. What was unique this year, Collins said, was how many political figures also made the cut.

"Not only is it an election year, it's a very important election year," she said, pointing out that, in addition to Michelle, women who made the list include Carla Bruni-Sarkozy, the wife of French president Nicolas Sarkozy and whose long list of prior suitors includes rock stars and other celebrities; and Diana Taylor, New York City mayor Michael Bloomberg's companion.

"Having the First Lady of France who was Mick Jagger's girlfriend is probably even more unpredictable than having a First Lady who is black. The twenty-first century has arrived!" Collins proclaimed. "They [the political leaders and their significant others] are the rock stars right now, they're the movie stars. It's a good moment for the business of politics."

And apparently fashion as well.

In the year and a half since her husband announced his presidential run, Michelle Obama became the talk of the fashion world.

In its April 2008 issue, *Vogue* magazine wrote, "Whether she's barnstorming in New Hampshire or stumping at the New York Historical Society, Michelle Obama . . . has cut a self-assuredly chic swath through the 2008 primary season with her sleek, spare separates, crisp white blouses, and smart tweed skirt suits." The article, called "Flash: It Girl Michelle Obama Lights Up the Campaign Trail, Proving That She Is a Fashion Force to Be Reckoned With," showed a series of photographs of Michelle wearing simple but elegant monochromatic dresses, blouses, skirts, and slacks, often with a strand or two of gumball-sized beads.[2]

There she is in Des Moines wearing a form-fitting black dress with three-quarter-length sleeves, white pearls draped around her neck. For an event in Beverly Hills, she sports a white blouse, tan pants, and a double-stranded necklace of turquoise beads, her hair drawn back into an elegant bun. She wears the same turquoise beads with a tan coat dress, accompanied by some stiletto-heeled brown suede boots, for a speech in Las Vegas. Campaigning in Des Moines on a hot summer day, she wears a white camisole top with a black skirt and black sunglasses (daughter Sasha is wearing a plaid sundress; husband Barack a blue dress shirt, sleeves rolled up, without a tie or jacket). Canvassing in New Hampshire with Barack, she dons a black knit top, black capri pants, and black ballet flats.

A June 8, 2008, article in the *New York Times* Sunday *Style* section said she "favors big beads, belts, and streamlined silhouettes that point to her image strategy." The article, entitled "She Dresses to Win," focused on one outfit in particular—the bright purple belted cocktail dress she wore when her husband proclaimed himself the victor in his drawn-out race against Hillary Clinton:

> *When Mr. Obama and his wife triumphantly took the stage in St. Paul Tuesday to claim the Democratic presidential nomination, the candidate, dressed in one of the crisp, neutral suits that have made him a GQ darling, was momentarily upstaged by his wife, and not just because she knuckle-bumped him in front of the world.*
>
> *What grabbed the eye was the sleeveless purple silk crepe sheath made for Mrs. Obama by Maria Pinto, the former Geoffrey Beene assistant who has long been an Obama favorite. Simple in silhouette and, at about $900 retail, not the kind of garment most working-class voters can reasonably aspire to, the dress was immediately subject to water cooler dissection.[3]*

Some remarked about the Azzedine Alaia belt, others about the oversized pearls. Some said it was the boldness of the color that grabbed them, others what she *wasn't* wearing. Mikki Taylor, beauty director and cover editor of *Essence* magazine, told the *New York Times*, "Every woman I talked to was saying how she has this confidence that is empowered—the purple dress, the legs that I have to believe were bare and not wearing the prerequisite suntan stockings, all say 'I'm here to do business.'"[4]

Indeed, Michelle's status as a fashion trendsetter was so secure by early August 2008 that one of the world's biggest fashion icons—Tyra Banks, the supermodel turned talk show host who also hosts the hit reality TV show "America's Next Top Model"—was photographed for *Harper's Bazaar* in a photo spread "imagining Michelle Obama as First Lady." As *New York* magazine's website said, "Barack Obama may not be the 'biggest celebrity in the world,' as last week's controversial McCain ad charged, but his wife's a fashion icon."[5]

What is perhaps even more noteworthy about all of this Michelle Obama as fashion icon stuff is that hers is a style all her own. "To the best of my knowledge, she does not use a stylist," Michelle's spokeswoman Katie McCormick Lelyveld said.[6] Indeed, asked what her fashion secret is, Michelle reportedly told *USA Today*, "Wear what you like."[7]

In an interview with *Ebony* magazine, she also said her favorite accessory is her husband. "Barack and I—as partners, as friends, and as lovers—we accessorize each other in many ways," she said. "The best thing I love having on me is Barack on my arm and vice versa, whether it's having him standing there smiling at me, or watching him mesmerize a crowd or talk to some seniors in a senior center."[8]

That particular accessory might be difficult for others to come by, but a woman wishing to emulate the would-be First Lady's sense of style would do well to go to a dress shop and purchase a simple sleeveless cocktail dress, the kind of look that helped crown Michelle the "Commander in Sheath" in *Vanity Fair*'s lineup of best-dressed people for 2008. According to the Women's Fashion section of About.com, a sheath dress "features a figure-hugging silhouette with a defined waist (no belt or waistband). This short (mid-calf or shorter) dress works well in sleeveless styles on well-toned bodies."[9]

Michelle certainly fits that bill. *Vanity Fair's* Amy Fine Collins said, Michelle "looks like a real woman. She's got a body there—a physicality. . . . You have to imagine a woman running in her clothes. You can imagine Michelle running after her children. It's not just a flat, snapshot look."[10]

As my journalist friend Ben Macintyre says, Michelle "is the most striking-looking woman. She has this incredible height and this poise. . . . If you were against her, you might think she was looking down her nose at you. Actually, she's just looking down at you because she's almost six feet tall!"[11]

Collins also said part of what makes Michelle's style so unique is her willingness to wear new and different colors, in shades that we haven't traditionally seen on political spouses (who tend to sport red, white, and blue for obvious reasons). "A lot of the strength is in the color," Ms. Collins said. "A lot of boldness in that—none of it is outside the boundaries of what is appropriate and correct, and yet it's a little more fun."

Again, there was that purple Maria Pinto dress she wore when Barack made his speech in St. Paul. *Washington Post* fashion editor Robin Givhan couldn't get enough of Michelle's getup that night:

> *The choice of violet stands out because it's not one of the primary colors so beloved by political spouses. Historically, it's regal. Today, it's fashionable. Michelle Obama seems to choose her hues based on what looks best on her, ignoring the political how-to manual. And so it's no surprise that we should see colors like violet—or chartreuse—that are atypical. She is not standard First Lady material. She is a black woman dressing to flatter her skin tone. Can shades of pumpkin or mustard be far behind?[12]*

One could look at her color choice—the color purple—and be reminded of Alice Walker's book (later a movie and musical) of the same name. Because it has been years since I read Walker's beautiful novel, I couldn't remember what the purple was supposed to symbolize. So I went to that quick and dirty resource—Wikipedia—and here is what I learned: The color purple in the novel *The Color Purple* derives from a conversation two of the main characters have about faith. "I think it pisses God off if you walk by the color purple in a field somewhere and don't notice it," one of the characters, Shug, says. When Celie, the other character, asks what God does after being so ignored, Shug says he creates something else for people to see and respond to. According to Shug, God just wants to be loved.[13] Taken in the context of the book, God must have been happy when Michelle Obama wore her purple dress—people certainly noticed.

Then there were the suggestions that, by choosing to wear purple, Michelle was sending a political, if subliminal, message. As every child knows and the *New York Times* even went so far as to point out, purple is made from mixing the primary colors red and blue. Could there have been any conscious thought behind the decision to wear a color that symbolically unites red and blue (as in red and blue states)? And at the conclusion of an interminably long and painful (as in "bruising"—also purple) *primary* battle?

In a pre–Independence Day piece that ran on July 2, Pam Adams of the *Peoria Journal Star* wrote, "Rather than red, white, and blue, shall we celebrate purple on the Fourth of July?"

"Specifically," she went on, "the splendid royal purple of Michelle Obama's dress on the night that her husband became the presumptive Democratic nominee for president of the United States. There was no mistaking the meaning of the color purple in her dress that night, the echoes of the speech her husband gave at the Democratic National Convention of 2004: 'The pundits like to slice and dice our country into red states and blue states: red states for Republicans, blue states for Democrats. But I've got news for them, too. We worship an awesome God in the blue states, and we don't like federal agents poking around our libraries in the red states.'"[14]

Remember the interview Michelle had with Katie Couric, when she discussed her husband being a unifier? The specific words she used were, "We need someone who can bring this country together. . . . You know, Barack is demonstrating an ability to reach across party lines and change blue and red states to purple in ways that potentially will help us build a working majority in Congress where we can get some of this stuff done."[15]

It is also interesting to note that, after Michelle famously donned her purple crossing-the-political-spectrum dress, others started sporting the color as well.

As *New York Times* writer Eric Wilson wrote in a late July article, "Cable news networks may never agree which program is fairer and more balanced, which talking head is the puppet of whose talking points. . . . But on one crucial point, the pundits have surprisingly taken the same position. Purple is in."[16]

Wilson was talking about neckties. Apparently commentator Keith Olbermann on MSNBC, Lester Holt and Al Roker on NBC, Bill O'Reilly and Kelly Wright on Fox, Charles Gibson and George Stephanopoulos on ABC, and even Jay Leno on NBC's *The Tonight Show* had all sported varying shades of the color purple around their necks. "In this election, the news media's objectivity has also been part of the story. . . . So rather than risk the appearance of favoritism by wearing red or blue, the press has gone purple," Wilson wrote.[17]

Wilson includes a comment from Tommy Fazio, the men's fashion director at Bergdorf Goodman. "I'm surprised to see it on so many people throughout this whole political season," Fazio told Wilson. "There are other ways of not being partisan."[18] The look continued to be popular right through the election in November. Almost any night you turned on the television, there it was—a pundit or host sporting a flashy, violet necktie.

With her purple dress, Michelle seems to have started a trend. Whether her choice of sheath color that night was intentionally symbolic or entirely coincidental, we may never know. But given the next outfit that brought Michelle as much—if not more—attention, you do start to wonder. When she appeared on ABC's *The View* on June 18, Michelle wore a black-and-white off-the-rack floral number from a store called—of course—White House/Black Market.

If the purple dress she wore the night her husband clinched the nomination created almost as much of a stir as the celebrated fist bump, the black-and-white *View* dress caused an absolute sensation, what one reporter even called a "frock frenzy." Almost the moment the show aired, the dress began selling like hotcakes, with several White House/Black Market stores across the country reporting that they were sold out. The dress's designer, Donna Ricco, who had been selling the frock for $99 from her website, DonnaRicco.com, sold every dress within hours. The store's website, WhiteHouseBlackMarket.com, featured a photo of the so-called "Samburu-style dress" on its homepage, coupled with a headline that read, "Road to White House Style."[19]

Like the purple number, the black-and-white floral dress was sleeveless, accentuating Michelle's unbelievably long and toned limbs. With a $148 price tag, it was nowhere near the cost of most dresses favored by political spouses—certainly more affordable than the purple mingling-of-the-primary-colors dress. A spokeswoman for the retail chain said the dress looks good on anyone, but it looked particularly flattering on Michelle's lean figure. As for Ricco, the dress's designer, orders for her line were suddenly up more than 35 percent. Perhaps more important, she was blessed to have a very high-profile, admiring client who might be able to give her some even more high-profile opportunities in the future. (Ricco confessed at the time that she was already dreaming about inauguration day in January 2009. . . .)[20]

Michelle had high praise for the designer. "Her clothes really capture the strength and grace of women," said Michelle, who reportedly had gone on *The View* precisely to show America how as a modern woman she can be, at once, both strong and graceful. She found the perfect vehicle in the floral number.[21]

In addition to winning kudos for choosing an off-the-rack outfit and wearing it so well, Michelle also won praise for her down-to-earth conversation on *The View*. After greeting her cohosts with her now-trademark fist-bump, she answered questions with her characteristic candor, but none of it was controversial or, as one reporter pointed out, even particularly newsworthy.

Asked by Barbara Walters if she was proud of her country, Michelle responded, "I'm a girl who grew up in a working-class neighborhood in Chicago—let me tell you, of course I'm proud. Nowhere but in America could my story be possible."[22]

What is her favorite breakfast food? Michelle confessed to being a bacon fan. Where does she enjoy shopping? Target (in addition to White House/Black Market, of course). Was she wearing pantyhose? No, she hates pantyhose and threw them out years ago.[23] (Is this the strong yet graceful woman's equivalent of bra burning?)

The appearance on *The View* and a subsequent cover story in *US Weekly* were reportedly attempts to introduce viewers and readers to the "real" Michelle, not the scowling woman who peered out at them from the cover of the *National Review* or the woman who proclaimed that she was proud of her country for the first time in her adult life. Certainly the floral print on her black-and-white dress brought a new, slightly more feminine dimension to her previously monochromatic, workmanlike color scheme. And her easy banter with her cohosts added to the impression.[24]

She was "the picture of graciousness, style, and extraordinary intelligence," Thyra Lees-Smith said in an entry on Michelle's Facebook page. "But what really impressed was that she managed to be all of those things without seeming snotty, distant, or unapproachable," she wrote. "As much as I love Jackie O., I think Michelle Obama takes the cake in terms of sheer class."[25]

On a *New Republic* blog Michelle Cottle wrote:

> *"Watched Michelle O on* The View *this morning. . . . She said nothing newsworthy, played nice with Hasselback [sic] [*The View's *conservative host] . . . and mentioned daughters Sasha and Malia every chance she got."[26]*

Responding to Cottle's comments, *Columbia Journalism Review's* Megan Garber wrote, "Again: *She said nothing newsworthy.* She was *pretty but not threatening.* Thus she did a *fine job.* That says a lot."[27]

If there was indeed a "softening" attempt—an attempt to introduce a Michelle who was "pretty but not threatening"—it appeared to be working. A *Newsweek* poll released on June 23, five days after her ABC television appearance, found that 71 percent of voters felt they had an opinion about Michelle, whereas half of the voters questioned said they didn't know enough about Cindy McCain to voice an opinion. Furthermore, respondents in the *Newsweek* poll said they thought Michelle would make a better First Lady than Cindy, with 31 percent supporting Michelle and 25 percent supporting Cindy McCain.[28]

Unlike Michelle, whom a majority of voters felt they knew, at least to some extent, Cindy was regarded as somewhat of a mystery. "Many know her only as the blond standing alongside her gregarious husband, lips fixed in a practiced smile, ice-blue eyes serene and adoring, but inscrutable," *Newsweek* said.[29] (It must be said that Cindy is always impeccably and expensively dressed, her hair always perfectly coiffed, nothing out of place. The one exception to this might be the very day Michelle appeared on *The View*. Cindy was in Vietnam at the time with Operation Smile, a group that brings American doctors to help children with cleft palates. Mrs. McCain is on the board and her adopted daughter, Bridget, was born with a cleft palate. For a television interview in which she spoke about what it meant to her to visit with needy children in the country where her husband had been imprisoned for so many years, she wore a baseball hat and a casual navy-blue shirt. Her hair was pulled back into a somewhat disheveled ponytail and her makeup wasn't perfect. There appeared to be a bit more life in her "ice-blue eyes" as she spoke about the emotional toll taken on military families. Perhaps the McCain campaign was also embarking on its own "softening" mission.)[30]

The *Newsweek* poll contradicted what, until then, had been the dominant trend in recent presidential elections: For the most part, voters in recent elections seemed to favor the more traditional (and generally the Republican) First Ladies. At this point in the 1996 presidential election, Elizabeth Dole was preferred over Hillary Clinton by 14 points, while Laura Bush was favored by 20 points over Teresa Heinz Kerry. Perhaps these dresses (and their subliminal messages?) were helping things to change.[31]

At the very least, the hoopla over the frocks made for a lot of newspaper and magazine sales. Just as women continued to line up in an effort to purchase the black-and-white dress, the media refused to let the Michelle Obama/fashion icon story die down. In a June 23 article about the dress, *Chicago Tribune* fashion columnist Wendy Donahue quoted online magazine *Slate*, writing, "Pundits will wonder whether it was a reference to 'ebony-and-ivory unity,' pointing out that the brand's name, White House/Black Market, points to Pennsylvania Avenue."[32]

"I'd put her in an Oprah sphere in terms of influence," Tom Julian, president of the Tom Julian Group, a New York–based brand consultancy, told the *Wall Street Journal*. Speaking to the Dish Rag, a *Los Angeles Times* blog, Julian said Michelle would "bring affordable American sportswear to the forefront," something that should be "very appealing to the middle American voter."[33]

NBC's *Today Show* said that Michelle Obama had initiated a "frock frenzy," and newspapers in foreign countries were even writing about Michelle Obama, the fashion sensation. The day after *The View* aired, the *New York Times* and other news outlets ran stories about *Vogue Italia*, the Italian version of the US fashion magazine, which for its July issue used almost entirely black models and focused on topics related to black women in the arts and entertainment. The magazine's editor, Franca Sozzani, said that she has been fascinated by the American presidential race and also been bothered by the lack of diversity on runways. Also in its July issue, American *Vogue* carried an article about the dearth of black models in the high-fashion world.[34]

Despite the media frenzy and even the results of the latest First Lady poll, though, not everyone had been won over. The weekend after *The View* aired, a friend came by our house to visit. Seeing a copy of the *US Weekly* magazine featuring Michelle and Barack Obama on the cover on my kitchen counter, my friend offered that her mother really disliked Michelle. "Why?" I asked.

"She hates having to see her bare arms all the time," my friend said. ("Heck, if I had arms like that I'd never put sleeves on," I told my friend.) My friend said she thinks perhaps the real, if unspoken, reason for her mother's disdain is that she's still upset about Hillary Clinton's defeat. An elderly New Yorker, my friend's mother had longed to see her senator become the first female president. Failing that, she at least had hoped to see her become the first female vice president. But as long as Michelle had a spot in the White House, she was figuring Hillary wouldn't stand much chance of finding her own place there. Not enough room for two uber-strong women. (I never learned if she was surprised or pleased when President Obama named her secretary of state.)

Ironically, in the summer of 1992 Hillary was in a similar position to the one in which Michelle found herself early in the summer of 2008. After having made some statements that led at least some voters to think she was an "uppity" wife, as one reporter called the type, Hillary found herself needing to soften her image. Like the Obamas in *US Weekly*, she and Bill and Chelsea posed for a cover story in *People* magazine, giving the world a view of the family side of Hillary and Bill, the power couple.

As Alessandra Stanley wrote in the *New York Times*:

> *Early on, Mrs. Obama was likened to Jackie Kennedy for her youth and fashion style, but lately, the strong and assertive African-American career woman is experiencing the kind of antifeminist hazing that Mrs. Clinton endured in the 1992 campaign when she made her "baking cookies" faux pas.*[35]

Stanley wrote that Michelle made an attempt to distance herself "from that model on *The View*, describing herself as a mother and not mentioning her law career or her views on policy." But she also made a point of praising her husband's former rival for the Democratic nomination, "framing Mrs. Clinton as a pioneer, asserting that sexism had been an issue in her bid for the presidential nomination and praising her gumption," Stanley wrote.[36]

Importantly, Michelle also took the time to thank Hillary Clinton for taking the lead and serving as an example for her daughters. "It's only when women like her take the hits and it's painful, it's hurtful, but she's taking them so that my girls, when they come along, won't have to feel it as badly," she said.[37]

Hmmm. . . . let's see . . . a purple dress representing the union of blue and red states . . . a black-and-white dress representing a union of black and white citizens. Might there be a dress somewhere—or perhaps a pantsuit—that could somehow represent a reunited, fully healed Democratic Party, one in which everyone works together in mutual respect and admiration without regard to gender? Did the green dress she wore the night she spoke at the convention do the trick? And what, one couldn't help but wonder at the time, would Michelle wear to an inauguration?

CHAPTER 8

Questions of Race, Gender, and Age

Letting Go of Fears

THE ELECTION OF 2008 WILL ALWAYS BE REMEMBERED AS AN ELEC-tion of firsts. This was the year the country could have elected its first African-American president, its first woman president, or the oldest first-time president in history. Whichever way it went, the result would be historic. And whichever way it went, people would inevitably see racism, sexism, and/or ageism at work.

The first major hue and cry over perceived discrimination came in the days after Barack Obama became the presumptive Democratic nominee. Even after Hillary Clinton had made her concession speech and urged her supporters to switch their allegiance to her former Democratic rival, several of her staunchest supporters were still saying no. And not just no, but @#%* no!

Supporters joined together in groups, such as the collection of fans who called themselves the PUMAs (for "Party Unity My Ass"); others collaborated on a website called JustSayNoDeal.com, created as more or less a clearinghouse for individuals angry at the Democratic Party over the way the primary campaign was conducted and, ultimately, con-cluded. There was the so-called Operation Donation Vacation, which was basically a call to send the Democratic National Party checks made out for zero dollars as a means of protest, as well as any number of other efforts aimed at punishing the party for perceived injustices against Senator Clinton.[1]

The litany of complaints was varied, but one common thread seemed to unite all the individuals who refused to fall in line behind Barack Obama: anger about the Democratic Party's failure to address repeated displays of sexism during the campaign.

Call it what you will—or won't (and there are many who won't; look at how people pounced on *CBS Evening News*'s Katie Couric after she said, "Like it or not, one of the great lessons of that campaign is the continued—and accepted—role of sexism in American life, particularly in the media")—the evidence that sexism was at play during the 2008 election is pretty hard to dispute. A few examples:

- On March 20, 2007, MSNBC's *Tucker* host Tucker Carlson said, "[T]here's just something about [Hillary Clinton] that feels castrating, overbearing, and scary."[2]

- On July 16, 2007, Carlson said, "When [Hillary] comes on television, I involuntarily cross my legs."[3]

- On January 9, 2008, on MSNBC's *Morning Joe*, Chris Matthews said, "I think the Hillary appeal has always been somewhat about her mix of toughness and sympathy for her. Let's not forget—and I'll be brutal—the reason she's a US senator, the reason she's a candidate for president, the reason she may be a front-runner is her husband messed around. That's how she got to be senator from New York. We keep forgetting it. She didn't win there on her merit." Matthews pressed even further, "She won because everyone felt, 'My God, this woman stood up under humiliation,' right?"[4]

- Mike Barnacle, an MSNBC panelist, said that Senator Clinton looked "like everyone's first wife standing outside a probate court."[5]

- On ABC's *Good Morning America* on May 30, 2008, CNN *Headline News* host Glenn Beck talked about listening to Senator Clinton. "We were watching one of her interviews, or whatever she was doing, or a speech. And she had that tone of voice, where she just sounds like [covers his ears]. I can't listen to it, 'cause it sounds like—it sounds like my wife saying, 'Take out the garbage.'"[6]

- Who could forget Rush Limbaugh's famous question, uttered on December 17, 2007: "Will Americans want to watch a woman get older before their eyes on a daily basis?"[7] (The implication being, I suppose, that it's somehow *easier* on the eyes to see a man age in front of us?)

The National Organization for Women created a space on its website—the Media Hall of Shame: 2008 Election Edition—to catalog what it saw as the most egregious examples of sexism in the media during the election (several of the above statements are listed on that website). As of early August, NOW's Media Hall of Shame: 2008 Election Edition had catalogued twenty-nine such examples. Twenty-three were specifically about Hillary Clinton; nearly all the rest were about Michelle Obama. These included Fox News's "Obama's Baby Mama" graphic; a diatribe about "angry black women" by columnist Cal Thomas (more on that later); a comparison of the potential First Ladies—Michelle Obama and Cindy McCain—by Gary Langer on ABC; and a statement by Lars Larson on MSNBC's *Verdict with Dan Abrams* that implied that Michelle Obama was handed her "college education on a silver platter." Larson also said she had a "do-nothing" job at a hospital.[8]

Explaining the website, NOW's president Kim Gandy said her members would continue to remain vigilant about any additional examples of sexism in the media, even though Hillary Clinton was no longer in the race. "We're going to keep watching because we think Michelle Obama will be the recipient of the same kind of attacks that Hillary was."[9] (By mid-October, Sarah Palin had made her way onto the list several times as well.)

In the wake of Senator Clinton's concession—and perhaps as a result of the outraged response of many of her supporters—Howard Dean, chairman of the Democratic Party, called for a "national discussion" of sexism.[10] In an interview with the *New York Times*, he admitted that the "media took a very sexist approach to Senator Clinton's campaign." He even went so far as to call it "pretty appalling," observing that Mrs. Clinton "got treated the way a lot of women got treated their whole lives." Mr.

Dean also admitted that, as someone who is not a regular viewer of cable television, he may have been slow to react.

As the *New York Times* pointed out in its June 13, 2008, article entitled "Media Charged with Sexism in Clinton Coverage," Hillary Clinton herself may have initiated the discussion about sexism in her concession speech when she said that "women deserve equal respect, along with equal pay, and that "there are no acceptable prejudices in the twenty-first century in our country." It is interesting to note that the *Times* inferred from Mrs. Clinton's "no acceptable prejudices" comment that she was alluding to what had "emerged as conventional wisdom during the campaign"— that sexism will be tolerated in this country, but racism will not.[11]

Which gets us to our second topic: the question of race and racism during the 2008 election. The "conventional wisdom" may have been that racism is no longer tolerated, but just as it's not difficult to come up with a litany of examples of sexism, there are any number of examples of racist remarks, images, and innuendos that cropped up during the 2008 presidential election.

Let's start with the "sexist" examples about Michelle Obama listed on the NOW website. Take "Obama's Baby Mama." We have already said that that is an urban slang term that generally refers to the unwed mother of a man's children. According to Wikipedia, the term originated in Jamaica and has generally been used in African-American circles, although the movie *Baby Mama*, released in summer 2008, is about a white woman and a white surrogate mother.[12]

Hip-hop artist Nas cited the "Obama Baby Mama" incident when he joined MoveOn.org and another website, ColorOfChange.org, in a drive to deliver 620,000 signatures to Fox News, demanding that the network end its "pattern of racist attacks against black Americans." One of Nas's songs, pointedly called "Sly Fox," warns people to be aware of what they are watching because "Fox" is supplying "toxins."[13]

It is worth noting that the network said an editor used "poor judgment" in using the "Baby Mama" headline graphic, so perhaps in the end it wasn't truly "tolerated." The graphic was, however, allowed to appear on national television, on a network that uses these words for its tagline: "Fair and balanced."

The next NOW example was a comparison of the potential First Ladies, Michelle Obama and Cindy McCain. It's a bit more difficult to read anything racist there.

Then there were the Lars Larson comments on MSNBC. Here is what he said as he spoke about Michelle's "do-nothing" job at the University of Chicago Hospitals: Michelle, Larson said, has "awful things to say about a country that gave her a first-class Ivy League education. . . . Earned it? What, outreach and diversity? It's a BS job." Sounds a bit like the sentiments Michelle and some of her African-American classmates perceived from their white counterparts back in college and law school— that sense that affirmative action may have given minority students a leg up at the expense of more-qualified nonminority candidates.[14]

Finally there was Cal Thomas's diatribe about "angry black women." Here is how that one came down: On June 14, some eleven days after her husband clinched the nomination, a video clip of Michelle's "proud of America" statement was aired in a segment on Fox News. News anchor Jon Scott showed his guest, who happened to be syndicated columnist Cal Thomas, the Mrs. Grievance cover from the *National Review* (the one featuring a scowling Michelle Obama), observing that some "pretty powerful people in the media" seem to have "already made up their mind about Michelle Obama" even before the general election had really begun.[15]

Scott's guest must have been one of the "people in the media" to whom he referred, because this was Mr. Thomas's response: "In this campaign, we are being asked to accept three things simultaneously, the first woman with a credible chance of being president, the first African-American with the chance to be president, and, however Michelle Obama is going to be styled, the angry black woman First Lady. This is an awful lot."

Thomas dug in even deeper, citing what he described as a pervasive image of the "angry black woman" on television. "Politically you have Maxine Waters of California, liberal Democrat," he says. "She's always angry every time she gets on television. Cindy McKinney, another angry black woman. And who are the black women you see on the local news at night in cities all over the country? They're usually angry about something.

They've had a son who has been shot in a drive-by shooting. They are angry at Bush. So you don't really have a profile of non-angry black women."[16]

Really? None? Not a single one? For anyone who wasn't yet angry, those statements might have inspired the sentiment.

There were many other examples that were not on the website:

- The allegations about the never-to-surface "whitey" tape. Roger Stone, a Republican strategist, alleged in a Fox News interview during the Puerto Rico primary that a tape existed showing Michelle uttering the term. Rumors began flying across the Internet, but Stone later admitted that he had not talked to anyone who had viewed the tape. As we know, the tape never surfaced and the Obama campaign denied she uttered the word and that the tape existed.[17]

- The hullabaloo over the fist bump. "A fist bump? A pound? A terrorist fist jab? The gesture everyone seems to interpret differently." That was how Fox anchor E. D. Hill introduced a segment on body language after the infamous Obama fist bump.[18]

- The provocative statement from conservative Fox anchor Bill O'Reilly after he learned about Michelle's "proud of America" comment: "I don't want to go on a lynching party against Michelle Obama unless there's evidence, hard facts, that say this is how the woman really feels," O'Reilly memorably said. O'Reilly later apologized for the lynching statement.[19] This was another example cited by the rapper Nas and others in the decision to join the protest against Fox. As James Rucker, executive director of ColorOfChange.org, said, "When Fox talks about lynching the woman who may soon be our First Lady and then refers to this wife and mother as a 'baby mama,' they are maligning not only the Obamas, but black women and black people across this country."[20]

- The allegation, promulgated most actively by businessman (and soon to turn politician) Donald J. Trump that Mr. Obama was not an American citizen.

It is interesting to recall that, early on in the campaign, Michelle Obama seemed to enjoy a brief period as a media darling. Think of the praise she garnered from her initial interview on *Larry King Live* and her performance on *The Colbert Report* to say nothing of the way news outlets reported on her ability to connect with voters and would-be donors.

Then, just as her husband's campaign gained steam, along came her "first time in my adult lifetime/proud of America" statement and her comments that America could be "downright mean" or that life for "regular folks has gotten worse over the course of my lifetime."[21]

On the face of it, many feel these were not such terrible things to say (particularly when looked at in the context of the points she was trying to make and, with the gift of hindsight, looking at what she had to say about the state of the economy). And yet, almost the moment she uttered those words, the rhetoric about her began to change. Suddenly she was "Obama's Bitter Half" and "Mrs. Grievance." Why?

In a June 23 opinion piece in the *Sacramento Bee*, Ruben Navarrette pondered the question and what he saw as its absurdity. "Introducing Michelle Obama, Angry Black Woman," Navarrette writes. "What an absurd caricature this is turning out to be. Not to mention a confusing one. Growing up on Chicago's South Side, Michelle Obama was probably accused of 'acting white' because she excelled academically and went off to the Ivy League. Now—abracadabra—she's a Black Panther."[22] And this was written almost a month before the infamous *New Yorker* cover (read on) appeared on newsstands and in mailboxes.

In his piece entitled, "Michelle Obama's Under Fire, But for No Good Reason," Navarrette asks the age old question: How did we get here from there? "How do you get from remarks about finally being proud of one's country to the assumption that one has something against white people and uses a word like 'whitey'?" he asks.

His answer? "You can't. Not unless you take a detour through prejudice and fear. Granted, that has become a familiar route in American politics. But it's also a dead end we'd be wise to avoid."[23]

Navarrette was hardly the only person asking the question "How did we get here?" and coming up with the same answer.

On June 25, a few days after a *Washington Post–*ABC News poll was released indicating that three in ten Americans admitted having "at least some feelings of racial prejudice," Michelle Martin ran a segment on NPR's *Tell Me More* about the way African-American women have been depicted in the media and, specifically, how Michelle Obama had been portrayed of late. Pointing out that Michelle had been called "arrogant, unpatriotic, and angry," Ms. Martin asked her guests from *Ebony* and *Essence* magazines if they had "ever seen an African-American who is not the principal, she is not the candidate, whose image has evoked this kind of response?"[24]

The answer from Harriet Cole, creative director at *Ebony* magazine, and Tatsha Robertson, news editor at *Essence,* was an emphatic "No."[25]

"I'd have to say no," Cole said. "I think what's happening now is that America—and perhaps the world—are in shock that there is an African-American Democratic nominee and with him a wife who is hardly Barbie. She is a powerful, tall, smart, clear-thinking, well-rounded woman."[26]

Robertson concurred. "I think there is something really interesting going on," she said. "The opponents of Barack Obama have not really been able to have their criticisms stick. I mean, there was the Reverend Wright issue, there was the flag pin—none of that really stuck." And so, Robertson offered, the opponents felt they needed to go after the next best thing, his wife.[27]

Race—specifically as represented by Michelle—may have also made her a target, Robertson said. "Barack Obama has sort of been able, not really to be raceless—of course not—but race is not a huge factor. All types of people can relate to him. . . . I really believe Michelle Obama is someone that the opponents are now focusing on."[28]

"Why?" Michelle Martin asked.

"They've got to do whatever they can," Cole responded.[29]

Others took this line of argument even farther. As Earnest Harris wrote in the *Huffington Post* on July 2, "To engage with the news since Senator Obama became the presumptive nominee for the Democratic Party, you would think that the member of the Obama family pitted against John McCain was Michelle."[30]

Harris said he believes it is always fair to take a close look at the spouse of a presumptive nominee, particularly one who takes an active role in a campaign, because he or she is a "good barometer of the candidate's judgment" and also may one day represent the country "at least in an unofficial way." And yet, "Why does [Michelle] spark such a high level of rancor from those on the far right?" he asks. Words such as "baby mama" and "angry black woman" go "very far beyond the line of decent and fair political discourse, even in its present state," he says.[31]

Why the rancor? The answer, according to Harris, has something—if not everything—to do with race. "I suspect that part of the focus on Michelle Obama is the fact that she has a double negative in the eyes of some. She is an intelligent, strong African-American woman, and I suspect for some this is really hard to handle."[32]

Remember Cal Thomas's words: "An awful lot"?

An article in the British newsmagazine the *Economist* also dissected the issue of race as it relates to perceptions of both the presidential candidate and his wife. In "Is Barack Obama's Wife His Rock or His Bitter Half?", the magazine describes the candidate's birth family as "exotic," with his African father having left when he was two and Barack having grown up in both Hawaii and Indonesia. Michelle's family, by contrast, had a more typically American story. Her family was "hard-up but intact," the article said. "It was also all-black, all-American, and rooted in the South Side of Chicago."[33]

This was not without some benefit for Barack Obama the candidate, the magazine said. For one thing, Michelle had deep connections in the African-American community of Chicago, which may have been useful to a husband with his political aspirations. The magazine mentions her childhood friend, Santita Jackson, Reverend Jesse Jackson's daughter.[34]

The *Economist* also suggested that the woman he married may have helped Barack overcome a perception that he was not African-American enough.

"When Barack was starting out as a politician, his rivals dismissed him as inauthentically African-American or even 'the white man in blackface,'" the *Economist* writes. "Having Michelle at his side helped reassure sceptical blacks that he was really one of them. Even the precise shade of her skin colour may have helped him at the polls."[35]

One segment of the population Michelle may really have helped Barack with, according to the British newsmagazine, is black women. "Famous black men often pick light-skinned or white wives," the magazine argued, and "some black women resent this." The fact that "Michelle is quite dark may have endeared Barack to black female voters who might have otherwise voted for Hillary Clinton," the *Economist* maintained.[36]

It may be interesting to note that Michelle herself dismissed questions about whether her mixed-race husband was "black enough" for African-American voters as "silly."[37]

Another British publication also weighed in on this question, however. In an opinion piece about Michelle Obama's so-called "make-over" (the attempt, denied by the Obama campaign but reported by several media outlets in June, to "soften" Michelle Obama's image), Rupert Cornwell tries to dissect the reasons she suddenly went from fashion-world "it" girl and media darling to the demonized Mrs. Grievance.[38]

In the June 22, 2008, piece published in the *Independent*, Cornwell initially attributes the almost obsessive, largely negative focus on Michelle to, well, boredom. Or at the very least, a lull in the normal election news cycle.[39]

"Like nature, news abhors a vacuum," Cornwell writes. By late June, the United States found itself in that strange "interlude between a thrilling primary season and the next big event when the two candidates announce their respective running mates." So what do they talk about in the meantime?

Cornwell maintains the choice was easy: "The hungry circling spotlight has lit upon Michelle Obama, and with very good reason. She might just make the difference between her husband winning and losing."[40]

Cornwell goes through a litany of explanations about why he thinks Michelle could be the linchpin for her husband: "her sarcasm, her fondness for bringing her husband down to earth." But that isn't all. As Cornwell writes: "And then, of course, she is black." Cornwell calls race "the wild card, the great unknown of this election."

As others have before him, Cornwell insists that Barack Obama himself "transcends race," likening him to Tiger Woods "and to a lesser extent Colin Powell."[41]

Cornwell calls Barack the "post-racial candidate, not black but African-American in its literal, not politically correct, sense. The son of a Kenyan father and a white American mother, he is not descended from slaves, nor was he shaped by the struggle for civil rights."

Cornwell even goes on to surmise that had Barack Obama, "like Woods," married a white woman, "the question of his race might never have arisen." (Really?) "But he didn't," Cornwell continued. "He married Michelle LaVaughn Robinson, product of the historically black South Side of Chicago, whose father worked in the city's water department, whose ancestors were slaves, whose family roots are in the deep south, in South Carolina."[42]

In a June 25, 2008, article on NPR's Political Positions blog, the president-elect of the National Conference of Black Political Scientists pondered this situation further, pointing out the differences between Barack Obama's mixed-race background and the more traditional African-American story to which his wife lays claim. Ultimately, the author, James Lance Taylor, finds that the reason Michelle Obama has become such a target—or "fair game," in spite of the fact that she's not one of the rostered players—is directly traceable to race and the particular history of African-Americans in the United States.[43]

"Like most Americans, Obama has had his hardships growing up as he has said, 'without a race,' without a father, without a sense of community," writes Taylor, associate professor of politics at the University of San Francisco in an article called "The UnAmerican Americans: Or, Why Michelle Obama Is 'Fair Game.'"[44] "Whatever personal alienation he may have felt growing up part African, part American, part abandoned by his African father, part Hawaiian, and part Kansan, no one in his ancestry was ever subject to the Supreme Court's Dred Scott ruling as were all Black people in the United States; none were subject to Jim Crow; and none lived in an American ghetto."

His wife is another story altogether. "Michelle Obama on the other hand would be the first American with a slavery ancestry to occupy the

White House; minus the slaveholding presidents," Taylor writes. "That her comments, 'for the first time in my adult lifetime, I am really proud of my country,' could be used to question her patriotism by fraudulent blogs, cable news programs, and print media despite the fact that the adverb 'really' actually heightens her sense of pre-existent pride in the country, is made possible in a place where Black Americans' patriotism has been trumped by the very fact of their blackness.[45]

"Michelle Obama represents parts of Black America in ways that Obama cannot; and that is her original political sin," Taylor concludes. "If Obama's Black 'half' is forgivable, his better half Michelle's is not."[46]

The questions about race and what is and what isn't "fair game" in the world of politics reached a crescendo in mid-July when the *New Yorker* featured the now-infamous cartoon on its cover depicting an Afroed, AK-47-toting Michelle Obama wearing military fatigues (and looking a lot like '60s radical Angela Davis) and her husband dressed in traditional Muslim garb (turban, gown, sandals). The couple, standing in an ovoid room (suggesting the Oval Office?), performs a fist bump. An American flag burns in the fireplace, over which hangs a painting, a portrait of Osama Bin Laden.

There is no question that the drawing, called "The Politics of Fear," was intended to poke fun at racial, religious, and political prejudices, but very few people were laughing.

David Remnick, editor at the *New Yorker*, the award-winning literary and culture magazine that is widely considered to be liberal-leaning (and which has, in fact, produced several positive articles about the Obama campaign, including a March 2008 profile of Michelle), said the drawing by the artist Barry Blitt "takes a lot of distortions, lies, and misconceptions about the Obamas and puts a mirror up to them to show them for what they are."[47]

In an e-mail to the *Huffington Post,* cartoonist Blitt said the cover was intended to point out how ridiculous some of the misconceptions are: that the Obamas are unpatriotic, that he is a Muslim, that their fist bump could have been a "terrorist fist jab." "It seemed to me that depicting the concept would show it as the fear-mongering ridiculousness that it is," he said.[48]

So why weren't people able to see the ridiculousness?

For one thing, it came on the heels of yet another *Newsweek* poll, this one showing that 12 percent of respondents continued to believe that Barack Obama was a practicing Muslim and that another 12 percent believed he was sworn into the US Senate with his hand on a Koran rather than a Bible. (Neither is true, as the Obama campaign's FightThe Smears.com pointed out in no uncertain terms.)

Although Obama himself said he had no comment when initially asked about the magazine cover, both his campaign and the McCain campaign objected to the satire almost immediately. A spokesman for the Obama campaign called it "tasteless and offensive," while Senator McCain called it "totally inappropriate."

But not everyone was rushing out to purchase a copy. On one of the *Chicago Tribune* blogs, Mark S. Allen wrote, "I will NEVER purchase or read the *New Yorker* magazine again!!! I found your current cover on the Obamas extremely insulting, hurtful, racist and not worthy of the reward of my continuing to purchase the *New Yorker*."[49] Meanwhile, Chuck-in-Wichita left a comment on the *Los Angeles Times* blog Top of the Ticket in which he vowed to "never even visit New York, let alone live there."[50]

Even *Al Jazeera*, the English version of the Arabic-language news agency, weighed in. In an article called "Obama Cartoon 'Insult to Muslims,'" the news agency reported on the controversy, quoting Senator Obama during an appearance on CNN's *Larry King Live*.[51]

"You know, there are wonderful Muslim Americans all across the country who are doing wonderful things and for this to be used as sort of an insult, or to raise suspicions about me, I think is unfortunate," Obama said.[52]

Still, ever the constitutional law professor, he defended the *New Yorker*'s right to run the artwork. "You know, it was their editorial judgment," he said. "And, as I said, ultimately, it's a cartoon."[53]

Obama also admitted that he had perhaps not been forceful enough in fighting some of the misconceptions about his religious positions. MichelleObamaWatch.com was also hot on the trail of news about the *New Yorker* cover. Gina McCauley, the creator of WhatAboutOur Daughters.com, MichelleObamaWatch.com's parent, said the *New*

Yorker satire was reminiscent of another image of Michelle Obama that appeared earlier on DailyKos.com. Like the *New Yorker* cover, the earlier image (which was digitally altered to depict Michelle Obama being savaged by the Ku Klux Klan) was intended to satirize "fear mongering and race-baiting." Also like Blitt's image, it was deemed tasteless by many. It was eventually removed.[54]

Some seemed surprised that people didn't get the *New Yorker* joke, particularly the people who were posting irate comments on liberal, pro-Obama blogs. "They sound so elitist," Art Spiegelman, cartoonist and former *New Yorker* staffer, told the *San Francisco Chronicle*. "The essence of what they're saying is, 'I get it, but I don't trust the people in Kansas to get it.'"[55]

So in the midst of all this, the Obama campaign and those who voiced their opposition to the cartoon received not a little criticism for essentially being humorless. In a column published July 16, *New York Times* columnist Maureen Dowd asked, "May we mock, Barack?" She referred to an article appearing in her newspaper that day by Bill Carter called "Want Obama in a Punch Line? First, Find a Joke." Apparently the writers for late-night television had been having some trouble finding things to joke about when it came to the Democratic nominee. As one writer of political jokes for late-night television said, "The thing is, he's not buffoonish in any way."[56]

In an "On the Media" column in the *Los Angeles Times*, James Rainey, when asked about the *New Yorker* cover, opined that Obama should have resorted to a little humor himself. "Instead of his terse no comment, he should have played one of his strongest cards—his cool—responding something like: 'Hey, I thought Michelle looked pretty good in camouflage.'"[57]

(Cool may be Obama's strong suit, but the gift for quick one-liners resides with his wife. If they were looking for humor, it's too bad no one asked Michelle her take on the *New Yorker* cover. No doubt, this woman who "always speaks the truth" and at the same time is the comedian of the household would have delivered a zinger.)

So, funny or not? Instructive or not? Helpful to the political discourse or not? Don't expect that answers about race and what is and isn't appropriate, what is and isn't funny, will be answered anytime soon. As Gina McCauley of WhatAboutOurDaughters.com said, "We're in new ground here with how we deal with two African-Americans running for the White House. It will test white liberals in ways that they have never been before. And it will test African-Americans, too. It's a process we have to go through as a country."[58]

The fact that race had emerged as an issue in the campaign did not come as a surprise to either the Democratic nominee or his wife. In late June, Barack Obama told supporters in Florida that he fully expected his opponents to use the question of race to create fear.[59]

"They're going to try to make you afraid of me," he said. "He's young and inexperienced and he's got a funny name. And did I mention he's black?"[60]

The senator said he was ready for attacks against his wife as well. "We know this strategy, because they've already shown their cards," he said. "Ultimately, I think the American people recognize that old stuff hasn't moved us forward. That old stuff just divides us."[61]

Michelle was sanguine about what she could expect. "As we've all said in the black community, we don't see all of who we are in the media," she said in an interview on ABC's *Good Morning America* in May 2007. "We see snippets of our community and distortions of our community. [Was she presciently thinking of those "angry black women" comments?] So the world has this perspective that somehow Barack and Michelle Obama are different, that we're unique. We're not. You just haven't seen us before."[62]

After airing on television, the statements were presented in an online ABC News article called "Michelle Obama: I've Got a Loud Mouth." A good title, perhaps, for an interview with a woman whose parents taught her to speak her mind, whose husband says she always tells the truth, and whose children have been encouraged to voice their opinions as well. Here is another quote from the interview:

> *I don't want to paint some unrealistic picture of who we are so that in the end, when it falls apart and if we haven't lived up to this unrealistic expectation, people feel let down in some way. This is who*

we are. I've got a loud mouth. I tease my husband. He is incredibly smart, and he is very able to deal with a strong woman, which is one of the reasons why he can be president, because he can deal with me.[63]

Maybe that's why her husband didn't seem to have too much of a reaction when asked about the *New Yorker* cover. Maybe it's just hard to get under his skin (probably not a bad trait for a commander-in-chief). And it would appear that, at least in part, we may have his teasing wife to thank for that.

But here's an idea for those woebegone comedy writers: If the late-night hosts are really desperate for material with which to skewer Obama—in a joking way, of course—they might do well to speak to his wife. (Or perhaps his daughters who showed an equal facility for teasing him about his taste—or lack thereof—in sweets, chewing gum, and clothing during the July 4 *Access Hollywood* interview. Maybe a few minty gum jokes?)

Then again, maybe the trick was to wait for someone else to come along. As Mike Sweeney, head writer for Conan O'Brien's *Late Night*, told the *New York Times* back in July, "We're really hoping he picks an idiot as vice president."[64]

Senator Biden did provide a lift when he joined the Obama ticket, but it was the introduction of McCain's running mate a few weeks later that really got late-night going. Two words sum up the gold mine Sarah Palin provided to late-night television: Tina Fey. And when the governor herself appeared on *Saturday Night Live*, it was even more of a boon for the comedy show: More than fourteen million people tuned in to watch her performance—the largest *SNL* audience since 1994.[65]

As Lorne Michaels, executive producer of NBC's *Saturday Night Live*, told the *New York Times*, "I think the gods smiled on us with the Palin thing. Like if he'd chosen Romney, I think it would be completely different."[66] *SNL* saw its ratings go up 50 percent among all viewers during the election season.

Late-night television never had trouble finding jokes based on the third "ism" of the 2008 election—ageism. Admittedly, compared to race and gender, this one seems a lot more benign, which is why, perhaps, the late-night crowd was feeling free to have a field day.

Even John McCain, who would have been seventy-two during the inauguration, making him the oldest president to take office for the first time, poked fun at his own relative maturity, describing himself as older than dirt with more scars than Frankenstein. Appearing on *Saturday Night Live* in May, Senator McCain gave the late-night hosts plenty of fodder.

"I ask you, what should we be looking for in our next president?" McCain said. "Certainly someone who is very, very, very old."[67]

As part of his sketch on *SNL*, he appeared in a fake campaign ad, in which his advanced years were again the brunt of the joke.

"Controlling government spending isn't just about Republicans or Democrats," he said in the gag ad. "It's about being able to look your children in the eye. Or in my case, my children, grandchildren, great-grandchildren, great-great-grandchildren, and great-great-great-great-grandchildren, the youngest of whom are nearing retirement."[68]

He didn't stop there. "I have the courage, the wisdom, the experience, and, most importantly, the oldness necessary," McCain said. "The oldness it takes to protect America, to honor her, love her, and tell her about what cute things the cat did."[69]

During the campaign, the media had fun pointing out all of the things that didn't exist way back in 1936, when John McCain was born. "So how old is John McCain?" an Associated Press article begins. "Six-packs, automatic transmissions, and the American Express card were all introduced after he was born—not to mention computers, which McCain admits he doesn't use."[70]

During the race for the Republican nomination, McCain and his fellow Republican candidates were famously asked whether they used PCs or Macs. When it was McCain's turn to answer, his response was "Neither. I am an illiterate who has to rely on my wife for all of the assistance I can get," he said.[71] These and other comments are highlighted on the website ThingsYoungerThanMcCain.com, started by a graphic designer named Joe Quint who says in the website's introduction, "Am I being ageist? Maybe. But maybe not. The world is a pretty complicated place right now and I'm thinking that it's not such a great time to elect our oldest president ever. So sue me."[72]

It should also be noted here that, in addition to Cindy, the McCains' daughter Meghan is computer-savvy. So savvy, in fact, that during the campaign she was running McCainBlogette.com, a blog of "Musings and Pop Culture on the Political Trail."

Most of the jokes and comments about the age question take a lighthearted approach, but the fact is that McCain's relative maturity and Obama's relative lack thereof was a serious part of the debate during the election, like race and gender.

An AP–Yahoo News poll found that 20 percent of voters questioned said "too old" describes Senator McCain "very well," while 14 percent strongly believed Senator Obama was "too young."[73]

At seventy-two, McCain would be the oldest new president to take office—Ronald Reagan turned seventy shortly after he was sworn in for his first term; however, he was almost seventy-four at the start of his second. Obama turned forty-seven in August 2008, making him some four years older than the youngest-ever president, John F. Kennedy.

Here is a sampling of some of the serious discussion about age that arose during the campaign:

- In an article called "How Smart is Grandpa? How Much Can You Expect from a Septuagenarian Brain," author Michelle Tsai said it all depends on the septuagenarian. Often, visual spatial skills decline "typically before the age of 40," followed by the ability to learn new things (and retain them in short-term and intermediate memory). On average, she writes, "People lose about a fifth of their working memory capacity between the ages of 40 and 70," but the amount varies. After memory "begins to slip away, we gradually lose the ability to make good decisions based on new information," Tsai writes. She does add, however, that "septuagenarians who start with high cognitive function— like McCain, perhaps—are less likely to experience mental deterioration as they age."[74]

- In a July 15 Associated Press article, Dr. William Thomas, a geriatrician and professor at the Erickson School of Aging Studies at the University of Maryland, Baltimore County, noted that the "presidential campaign is full of chatter—much of it misinformed—about the role of aging." "People in old age are fully capable of imaginative and skillful work," he continued. "A person's age is not a block to doing fantastic work."[75]

- In that same article, Dr. David Reuben, chief of geriatrics at UCLA's David Geffen School of Medicine, said McCain appears to be in fine form. "As a clinician, I look at whether they appear to be robust, whether their sentences flow, whether their thoughts connect, whether they are easily distractible. McCain appears to be quite robust."[76]

While the general consensus seemed to be that age—either too advanced or too premature—was not a major stumbling block during the election, the fact that it was so readily discussed shows that, at the very least, it was on people's minds.

And to many the jokes about McCain's advanced years ceased to be funny when people began to point out that his chosen running mate— the person who was a heartbeat away—had little economic experience, limited experience with the nation as a whole, and practically no foreign policy experience.

"You do the actuary tables, there's a one out of three chance, if not more, that McCain doesn't survive his first term, and it'll be President Palin," actor Matt Damon said during the Toronto Film Festival. "I don't understand why more people aren't talking about how absurd it is. It's a really terrifying possibility."[77]

And so where do we go from here? How will we regard the 2008 election when we look back on it years from now? To be sure, it was a campaign period that was rife with evidence of sexism, racism, and ageism, to say nothing of unforgettably fierce competition with a few lighthearted moments thrown in. And yet, the three central characters— Barack Obama, John McCain, and Hillary Clinton—with their personal stories (first African American, oldest man, first woman) made it utterly groundbreaking. Sarah Palin's arrival on the scene—with the near simultaneous meltdown in the financial markets—added to the sense that we had entered an entirely new world. So what can we expect next?

Once again, Michelle Obama herself might provide the best clue. While visiting with reporters and voters in Pittsburgh in April 2008, she talked about the controversy that arose after Reverend Jeremiah Wright's lambasting sermons were aired and her husband gave what is now called his race speech.

Describing her husband's words as both "honest and powerful," Michelle said, "What Barack Obama did in his speech was give voice to every emotion I have." Perhaps as prescient as she is truth-telling, she said we can all expect more of these moments that really touch our emotions.

"This stuff doesn't happen in a vacuum," Michelle said. "There's some hard work, and there's gonna be some tears. Change is going to be hard. It's going to require moving out of our comfort zones, away from our divisions. Letting go of fears."[78]

Toward the end of the race, a few weeks before the general election, Michelle offered what she saw as evidence that things were, indeed, changing. Asked during an interview with *Good Housekeeping* magazine whether she thought the campaign had changed perceptions of race in America, Michelle said, "I think it absolutely has. We are talking about issues that we have never talked about before out in the open. The good and the bad.

"I think that at least for the kids I know—not just African-American kids—seeing different images of what is possible means something," she continued. "So many kids—because of their race, their economic background, or where they live—don't see themselves [reflected in this world]. And when kids don't see themselves, they don't see their possibilities. As young people have watched Hillary Clinton and Barack Obama being treated as serious, viable candidates—people who could be President of the United States—it changes everything."[79]

For some reason, Michelle's words about change, about moving out of our comfort zones and letting go of our fears, called to mind a vision from John Milton's *Paradise Lost*. At the end of Milton's classic seventeenth-century epic poem about Adam and Eve and their expulsion from paradise, the young couple wanders off to face their uncertain future. There is a sense of foreboding as our first ancestors prepare to take on the burdens of all humanity. (In America-2008 terms, this would include a devastated economy, fearful citizens, and wars being fought on several fronts.) And yet, there is also a sense of optimism, as, together and hand in hand, they move forward to face the challenges that await them, the triumphs and the defeats, on this imperfect earth:

> The world was all before them, where to choose
> Their place of rest, and Providence their guide.
> They, hand in hand, with wandering steps and slow
> Through Eden took their solitary way.

In the end, regardless of who won on November 4, who would take the oath of office on January 20, 2009, this country had moved somewhere, thanks to John and Cindy McCain, Hillary and Bill Clinton, and Barack and Michelle Obama (and yes, Sarah Palin and Joe Biden). The steps may have been both wandering and slow (and sometimes accompanied by bitter and nasty rhetoric and/or tasteless, infuriating imagery), but changes had undeniably been made. People had moved—at least a short distance—out of their comfort zones. Will these changes ultimately lead people to let go of fears and away from divisions? Only time will tell. (So far, we're clearly not there yet. As Milton said, "Wandering steps and slow . . .")

CHAPTER 9

A New Landscape

New Players, New Tools, New Conversations

So maybe the *Paradise Lost* analogy is just a wee bit hyperbolic. But the fact is, like the world in which Adam and Eve found themselves after their expulsion from Eden, the 2008 election ushered in an entirely new landscape.

There were the obvious changes that have already been stated: the fact that, for the first time, a woman and a black man were among the country's top three choices to lead its citizens through the next, undeniably tricky phase of its history. With two wars being fought overseas, a third war being waged against terrorism, and an economy teetering on the brink of disaster, the choice of who would be the next—and best—leader was of no small significance. Nor was it insignificant that two of the three finalists for the job represented interest groups that had never before appeared in such a high-profile way on the national stage.

Then there were also the changes that, though perhaps less obvious, had the capacity to alter the future almost as much as the new profiles of the would-be presidents.

First among those is the way the Obama campaign attracted, connected with, and organized its supporters (and how it collected the great bulk of its money). If Howard Dean is credited with introducing the Internet to the political campaign, Barack Obama will be credited with revolutionizing the one through the use of the other. Or, to quote Joe

Trippi, the web expert behind Dean's 2004 campaign, "We were like the Wright brothers." The Obama campaign "skipped Boeing, Mercury, Gemini—they're Apollo 11, only four years later," he said.[1]

From social networking innovations that allowed supporters to organize and communicate, to fund-raising vehicles that allowed the campaign to raise record amounts of money from a wide variety of people, including thousands of small, first-time donors, the campaign's use of the Internet transformed the way elections have been—and no doubt will be—run.

Because I'm on the My.BarackObama.com list, I received an e-mail from the campaign in mid-July that read, in part:

Elizabeth—

We have some big news to share with you.

Because of your generosity and commitment we're reporting to the press today that this campaign is in a very strong financial position.

In the month of June, supporters like you helped raise $52 million.

But more impressive than that number is how you did it. Hundreds of thousands of ordinary people contributed to building our campaign for change. Many were first-time donors, giving only what they could afford—and the average gift was just $68.

Fifty-two million dollars from donors whose average gift was just $68! How do you do that? Just read on. . . .

As one might expect, the great news about the $52 million is accompanied by a second message, which came in the form of a bit more background information followed by an "ask." Sent from Obama's campaign manager David Plouffe, the e-mail talked about the remarkable resources at John McCain's and the Republican National Committee's disposal. It claimed that neither the Obama campaign nor the Democratic National Committee accepts donations from Washington lobbyists and special interest PACs, but that "John McCain and the RNC have no such standards."

And then came the real point: "I know this isn't the first time we've asked you for money, and it won't be the last," the e-mail said. "Please give $250 now.... We can't do this without you."

As always, there was that attractive bright-red button that seemed to scream "Donate!"[2] (And the whole thing could be done online, securely, with a few clicks of the mouse and a credit card number.)

As any great marketing document will do, the e-mail was also tailored to include a personalized message ("Dear Elizabeth") and a personalized amount of requested money (I'm sure there were others who were asked for far more), not to mention the flattering message that, as an insider, I was being given this information before—or at least not after—the press was.

No doubt, untold numbers of people who received similar e-mails responded the way the campaign hoped they would.

So how did this come about? How was Barack Obama able to so effectively tap into the resources the Internet was capable of unleashing?

For one thing, as a man in his mid-forties, he had lived the Internet revolution and he had an idea about how it could be used. This was clearly an area where his relative youth was a plus, particularly when you think about John McCain's Luddite-like response when asked about whether he uses a PC or Mac. Remember? His answer was "Neither. I am an illiterate who has to rely on my wife...." McCain's response may have been both amusing and honest, but his campaign loses out if they don't know how to capture the social networking and fund-raising benefits available in the online world.

It was also Obama's good fortune that his message appealed to young and Internet-savvy supporters. One such supporter, Chris Hughes, one of four founders of Facebook, was such a believer that he left his job at the company to help the Obama campaign with its new media operations.[3]

By mid-summer, Hughes and his team had helped the Obama campaign raise nearly two million donations of under $200 each. It also helped organize supporters to come together, attend rallies (remember the campaign's e-mail about the Hartford rally?), listen to and share information (remember Michelle's e-mail about the will.i.am video?), and attract others to the cause. By mid-July, nearly one million members had signed up as members on My.BarackObama.com.[4]

Perhaps even more interesting, on June 17, Chris Hughes announced on his blog on the Obama website that more than one million supporters had signed up for Barack Obama on Facebook. As Hughes said in his blog, "The Obama page has by far more supporters than any other page—whether it's a politician, celebrity, or band—on all of Facebook."[5] And we wonder why Obama has attracted so much of the youth vote?

The tools Hughes and others set up were a "big part" of what enabled Obama to win enough votes to lay claim to the Democratic nomination, the candidate himself has said.[6]

Among the principles Hughes brought with him from Facebook was the rule: "Keep it real and keep it simple." These meshed well with Obama's own ideas: "One of my fundamental beliefs from my days as a community organizer is that real change comes from the bottom up," Obama told the *New York Times*. "And there's no more powerful tool for grass-roots organizing than the Internet."[7] (Again, visions of Rudy Giuliani sneering about Obama's community organizing days and Sarah Palin's mockery of the same subject come to mind.)

The Internet has also revolutionized the way information about a campaign is spread and reported. Andrew Rasiej, cofounder and publisher of TechPresident.com, told the *San Francisco Chronicle* that he believes the 2008 election would be a "watershed year in the evolution of the Internet." Partly this is due to the ability of everyday people to access vast amounts of political information online, and partly it is because media professionals are able to use the Internet to cover the campaigns.[8]

As Rasiej pointed out, "So many of the stories in print, on TV, and on the radio about the campaigns are originating online. In addition, 2008 was shaping up to be the year where voter-generated content primarily through video will play an even bigger role in changing the dynamics of the campaign and continue to erode the candidates' attempt to control their message."[9]

During the campaign, we saw the risks inherent in this new online world, as the Obama campaign struggled to deal with things like the GOP

YouTube ads that questioned Michelle's patriotism or the rumors circulating the Internet about "whitey" and/or Barack's alleged Muslim identity.

We also saw the way the campaign was able to use the Internet to forge its own counterattack against some of those pernicious rumors that threatened to squash the campaign's momentum the way the Swift Boat Veterans for Truth did for Kerry back in 2004. Although it is more difficult to monitor the success of something like FightTheSmears.com than it is a site whose purpose is something measurable like fund-raising or membership numbers, at least the campaign was able to combat the online rumor war with some e-weapons of its own.

One thing was clear: The Obama campaign appreciated what a difference the online world can make. So much so, in fact, that if elected, Barack Obama said he would hire a chief technology officer.[10]

A second fundamental shift came in the discussion of race—in the mere fact that race was being discussed at all, sometimes very, very loudly, and not simply swept under the rug. Remember how in her concession speech Hillary Clinton said that "women deserve equal respect along with equal pay," and that there "are no acceptable prejudices in the twenty-first century"? Remember that the *New York Times* took this to mean that she was saying some people still believe it is okay to be sexist but not racist?

Just as Hillary did with sexism, the Obama campaign seemed to have opened up a whole new discussion about race and prejudice, intentionally or not. Take the Barack and Michelle Obama *New Yorker* satire. On the front page of the Commentary section of the *Hartford Courant* the Sunday after the satirical cover was published, there were two opposing articles. One, by Gina Barreca, a professor of English and feminist theory at the University of Connecticut, ran with the headline, "A Childish Stunt that Only Shocks and Offends." The second, by Irene Papoulis, a writing teacher at Trinity College, bore the headline, "Cover Makes Us Squirm, But It Forces a Discussion."

Most people I spoke to looked at the question the way Barreca did, though I didn't find anyone else who used her particular analogy. In Barreca's words, "The *New Yorker* cover depicting Barack Obama as a

Muslim and his wife as some kind of armed black separatist was about as sophisticated a piece of satire as a penis drawn on a desk. . . . It is, on every level, one-dimensional."[11]

Papoulis, meanwhile, came at it in a more roundabout way. She wrote about seeing the cover for the first time and immediately experiencing feelings of outrage. She wrote about watching television pundits arguing the artwork's merits—or in almost every case, lack thereof. She described being stunned when one of the pundits—whose name she didn't catch—called it "brilliant, brilliant satire." As Papoulis wrote, "Whaaaaaaaaaaat?"

"The host, and the rest of the panel, condemned him. How could he be so wrong?" she wrote. She then went on with her day, but the pundit's view kept coming back to her. Mulling the topic over and over, she allowed herself to think, "But what if the cover works best solely because of the discussion it fosters? What if it is forcing people, whether dense or not, to confront their—our—usually unspoken attitudes about the Obamas? Do some of us see them as 'other'? If so, how?"

She went on to state that the cover "almost insists that you talk about it with someone, and all the public talking can make people shift their perceptions. The cover's satire invites us as a country to confront our secret biases, and to discuss them." There is something, she said, about art that can "work profoundly when it simultaneously makes us squirm and forces us to have a conversation."[12] The *New Yorker* cover most certainly did that. The presence of the Obamas did too.

Which is not to say there wasn't still a lot of work to be done. A New York Times–CBS News poll published on July 16, 2008, found that Americans were still "sharply divided by race" as the country headed into the election. (Ten years later, the need to do this work only feels more urgent.) According to the 2008 poll, nearly 60 percent of black respondents "said race relations were generally bad, compared with 34 percent of whites." In addition, some four in ten black respondents said "there has been no progress in recent years in eliminating racial discrimination" while "fewer than two in ten whites" said the same thing.[13]

And yet, at exactly the same time, CNN was running a series called "Black in America," which marked both the fortieth anniversary of the assassination of Reverend Dr. Martin Luther King and a year in which an African-American man rose to become a candidate for president.

"I think people are very interested in a conversation about race; part of it is Barack Obama, part of it is [Hurricane] Katrina," said Soledad O'Brien, the CNN anchor who reported the programs and who, with a white father and black mother, is biracial herself. "Especially among young blacks we interviewed who considered themselves leaders, they said it's time to take the reins and figure out where we go from here."[14]

The series was born out of a desire to show a broader view of the story of race in America. "We question ourselves; we look at the stories we are doing," Mark Nelson, vice president and senior executive producer for CNN Productions told the *New York Times*. "What's a more complex story in America than race?"[15]

Indeed, one of the biggest complexities in the story of race was exposed—however unintentionally—during an unguarded campaign moment that happened to be captured on television. When, during a break in an interview with Fox News, former presidential candidate Reverend Jesse Jackson made his now-famous comment about wanting to "cut [Obama's] nuts out," America was alerted to what some perceived as a rift between the new and the old guard in the African-American leadership. Reverend Jackson, who made his statement when he presumed the microphone had been turned off, was voicing a concern that Barack Obama had been "talking down" to black people. Essentially, the 1984 and 1988 presidential candidate seemed to object to comments Senator Obama had made in his Father's Day speech about black men needing to take responsibility for their children and the ability of faith-based initiatives to help address things like crumbling schools and high unemployment.[16] Where, some assumed Jackson was asking, was the government's responsibility to help address inequalities?

It is important to remember that both Barack Obama and Jesse Jackson are products of the same Chicago political world and that Jesse Jackson Jr. served as the national cochair of Obama's campaign. Michelle Obama and Santita Jackson are childhood friends, and Santita is Malia Obama's godmother.

When he realized his words had been recorded, Jackson issued a public apology, as well as a private one to Obama, and said he was committed to supporting Obama's campaign in every way. Jesse Jackson Jr., meanwhile, issued a statement saying he was "deeply outraged and disappointed in Reverened Jackson's reckless statement." He went on to say, "Reverend Jackson is my dad and I'll always love him." Many attributed Jackson's comments and any perceived rift to a generational divide, although Jackson himself said that claim was nonsense. "This is not an old-vs.-young showdown," he told the *Washington Post*. "That's trivial."[17] Sheryll Cashin, a Georgetown University law professor who writes about race, told Kevin Merida of the *Post* that Jackson's comments "made me wonder if there was some personal jealousy," adding that "it must be hard for a generation of black men who came up in an era when nothing was easy to see this young man rise, almost effortlessly."[18]

Others pointed out that Obama wouldn't be where he is without the influence of Jackson and the many other African-American leaders who came before him in the struggle for civil rights. As Jackson himself said, citing such milestones as the school desegregation ruling and the Voting Rights Act and reiterating his pride and excitement, Senator Obama is "running the last lap of a 54-year tag team race."[19]

"Man, there's excitement to see this in my lifetime. . . . If you're part of a team, whoever scores a touchdown, the victory goes to the team," he said.[20]

Donna Brazile, who was Jackson's field director in 1984 and later Al Gore's campaign manager, also pointed out what an integral part of the team Reverend Jackson was, unguarded comments or not. "He made it possible not just for blacks to sit at the black desk, but to sit at every desk," she told the *Post*. "He is my political father."[21]

In addition to the discussion about race and "political fathers" that emerged during the election, people were also talking about Michelle Obama and how she figures into the storyline of African-American women.

In an article titled "Black. Female. Accomplished. Attacked." that appeared in the *Washington Post*, Sophia A. Nelson wrote that there was nothing new about the *New Yorker*'s caricature of Michelle Obama as a gun-toting radical. The mischaracterization of Michelle Obama "hit the rawest of nerves," but it was not a surprise. "Welcome to our world," wrote Nelson, a corporate lawyer who is president of IASK, Inc., an organization for African-American professional women, about the cover, which appeared as she and friends gathered in Washington for the 100th anniversary of the Alpha Kappa Alpha sorority, the first Greek-lettered sorority established by African-American women.[22]

"We've watched with a mixture of pride and trepidation as the wife of the first serious African-American presidential contender has weathered recent campaign travails," she wrote. "Being called unpatriotic for a single offhand remark, dubbed a radical because of something she wrote more than 20 years ago and plastered with the crowning stereotype: 'angry black woman.' And then being forced to undergo a politically mandated 'makeover' to soften her image and make her more palatable to mainstream America."[23]

But what Michelle Obama has gone through is "nothing new to professional African-American women. We endure this type of labeling all the time," she wrote, describing some of the stereotypes of African-American women—"ignorant and foolish servants such as Prissy from *Gone with the Wind*" or the "ever-smiling housekeepers, workhorses who never tire, like the popular figure of Aunt Jemima." There are also the "aggressive, violent, and often grossly obese" women from movies like *Norbit* and *Big Momma's House*.[24]

She talked about all that black professional women have accomplished, and yet the fact that they are somehow "invisible." She mentioned statistics that show that 70 percent of black professional women were unmarried and that black women were five times more likely than white women to be single at the age of forty.

What she really hoped, she wrote, is that Michelle Obama will "defy the negative stereotypes about us" and show all that a strong professional black woman can be. Nelson finished her piece by quoting a friend, whom she described as a married professional mother of three. As her friend wrote to her recently: "I think one of the most interesting things about Michelle Obama is that what she and her husband are doing is pretty *revolutionary* these days—and I don't mean running for president. For a black man and woman in the U.S. to be happily married, with children, and working as partners to build a life—let alone a life of service to others—all while rearing their children together is downright revolutionary."[25]

As Nelson said at the time, "Our hope is that if Michelle Obama becomes First Lady, the revolution will come to us at last."[26]

Talking about real or perceived rifts in the world of African-American political leaders, talking about the realities of being a professional African-American woman and the need for change, a CNN program focusing on what it means to be "Black in America"—these open, frank discussions represented something new. And as Sheryll Cashin, the Georgetown law professor said, the African-American community should just keep them coming.

"The black community needs more than ever for a self-reflection, places where we can talk seriously about our own responsibility to our children and the values we want for our children," Cashin said. "We don't have enough places where we can be brutally honest about how we parent or why it is that so few of us are married."[27]

Do these perceived changes within the black community mean there will be changes in the community at large?

I do think of the telephone conversation I had with Louise Ambler Osborn, who had been in Michelle's class at Princeton but who—like all the other white classmates I spoke to—hadn't known her.

"What I see in my kids is that they're definitely in a better place, definitely more open-minded and have had a lot more experiences growing up than I ever did," Louise said. "Hopefully the new generation coming up is more comfortable and clued in as much as anything."[28]

My thoughts turn again to the little girl Michelle Obama talked about during her primary campaign speeches, that little girl in the South Carolina hair salon who told Michelle that, if her husband is elected president, "it means I can imagine anything for myself."

I have my own story.

As I was in the midst of writing this book, I had to pack up my bags—and my rough draft—one weekend and drive with my fifteen-year-old daughter to a two-day soccer tournament in another state. This tournament was basically a college showcase, an event to give college coaches a chance to identify potential talent.

As we tend to do for some of these tournaments that are farther away, we carpooled with another player and her mother. Like Barack Obama, this girl has a father who is black and a mother who is white. Her family, too, had been following the election closely and had, we discovered, been at the same Obama rally we had attended in Hartford in January.

Because my deadline was fast approaching, the Obamas were much on my mind during the tournament. And so when, just before one of the girls' first games, my daughter and her friend said they needed to hear some "pump-me-up music"—and when upstate New York radio failed to provide any songs that fit the bill—I suggested I read a paragraph from the manuscript I had sitting in front of me waiting to be edited. There was a quote from Michelle Obama that I thought might have the same effect as some loud, thumping music.

I opened it up to near the end of Chapter One, where Michelle talks about what, in our house, we have come to call "the table quote." You know, the one about ignoring the naysayers and simply making it happen.

"We are confronted with doubters," I read, trying to put emphasis in all the places I imagined Michelle would have. "People who tell us what we can't do. You're not ready. You're not good enough. You're not smart enough. You're too tall.

"Each and every one of you here has heard and felt those ceilings, somebody pushing you down, defining your limitations, who are you? You know damn well what you are capable of doing," I read, trying to increase the volume and cadence to reach a sort of crescendo toward the end.

"This election is just as much about that as it is about change because the truth is there are millions of shining lights just like me all over the country. Kids living in shadows, being told by their own communities what they can and cannot do. This is an opportunity for all of us to send a different message to those shining lights.

"You know, every time somebody told me, 'No, you can't do that,' I pushed past their doubts and I took my seat at the table!"

I exhaled, put down the manuscript, and looked up at the girls, anxious to see their inspired faces, sure that the quote would work just as well as any old pump-me-up song. My daughter, who as a second child came out of the womb ready to take on her older brother, if not the world, totally got it. A child who is, by nature if not by birth order, absolutely full of fight, she emerged from the car ready to knock over the next defender who came her way. (One of the fathers on the team nicknamed her "the wrecker" during the tournament.)

My daughter's friend, who is an only child and an absolutely beautiful soccer player (not to mention a beautiful girl), looked completely sick to her stomach. "That made me nervous," she said, her voice quavering. "It's too intense." Before the next game she asked me to please not read it again.

At the time, I was puzzled that she found Michelle's words too intense. To me it was the best pep talk ever. But then I thought about what those words could mean to a young girl of African-American heritage, the only girl of African-American heritage on the soccer team, one of the few at the tournament, a minority in her Connecticut town. "We are confronted with doubters. People who tell us what we can't do. You're not ready. You're not good enough. You're not smart enough. You're too tall. Each and every one of you here has heard and felt those ceilings, somebody pushing you down, defining your limitations, who are you?"

I started to get it. What if you really had heard those things—or thought perhaps you were hearing those things—all your life? What if it wasn't just in the context of being your brother's younger sister? What if you knew that, even if you weren't the recipient of those particular messages on a regular basis, people just like you, throughout history, had been? What kind of load would that be to carry?

Off the girls went to the game. The whistle blew and the action started. My daughter and her friend were both playing together up front. They passed, ran with the ball, passed again, took a few shots on goal. My daughter's friend got called for a foul after what looked to the parents on the sidelines like a clean slide tackle, and she was issued a verbal warning by the referee. (My daughter is usually the one who is issued the warnings.)

Sometimes a warning will keep a player, particularly one who is less assertive than my daughter, from trying a move again. Not my daughter's friend, not this time. She found another opportunity and performed a beautiful slide tackle, kicking the ball away from an opponent. No call. Our girls scored.

Coaches with clipboards began to appear at the field. At this game, and then the next, and the next. My daughter's friend scored and had several assists. She played absolutely brilliantly, a bright shining light in every way.

When we got home, we learned that she had received phone calls or e-mails from at least five college coaches.

I wish I could tell her—and that she would believe me when I did—that she really can do anything she chooses.

Instead, at the risk of being both too intense and repetitive, I give her the words of Michelle Obama:

"You take your seat at the table!"

Chapter 10

Michelle Obama Everywhere

A View of the Election in Early August 2008

It had been a week since I handed in my initial draft, and Michelle Obama appeared to be everywhere—on television, in the newspapers, on magazine covers, in every conversation. As one political blog post said, it's "All Michelle Obama, All the Time."[1] Which made it very hard to put this thing to bed.

The day before my first draft was due to my editor, I received an e-mail from Michelle Obama via info@barackobama.com:

Elizabeth—

Barack likes to tell a story about the two of us standing backstage before his speech at the 2004 Democratic Convention. The way he tells it, he was too busy in the days before the convention to feel any pressure—but about an hour before the speech, I could tell he was getting a little nervous.

To break the tension, right before he went out on stage I leaned in close and said, "Just don't screw it up, buddy."

We laughed. And then Barack brought the house down.[2]

Michelle goes on to talk about the much bigger house that her husband would be speaking before a few weeks later, when, during the 2008 Democratic Convention, "more than 75,000 people will be in Denver to be part of this important moment." She talks about what an opportunity it will be to attend the event and, of course, asks for a donation, which would make the donor eligible for a drawing to be one of ten people chosen to go backstage with Barack at the convention.[3]

An interesting technique for raising money, but not what interested me about the e-mail. What interested me—yet again—was Michelle's voice, her singular honest, down-to-earth voice. "Just don't screw it up, buddy."

Around the time that e-mail arrived in my inbox, I accompanied my daughter, one of her friends, and her friend's mother to Toad's Place, the legendary club in New Haven where everyone from the Rolling Stones to Bob Dylan, Bruce Springsteen, and U2 has performed, so the girls could hear the hip-hop artist Nas. To be honest, when my daughter first broached the subject, I wasn't sure who Nas was and I was inclined to say no to the concert idea. But then I read about the rapper—who happened to be called Nas—who had joined a protest against Fox News on behalf of Michelle Obama. I figured this meant my daughter had to go, and I just had to be her chaperone.

As it turned out, Nas is so popular that the concert was totally sold out and we were unable to purchase tickets at the door. For what seemed like hours we stood outside, hoping that maybe we could buy a ticket if there were no-shows. No dice. The line snaked out the door and around the block. Hundreds of people slowly streamed in.

Still, we had come this far, so we decided to wait on the sidewalk with a bunch of Nas groupies on the off-chance that the artist would give us a word before going in to perform. We waited a long time. Sometime after midnight the famous rapper appeared in a big, fancy coach bus with his name painted on the side. We tried to catch his attention as he entered the club, but a phalanx of security people and fans surrounded him and he was ushered right in. No quote about Michelle Obama or Fox. Nothing real to show for our efforts.

And yet it wasn't a totally wasted evening. While waiting for hours with this multi-age, multiracial crowd, we spoke to some of the others in the patient throng. There was an older man who asked me about my notebook and pen (I told him I was waiting to see Nas because I was writing about Michelle Obama). We spoke about the election. I asked him if he was a fan. I'm not sure if he thought I meant a fan of Barack Obama or Nas, but it didn't really matter. "The only person whose autograph I'd ever seek is Nelson Mandela," he said.

We met a young man from a magazine called *Oneself.* Produced in Hartford, the magazine's tagline was "One World, One Life, Oneself." In its literature, the magazine featured this quote: "Today's world is changing. It is driven by the undeniable culture of hip hop and the people who live it." The man we met, who was there to try to photograph Nas, told us he writes a lot of self-help articles. According to the magazine's website, its features have included: "Build Oneself," "Tycoon Tips," "Each One Teach One," "Local Reviews," "Career Savvy," and "Booked Market."

The friends we had come with—who are, in fact, the soccer-playing pal and her mother I wrote about earlier—are Nas aficionados. They told us about their favorite Nas song, "I Can." Its lyrics tell the listener to study hard and believe in yourself, and work to change the world. In the Nas lyrics, we heard echoes of Michelle Obama. "Take your seat at the table!" Michelle Obama's singular voice.

A few days later I handed in my first draft (sans this chapter and a chapter on the election results). As fate would have it, after the due date I kept meeting people who were friends and/or acquaintances of Michelle Obama. If I could distill those conversations into one sentence, it would be this: "Michelle Robinson Obama is the most honest, down-to-earth, intelligent, hardworking, *funny* woman you will ever meet."

"Just don't screw it up, buddy." Her singular voice.

The Sunday after I handed in my draft, I opened the *New York Times* to see Maureen Dowd's column, "Mr. Darcy Comes Calling" in The Week in Review. The headline might not mean much to many readers, but I am a *Pride and Prejudice* nut—one of those women who can practically recite whole paragraphs from Jane Austen's famous comedy of manners, in part because I've read it so many times and in part because I have watched the BBC version, all five hours of it, at least twenty times.

Needless to say, I dove right into the Dowd column. If I could paraphrase it, "Mr. Darcy Comes Calling" rested on a couple of ideas and interpretations. First, Barack Obama is a latter-day Fitzwilliam Darcy, the male protagonist of *Pride and Prejudice*. Second, Elizabeth Bennett, the vivacious, outspoken female protagonist Darcy woos and wins during the course of the novel, represents America.

On the first note, I got where Dowd was going. Quoting Austen, Dowd writes that Obama, like Darcy, can draw "the attention of the room by his fine, tall person, handsome features, noble mien." Got it. A real connection.

Dowd went on to present Austen's description of Darcy on the first evening we meet him. "He was looked at with great admiration for about half the evening, till his manners gave a disgust which turned the tide of his popularity; for he was discovered to be proud, to be above his company, and above being pleased," Dowd wrote, quoting Austen.

"The master of Pemberley 'had yet to learn to be laughed at,'" she wrote, drawing a parallel to Obama, "and this sometimes caused a 'deeper shade of hauteur' to 'overspread his features.'"[4]

As evidence of Obama's "hauteur," Dowd pointed to things like Obama's comment during the New Hampshire debates when he said to Hillary Clinton, "You're likeable enough, Hillary." (I remember the line, and I also remember the way his mouth tightened as he said it; he did seem to be battling a feeling that he was "above being pleased.") Dowd also pointed to the note Senator Obama left on the Western Wall in Jerusalem, in which he reportedly wrote a plea to the Lord to "help me guard against pride."

Would Darcy have done the same? Not, I would argue, until *after* he had met and won his Elizabeth Bennett.

Which gets me to my point. I don't think, as Dowd asserted, that the American voters represent Elizabeth Bennett, Austen's vivacious heroine who teaches Darcy to laugh at himself, who, in essence, brings him down to earth.

In my opinion, if anyone represents Elizabeth Bennett it is, without question, Michelle Obama. When Darcy meets Elizabeth at the beginning of Austen's beloved novel, he at first dismisses her until he begins to notice how her face "was rendered uncommonly intelligent by the beautiful expression of her dark eyes." (Remember the young summer associate's description of his Sidley & Austin mentor's eyes?)

Darcy also makes note of Elizabeth's manners, which "were not those of the fashionable world," but he was "caught by their easy playfulness." (Is anyone more playful than Michelle? Remember the socks? The *Access Hollywood* interview? Remember Obama's response—laughter and an easy self-deprecating humor all his own?) Despite the difference in their social status—Darcy is the wealthy owner of Pemberley, while Elizabeth is one of five daughters of a country gentleman whose property is entailed away—Darcy spends the bulk of the novel attempting to win his bride. In the process, they both learn a thing or two: Darcy about humility, Elizabeth about not prejudging people.

Without going into the entire comedy of manners with all of its twists and turns, subplots and minor characters, I would argue that—if we want to draw parallels—Barack Obama represents the post-courtship Darcy and that Michelle is the post-courtship Elizabeth.

"Now be sincere," Elizabeth says to Darcy at the end of the novel, when the two are about to be married, "did you admire me for my impertinence?"

"For the liveliness of your mind, I did," her intended responds.

Remember: "To break the tension, right before he went out on stage I leaned in close and said, 'Just don't screw it up, buddy.' We laughed. And then Barack brought the house down."

The same morning that I opened the *Times* to find Dowd's column, which received so many responses online that the newspaper stopped accepting them (and which several friends and family members felt compelled to send my way), I delivered fifteen pounds of coffee to people I had dined with the night before.

Some neighbors had invited me to join a group of friends who were visiting from New York. Among my fellow diners that night were several hard-core Obama supporters. Over dinner, I told them about a blend of coffee one of our local farms was producing in honor of the election.

I explained that I learned about the coffee during our town's little Fourth of July parade, when people manning a float from Ashlawn Farm threw out the requisite candy to spectators as well as some small shiny silver packets. The packet that came flying our way was a tiny container of coffee. Its label read: "Obama Blend. A sweet, balanced blend of dark and light roasted coffees from Kenya, Java, and the Americas. Try it for a change." The label featured a photograph of a pensive-looking Barack Obama with a red, white, and blue background.

The farm was also producing American Hero Coffee. Featuring a photo of Obama's presidential opponent John McCain, the label for that blend says: "A light-roasted, highly caffeinated coffee. This edgy, strong, and reliable single origin is grown in the hills of Vietnam."

The guests at the dinner placed orders for at least fifteen bags of Obama Blend, so I dutifully went off in pursuit. Carol Adams, who roasts the coffee, got up early to package my order. Carol told me that they had come up with the idea for Obama Blend because "it seemed like his history and his background lended itself so much to a coffee blend." So far, she said the Obama blend had been outselling the American Hero Coffee, by quite a bit. "If this were a poll, [Obama] would be winning by 90 percent," she said. (To check out the coffee, go to FarmCoffee.com.)

At my friends' house, where several of the guests were gathered that Sunday morning, I made my delivery and they proceeded to brew some Obama Blend. It was sweet, but also very strong. One of the guests, an octogenarian African-American woman who, when told about the book I had just written, said, "Oh, the wifey," slowly slipped her Obama Blend. We had had a conversation about what her life was like as an African-American professional woman raising children in New York. She talked about her son and daughter—now extraordinarily successful adults—and how her son recently told her he is who he is because of his mother. "I couldn't believe it," she said. "Because of me? I just always told them they could do whatever they wanted to do."

"Take your seat at the table." Echoes of Michelle Obama's singular voice.

The next week Michelle Obama really seemed to be everywhere, and not just figuratively. She was interviewed by Robin Roberts on ABC's *Good Morning America*, and later appeared on *Nightline*. We learned that in addition to appearing—via an impersonation by supermodel Tyra Banks—in the September issue of *Harper's Bazaar*, Michelle Obama herself was slated to appear on the covers of *Ebony*, *Essence*, and *Ladies' Home Journal* (alongside her husband in the latter).

A blog called "Michelle Obama: Cover Girl, Cover Girl, Cover Girl" presented a preview of the *Ladies' Home Journal* article.

"Michelle is one of the smartest people I know," Barack Obama says in the article, answering a question about Michelle's plans, should he become president. (Remember Darcy admiring the "liveliness" of Elizabeth's mind?) "She is my chief counsel and adviser. I would never make big decisions without asking her opinion."[5]

The would-be president then goes on to say, "My sense is—and I'll let her speak for herself here—that she'd probably be more interested in having a set of projects that were driven by her interests and her desires, as opposed to me handing her some sort of portfolio, and saying, 'Here, do this.'"[6]

His wife concurs. "There are tons of issues that I care deeply about. But the notion of sitting around the table with a set of policy advisers— no offense—makes me yawn," she says, frank as ever.

"I like creating stuff. I'd love to be working with young people. I'd love to be having more conversations with military spouses. I've learned not to let other people push you into something that fundamentally isn't you."[7]

In the August 7 interview with Robin Roberts, Michelle touched on a lot of themes, from life in the public eye to subjects that interest her. The interview ended on a typical Michelle note.

"Despite the whirlwind days of the campaign and the media frenzy that ensues, she still remains grounded," Roberts said.

To which Michelle responded, attempting to encapsulate herself: "I am Michelle Obama. I live in Chicago. I'm married to this guy Barack. That's about it. That's about how I see myself."[8]

Simple as that. No silver spoons. Down-to-earth. Witty. Honest. One-of-a-kind.

CHAPTER 11

The Home Stretch

A Sprint to the Finish

LATE AUGUST AND EARLY SEPTEMBER 2008 BROUGHT THE CONVEN-
tions, and for a while it seemed as though America might actually be in
for a journey along the high road, with the two parties energized behind
candidates who offered change from an increasingly dismal status quo.
Barack Obama symbolized change by his very presence at the top of the
Democratic ticket—as Roger Cohen wrote in a *New York Times* op-ed
piece titled "American Stories," Obama's "very identity represents an act of
reconciliation"—while John McCain showed that he fit his maverick billing by doing something few had expected the conservative establishment
to do any time soon: invite a woman to join him as his running mate.[1]

Michelle Obama set the tone for the Democratic Convention,
delivering a prime-time speech to seventeen million viewers in which
she showed how—in the campaign's words—she was "one of us." She
uttered many memorable lines during her twenty-minute speech, but
she expressed the one message she needed to get across in no uncertain
terms: "That is why I love this country."

Michelle was radiant that night, eloquent, warm, and elegant in a
form-fitting green dress, as she spoke about her parents and brother,
about how both she and her husband were the embodiment of the
American Dream, about the men and women who paved the way for her
husband's path to the White House, about the "thread that connects our
hearts"—and there was absolutely no shred of bitterness.

Toward the end of her speech she spoke about herself and Barack as parents and the way their hopes and dreams for their own daughters mirror the hopes and dreams all parents have for their children. At night, as she tucks her daughters into bed, Michelle said she thinks "about how one day, they'll have families of their own. And one day, they—and your sons and daughters—will tell their own children about what we did together in this election. They'll tell them how this time, we listened to our hopes instead of our fears. How this time, we decided to stop doubting and start dreaming. How this time, in this great country—where a girl from the South Side of Chicago can go to college and law school, and the son of a single mother from Hawaii can go all the way to the White House—we committed ourselves to building the world as it should be."[2]

The accolades came flying in. As Obama chief strategist David Axelrod said, "Things changed instantly when she had the platform to really introduce herself."[3] On Fox News, Juan Williams, who has been critical of the Obamas, called Michelle's speech "breathtaking." On CNN, David Gergen said that Michelle "rescued the night—the Democrats should be enormously grateful to Michelle Obama." The verdict from Arianna Huffington of *The Huffington Post*? "A home run ... emotional, heartfelt, and very authentic."

Byron York, the White House correspondent for the conservative *National Review*, seemed less convinced by the "authenticity" of her message, although he apparently believed Michelle had accomplished her mission. "So here in Denver, Mrs. Obama had a job to do," he wrote. "It wasn't just to introduce Americans to the Obama family or show another side of her husband's personality. It was to rehabilitate herself, to take the edge of anger and resentment from her public pronouncements and embrace a wholesome, country-loving, American Dream-living image. And that's what her speech at the convention was about."[4]

Michelle wasn't necessarily saying anything different—her message had always been about the American Dream and what, together and through hard work, Americans can accomplish—but she had perfected her delivery. I thought back to what she had said in June on *The View*—that she was taking some cues from First Lady Laura Bush, that "there's a reason why people like her. It's because she doesn't ... fuel the fire."

Of course many other memorable speeches followed, including powerful performances by both Clintons, vice presidential candidate Joe Biden, and the speech by Senator Obama himself, delivered to an audience of more than seventy-five thousand, forty-five years to the day after the Reverend Dr. Martin Luther King Jr. shared "I Have a Dream."

And then, the day after the Democratic Convention concluded, Senator McCain introduced the world to his surprise running mate, the previously little-heard-of governor of Alaska, Sarah Palin. This woman who described herself as a hockey mom brought a whole new tone to the arena. Gone were the fake Greek columns and the lofty rhetoric. Instead, we began to hear about the two Joes (Sixpack and Plumber), pit bulls, and lipstick. We heard sarcastic lines about community organizers and darker ones about people who "pal around with terrorists," lots of "You betchas," and "Darn rights!" and "Drill, baby, drills!"

As the economy began to tank, the rhetoric got edgier and the sentiment among the crowds at rallies grew more heated. There were the shouts of "Terrorist!" "Off with his head!" and "Kill him!" Suddenly the stakes felt very high. Suddenly it all threatened to reach a boiling point.

The debates added to the sense that things were reaching a crescendo, particularly the "Town Hall" debate in early October, when Senator McCain couldn't seem to sit still and appeared unwilling to make eye contact with or speak directly to his opponent, referring to him as "That one."

When the debate was over, the wives joined their husbands on stage. Both Obamas milled about, shaking hands and talking with people in the audience; the McCains, by contrast, left abruptly after Senator McCain had shaken a few hands (his wife stood behind him, hands clenched behind her back).

"McCain leaving right afterward was pretty shocking to me—even some of the big McCain fans among us were really surprised that he did that," Ingrid Jackson, an independent in the audience, told the *New York Times*. "I thought the Obamas came off like real people much more in the end."[5]

Meanwhile, the campaigns were spewing out ads that were increasingly negative, the stock market was fluctuating wildly even after the government had agreed to the largest bailout in history, and the general atmosphere felt utterly combustible.

Tuning into NPR's *Talk of the Nation* one afternoon, I heard a caller named Susie say she was disturbed by the negative tone of the campaigns and the state of the rhetoric she had observed at political rallies and, presumably, in conversations all around her. "We need to learn how to behave better," she said.[6]

Perhaps if both sides had exuded the same degree of intensity, things really would have boiled over. But through it all, Senator Obama remained unruffled. As *New York Times* columnist David Brooks, a conservative, wrote, "We've been watching Barack Obama for two years now, and in all that time there hasn't been a moment in which he has publicly lost his self-control. This has been a period of tumult, combat, exhaustion, and crisis. And yet there hasn't been a moment when he has displayed rage, resentment, fear, anxiety, bitterness, tears, ecstasy, self-pity, or impulsiveness."[7]

The same could be said of his wife. Michelle Obama, previously excoriated for her "bitterness" and for seeming "angry," was likewise entirely composed during this combustible stretch, even in the face of people shouting threats about her husband. Asked during an interview on *Larry King Live* whether she had been offended when Senator McCain called her husband "That one," Michelle said "no."

"They don't care about the back and forth between the candidates," she said. "They want real answers about how we're going to fix this economy and get the health care benefits on track." (Listening to her, I was reminded of the criticism she drew months earlier when she said life had gotten worse for regular folks during the course of her lifetime. A month before the election, those comments were not looking so bitter. If anything, they looked both prescient and spot-on, particularly when compared to claims by others that the economy was "still fundamentally sound.")

When King asked her whether it made her mad to see clips of Governor Palin talking about how her husband "pal[s] around with terrorists who targeted their own country," Michelle said, "I don't watch it."

Asked what she thought of Governor Palin running for vice president given her family responsibilities, she again refused to pounce.

Instead, she praised the Alaska governor for taking on her juggling act, saying that that was one of the main reasons she and her husband had chosen to embark on this race: so that all women would be able to make the kinds of choices she and Sarah Palin have.[8]

Others weren't so generous. The liberal blogosphere was full of scathing pronouncements about what many saw as the hypocrisy inherent in the Republicans' acceptance of those choices when made by one of their own. In a roundtable discussion reported in *USA Today*, a woman who identified herself as Cynthia expressed it far less bluntly than did some of the blogs: "I just wonder how Obama would be treated if he had a teenage daughter and she was pregnant? Or how Michelle would be treated if she had a [child] with special needs and left him with nannies so she could go out on the trail? . . . . I think there is a huge double standard and people haven't asked those questions."[9]

Fortunately, humor is always an outlet, and in the final days—in addition to the rancor—there was no shortage of laughter. The same evening she appeared on *Larry King Live*, Michelle also made an appearance on Jon Stewart's *The Daily Show*. Michelle reiterated some of the comments she had made earlier with King, such as that she doesn't watch the GOP rallies where people in the crowds had begun to scream violent epithets about her husband. She told Stewart she had "stopped reading and watching a lot of stuff," leading him to quip, "So you're a lot like Sarah Palin?" "Perhaps," Michelle responded as the audience laughed.

She also admitted that it has been a long and grueling campaign (she spent the last weeks of the election traveling relentlessly across the country, visiting primarily battleground states, and headlining dozens of events, many with military families), and said she sometimes welcomes nights off so she can just watch *The Dick Van Dyke Show*.[10] "It's been 20 months," she said, pointing to her cheek. "It brings a tear."[11]

Of course there were other moments of humor toward the end. Who could forget the roasts by Senators Obama and McCain during the Al Smith dinner or the long stream of hilarious *Saturday Night Live* skits? Maya Rudolph and Fred Armisen as Michelle and Barack Obama singing, "Our lead is solid, solid as Barack"? John McCain appearing alongside Tina Fey/Sarah Palin selling campaign memorabilia on QVC (with a guest appearance by wife Cindy as a perfect Carol Marol figure selling "McCain Fine Gold")? Sarah Palin as herself (appearing with Tina Fey-as-Sarah Palin) in a skit with Alec Baldwin? Pumping her arms in the air as *SNL*'s Amy Poehler rapped, "All the mavericks in the house put your hands up"? Governor Palin may not have won any points in the argument about whether she was prepared to be the president-in-waiting, but most who watched her on *SNL* that night (and there were some fourteen million of them) agreed that McCain's running mate was every bit as entertaining as she was game. As Alessandra Stanley of the *New York Times* wrote, "One thing everybody can agree on is that Gov. Sarah Palin is qualified—to someday host her own television show."[12]

Meanwhile, the early voting had begun, and the crowds lining up outside polling booths across the country were unprecedented. I heard one woman in Los Angeles describe on NPR how she had to wait in line for six hours before casting her vote, and she was happy to do so. Back in February, when Michelle made her famous "proud of America" statements, she explained that what she meant to convey was that she was excited that so many Americans were engaging in the political process. Watching the lines outside polling stations, we got it. As an American— regardless of political affiliation—it was hard to watch that footage and not feel moved by the notion that we each have a voice and that, this time, so many were choosing to use it.

In addition to the humor, the rancor, the nonstop campaigning, the polling, the early voting, and the angst about the economy, the final days of the campaign also brought the endorsements. The day after Palin made her *Saturday Night Live* debut, former secretary of state Colin Powell announced on NBC's *Meet the Press* that he planned to throw his support behind Senator Obama. Powell, a Republican and an African American who once considered a run for the White House himself, had previously donated to John McCain's campaign, and he admitted it was difficult for him to "disappoint Senator McCain in the way that I have this morning."[13]

But the retired Army general said he objected to some of the McCain campaign's tactics, particularly the one linking Senator Obama to William Ayers. Mostly, though, he said he had been moved by the force of character and intellect Obama had exhibited in the weeks and months leading up to the election, calling him a "transformational figure."

"I come to the conclusion that because of his ability to inspire, because of the inclusive nature of his campaign, because he is reaching out all across America, because of who he is and his rhetorical abilities . . . he has met the standard of being a successful president, being an exceptional president," Powell said. He predicted that an Obama victory would "not just electrify our country, it would electrify the world."[14]

On October 20, the *Los Angeles Times* endorsed Senator Obama, writing: "We may one day look back at this presidential campaign and wonder. We may marvel that Obama's critics called him an elitist, as if an Ivy League education were a source of embarrassment, and belittled his eloquence, as if a gift with words were suddenly a deficit. In fact, Obama is educated and eloquent, sober and exciting, steady and mature. He represents the nation as it is, and as it aspires to be."

On November 1, supermodel turned TV star Tyra Banks endorsed Obama—no great surprise, given her choice to pose as Michelle in *Harper's*—but endorsements also came from less expected quarters.

For the first time in its 161-year history, the *Chicago Tribune* endorsed a Democrat for president of the United States. "We are proud to add Barack Obama's name to Lincoln's in the list of people the *Tribune* has endorsed," the newspaper wrote. "It may have seemed audacious for Obama to start his campaign in Springfield invoking Lincoln. We think, given the opportunity to hold this nation's most powerful office, he will prove it wasn't so audacious after all."[15]

And then there was the British newsweekly the *Economist*. One afternoon in late October, as I retrieved the mail from our mailbox, I was struck by the plain, bold cover that greeted me. Showing a picture of a striding Barack Obama, head down, wearing a dark suit and red tie against a plain, white background, the cover read simply: "It's time."

On top of the grueling presidential race with all of its twists and turns, the Obamas also had to deal with the ups and downs of regular, old life. Ten days before the election, the Obama campaign announced that the candidate would take a few days off so he could fly to Hawaii to visit his gravely ill grandmother. Obama spokesman Robert Gibbs told reporters that the senator's eighty-six-year-old grandmother Madelyn Dunham "has become ill and in the last few weeks, her health has deteriorated to the point where her situation is very serious."[16]

Some questioned the wisdom of taking a break from the campaign during such a critical juncture, while others said it was a no-brainer. When a loved one is ill, you go. Senator Obama had made a different decision when his mother, Stanley Anne Dunham, died of ovarian cancer in 1995, a decision he came to regret deeply. He apparently was not willing to take that chance this time around.

Fortunately for the would-be president, he had a top-notch, wholly trusted stand-in. The campaign announced that in her husband's absence Michelle Obama would headline the scheduled events in the critical swing state of Ohio.

A week later, the Obamas again allowed regular, old life to intervene. On October 31, Senator Obama flew home to Chicago so he could help his daughters celebrate Halloween. Yet again, some said leaving the campaign trail even briefly would be foolhardy, but he ignored the naysayers and joined his girls for their holiday.

Not everyone was willing to let the Obamas celebrate like a normal family, though. As the candidate walked to a Halloween party with a costumed Sasha (she was dressed as a "corpse bride" while Malia was an "evil fairy," Michelle disclosed on the website Blogher.com), a swarm of photographers began clicking away. Obama asked them to back off, and when they refused, he and Sasha literally sprinted off down the sidewalk, Secret Service agents in pursuit, leaving the camera-laden photographers to sputter about the candidate's uncharacteristic "testiness."[17]

The family was together for the weekend, the girls joining their parents on stage in Cleveland, Ohio, for a rally with Bruce Springsteen. Before breaking into his classic "The Rising," the Boss delivered an inspiring introduction about America still being a "repository for people's hopes and dreams," and urging the audience to vote on Election Day.

Suddenly the skies opened and it began to rain—hard. But Mother Nature didn't deter the Obamas any more than the naysayers had. "Sunshine is on the way," the candidate insisted. "We've just got two more days of these clouds."

Sadly, the next day—election eve—brought a major cloud. Senator Obama learned that his beloved grandmother had lost her battle with cancer.

In her last appearance of the campaign, a tearful Michelle asked her audience in Littleton, Colorado, to say a prayer for the woman her husband called "Toot." "Thank her for raising Barack," Michelle said. "I think she did an amazing job."[18]

Senator Obama also choked back tears as he spoke to a crowd in Charlotte, North Carolina, explaining how his grandmother had inspired him through her hard work and sacrifice. "In just one more day we have the opportunity to honor all those quiet heroes all across America," he said. "We can bring change to America to make sure their work and their sacrifice is honored. That's what we're fighting for."[19]

CHAPTER 12

Crossing the Finish Line

The Triumph of Hope—November 4, 2008

DESPITE THE SAD NEWS OF THE DAY BEFORE, ELECTION DAY GOT OFF to an auspicious beginning for the Obamas. In Dixville Notch, New Hampshire, the twenty-one registered voters cast their ballots simultaneously just after midnight. A few minutes later, the results were announced: This minuscule New England town—which hadn't gone Democratic since 1958—voted 16–5 in favor of Barack Obama and Joe Biden over McCain-Palin.

The rest of the day went much the same way. Voter turnout was high, and despite long lines that kept people waiting for hours at polling stations across the country, there was a palpable excitement in the air, including at the school in the Hyde Park neighborhood of Chicago where the Obama family went to vote. After casting his ballot with a smiling Malia at his side, Senator Obama called to the waiting voters, "I voted!" The crowd erupted into a cheer.

The anticipation continued to build as polls started to close and when, around 11:00 p.m., it became clear that Senator Barack Obama had been elected the forty-fourth president of the United States, the world went wild. There was dancing in the streets in Harlem and Washington, DC, and Kisumu, Kenya, Obama's grandmother's hometown. There were shouts and screams from houses across the country, including ours.

I will never forget the sight of Jesse Jackson Sr. standing in the crowd in Chicago's Grant Park, tears streaming down his face, chewing the tip of his finger, as he watched the first African-American First Family take the stage and the first African-American president-elect address his nation.

I will never forget the unabashed affection the president-elect displayed as, with the whole world watching, he said to his beautiful family, "I would not be standing here without the unyielding support of my best friend for the last sixteen years, the rock of our family, the love of my life, the nation's next First Lady, Michelle Obama."

"Sasha and Malia," he went on, "I love you both more than you can imagine. And you have earned the new puppy that's coming with us to the White House."

I will never forget the almost somber expression on his face as he said, "If there is anyone out there who still doubts that America is a place where all things are possible, who still wonders if the dream of our founders is alive in our time, who still questions the power of our democracy, tonight is your answer."

I thought about the little girl Michelle had described months earlier—the ten-year-old in the beauty parlor who had told her that if her husband was elected president, it meant that she could imagine anything for herself. I thought of my daughter's soccer-playing friend and what an Obama victory would say to her about her absolute right to take her seat at the table. I thought of the twenty-year-old Michelle Robinson, who wondered in her college thesis if she would always feel like an outsider. I thought of the Michelle Obama who said she was really proud of her country for the first time because it seemed that hope was making a comeback.

The future is full of challenges. Or, as the president-elect said on Election Night, "The road ahead will be long. Our climb will be steep. We may not get there in one year or even in one term. But, America, I have never been more hopeful than I am tonight that we will get there. I promise you, we—as a people—will get there."

Back in January, when the primaries were just heating up, I received an e-mail from my high school principal, a man who later became the principal at my children's elementary school and then went on to another school. He wrote that, because of Barack Obama and his message of hope, he was excited in a way that he hadn't been since "the days of Jack, Bobby, and Martin."

In September, he called me out of the blue. He had retired and was spending most of his time volunteering for Obama. After we spoke, he sent me an e-mail with a link to a song. The subject line of the e-mail said, "Check out My American Prayer even if you're not religious." His e-mail read, "Any time I need a bit of hope and inspiration, I bring it up on my iMac."[1]

I clicked on the link. In an introduction to "My American Prayer" singer/songwriter Dave Stewart wrote that he had coauthored the original song in 2002 with U2's Bono. While recording a new version this year, its lyrics "seemed to take on a whole new resonance," he said.

"The song always contained one of my favorite passages from Dr. King, which was hauntingly delivered the night before he was assassinated," Stewart explained. In that final speech, Dr. King famously said, "Like anybody I would like to live a long life. Longevity has its place. But I'm not concerned about that now. I just want to do God's will. And He's allowed me to go up to the mountain. And I've looked over. And I've seen the Promised Land. I may not get there with you. But I want you to know tonight, that we, as a people, will get to the Promised Land."

(Again, Barack Obama on Election Night: "Our climb will be steep. We may not get there in one year or even in one term. But, America, I have never been more hopeful than I am tonight that we will get there. I promise you, we—as a people—will get there.")

Stewart writes that when he set out to make a video for the new version, it wasn't so much an endorsement for Barack Obama as it was a celebration of the people who had been moved to work together for change. "I wanted to honor all those millions of people, especially young people, who are, for the first time, feeling empowered to voice their beliefs."

Like the will.i.am video that Michelle Obama introduced me to with her e-mail, "My American Prayer" incorporates guest appearances from a large cast of characters—people like Forest Whitaker, Macy Gray, Cyndi Lauper, Barry Manilow, Joan Baez, Sergio Mendes, and Herbie Hancock.

It incorporates an array of American images, from immigrants arriving at Ellis Island to footage of the Obamas, and scenes of New Orleans in the aftermath of Hurricane Katrina. It ends with a simple graphic and four letters: an illustration of Obama's face followed by the word "Hope."

On November 4, 2008, hope did not just make a comeback. Hope won. And presumably hope—coupled with hard work—will carry us through to the next chapter.

CHAPTER 13

The First Lady's Accomplishments

Eight Years as Our Mom-in-Chief

IN LATE 2008, AS HER HUSBAND PREPARED TO ASSUME THE TITLE OF commander-in-chief, Michelle Obama raised some eyebrows when, looking toward her future as First Lady, she described her forthcoming role as "mom-in-chief." At the time, many observers assumed her self-described title meant that, as First Lady, she planned to spend the bulk of her time helping her daughters navigate their lives in the nation's capital, leaving public initiatives to others. After all, in her widely lauded speech at the 2008 Democratic National Convention, she had characterized herself as "a mom whose girls are at the heart of my heart and the center of my world—they're the first thing I think about when I wake up in the morning, and the last thing I think about when I go to bed at night."[1]

That mom-in-chief designation disappointed some observers, who had hoped to see this Princeton- and Harvard-educated lawyer use her immeasurable skills, experience, and education to influence policy and advocate for the common good. They needn't have worried. After all, the next sentence in her convention speech was this: "Their future [meaning Malia's and Sasha's]—and ALL our children's future—is my stake in this election."[2]

So how did her stake in the election unfold? As mom-in-chief, Michelle did initially focus on getting Malia and Sasha settled. She helped move them into the White House and let them decorate their new rooms. She enrolled them in their new school, Sidwell Friends, and invited their friends over for White House sleepovers. She and their father surprised the girls with a new play structure, the White House's first-ever play structure, featuring an array of swings, a climbing wall, a fort, and climbing ropes. And, with the help of Senator Ted Kennedy, she also saw to it that, as promised, her daughters got their White House dog, Bo.[3]

But even as she focused on getting her daughters settled, she also began working on behalf of all children. On March 20, 2009, the first day of spring and just two months after she and her family moved into their new home, she welcomed twenty-three fifth graders from Bancroft Elementary School in Washington, DC, to join her on the White House South Lawn. Together, the First Lady and the students used shovels, pitchforks, and wheelbarrows to break ground on what would become the White House Kitchen Garden.

Although the garden had its practical purpose—to provide fresh produce for White House inhabitants and visitors—it had another purpose as well. "As both a mother and a First Lady, I was alarmed by reports of skyrocketing childhood obesity rates and the dire consequences for our children's health," she wrote in her book, *American Grown: The Story of the White House Kitchen Garden and Gardens Across America*. "And I hoped this garden would help begin a conversation about this issue—a conversation about the food we eat, the lives we lead, and how all of that affects our children."[4]

The idea for the garden had actually begun to take shape months earlier, well before the election, as Michelle sat in her Chicago kitchen, musing with Sam Kass, her family's chef, about what her role might be, should her husband actually be elected president. Their conversation turned to the growing problem of childhood obesity, and Michelle started to envision a garden and how a movement could grow from there.[5]

The fifth graders who had joined her to dig the garden in March returned in April to plant it, all the while talking about healthy food and the value of eating fresh fruits and vegetables. And thus was born Michelle Obama's first major initiative, Let's Move! Officially launched on February 9, 2010, with the stated purpose of ending the epidemic of childhood obesity within a generation, the Let's Move! campaign encouraged children to be more physically active and their families to be more knowledgeable about nutrition. At the same time, it called upon companies to market healthier foods and schools to provide healthier choices to students.[6]

Sam Kass, who had moved to Washington to serve as assistant chef at the White House, became executive director of the Let's Move! campaign and the president's senior policy adviser for nutrition policy.

Let's Move! led to the creation of President Obama's Task Force on Childhood Obesity, for which her husband announced the First Lady's role in leading public awareness, an assignment she took to heart (and to the airwaves). Who will ever forget some of the cameo appearances she made to gain attention for Let's Move!? There was the "Uptown Funk" dance-off with Ellen DeGeneres and the *So You Think You Can Dance* crew to celebrate the fifth anniversary of Let's Move! There was the Let's Move! focus group she conducted with a group of children and comedian Will Ferrell and the absolutely hilarious *Evolution of Mom Dancing* scenes she performed with Jimmy Fallon to promote exercise. There were the appearances on shows like *Sesame Street*, where she joined Big Bird to discuss the importance of eating healthy food, and the PSA with members of the NBA Champion Miami Heat to discuss nutrition.[7]

Among the initiative's achievements were creating the Healthy, Hunger-Free Kids Act, which updated school nutrition standards and increased the number of children who could get school meals at reduced or no cost; modernizing the Food and Drug Administration's Nutrition Facts Label for packaged foods; and increasing access to fruits and vegetables through Salad Bars to Schools. Efforts were also made to increase opportunities for physical activity through such programs as Let's Move! Active Schools, which equipped schools with plans to create active learning environments; a partnership with the US Olympic Committee to provide free or low cost athletic programming; and an update of the President's Challenge Youth Fitness Test to promote active, healthy lifestyles rather than athletic performance and competition. Let's Move! Outside was created to encourage families to take advantage of our country's outdoor resources and federally managed lands. To support healthier lifestyles, the initiative engaged 225 corporate commitments and partnerships with the First Lady as chair of the nonprofit Partnership for a Healthier America. The campaign launched marketing campaigns encouraging Americans to consume more fruits and vegetables and to drink more water and extended its reach by encouraging child care centers to commit to improving the nutritional quality of snacks and meals, increasing opportunities for physical activity, and limiting screen time. The campaign even encouraged burgeoning chefs to create original, healthy, affordable recipes and then prepare and serve the food at Kids' "State Dinners" at the White House.[8]

During the official dedication of the White House Kitchen Garden on October 5, 2016, Mrs. Obama recited some impressive statistics. "Today, 81 million Americans woke up in a Let's Move! city, town, and county," she said. "Fifty million kids had access to healthier meals and snacks at school; 11 million kids attended a Let's Move! Active School where they can get 60 minutes of physical activity a day; 1.6 million kids attended a Let's Move! Child Care program, where they're eating 225 million healthy meals and snacks a year; 8.1 million people in underserved areas had somewhere to buy healthier food."[9]

Of course it remains to be seen how many of those statistics will hold in the face of a new administration with wildly different priorities. Already there have been discussions about rollbacks in key portions of the initiative, such as a relaxation of the Obama-era school lunch nutrition rules (in a statement posted on the USDA website, President Trump's agriculture secretary Sonny Perdue famously said "It doesn't do any good to serve nutritious meals if they wind up in the trash can").[10] But at least one element remains in place: the White House Kitchen Garden itself.

Part of that may be due to Michelle Obama's foresight. During the summer of 2016, a year and a half before she and her family would have to vacate their home of eight years, she engaged a team from the University of Virginia's School of Architecture to help design an outdoor gathering space for the White House Kitchen Garden. The ultimate design conveyed permanence, with stone and steel features, along with some beautiful wooden structures firmly cemented into the ground. Perhaps more important, the garden secured funding from the W. Atlee Burpee home gardening company and The Burpee Foundation to cover maintenance for at least seventeen years. The $2.5 million donation was contributed to the National Park Foundation for that purpose, ensuring that, for now anyway, the garden will stay in place—and keep growing—without having to dip into taxpayer money.[11]

The new First Lady, Melania Trump, showed initial willingness to continue the garden initiative, in spite of her husband's well-documented preference for fast food. During her first autumn in the White House, she donned a plaid flannel shirt and red gardening gloves and invited local students to join her as they harvested produce from the garden. "I'm a big believer in healthy eating, because it reflects on your mind and your body," she told the students. "I encourage you to continue to eat a lot of vegetables and fruits, so you grow up healthy and take care of yourself."[12]

In October 2016, during the official dedication of the White House Kitchen Garden, Mrs. Obama stood under the new arbor, made from wood sourced from the estates of Thomas Jefferson, James Madison, and James Monroe, and from the birthplace of Martin Luther King Jr.[13]

After thanking everyone who had joined her in the effort to create the garden and everything that followed it, the First Lady said the lessons they had learned are timeless:

> *This garden has taught us that if we have the courage to plant a seed, just be brave enough to plant it, then take care of it, water it, tend to it, invite friends to help us take care of it, weather the storms that inevitably come, if we have the courage to do that, we never know what might grow.*[14]

The garden—and the Let's Move! initiative it inspired—was just the first of many undertakings launched by this active mom-in-chief during her eight years in the White House, but it really stands as a metaphor for everything that followed. Plant those seeds, tend them, invite others to join in, weather the storms, and watch beautiful things grow.

Other major undertakings initiated and championed by this First Lady mom-in-chief included:

- The Joining Forces campaign, launched in 2011 by the First Lady and Dr. Jill Biden, the wife of Vice President Joe Biden, to support service members, veterans, and their families. Joining Forces engaged both the public and private sector to provide education, wellness, and employment opportunities to service members, veterans, and their families.

- The Reach Higher initiative, established in 2014, which encouraged young people to continue their education past high school, whether through professional training programs, community colleges, or four-year institutions.

- Let Girls Learn, an initiative the First Lady launched with President Obama in 2015 to help girls around the world go to and stay in school. As part of this effort, she called on all countries to help educate and empower young women and shared stories about the struggles of these young women, hoping to inspire students in the United States to commit to their own educations.[15]

Mrs. Obama also found other ways to help children learn and grow. During her first year as First Lady, she started a leadership and mentoring program for girls, pairing twenty Washington, DC, area high school girls with administration officials. Each month, the girls would come to the White House, meeting with their mentors and learning about their work. "I wanted [the students] to experience this notion that if you can walk [through] the doors of the White House once a month and sit down with the First Lady and her Chief of Staff and some other senior officials, and they're talking to you and you get used to hearing your voice in the space, then it becomes not a big deal," she said.[16]

Mrs. Obama made use of some of her connections within the arts community for another key initiative. The Turnaround Arts program, founded in 2011, utilizes the power of the arts to boost academic achievement and better engage students at struggling schools. Operating in various locations across the country, Turnaround Arts brings top-notch music, visual arts, dance, and theater to underperforming schools, engaging scores of artists—from Dave Matthews to Smokey Robinson, Yo-Yo Ma to Paula Abdul, Kerry Washington to Tim Robbins—to volunteer alongside students and teachers. Founded by the President's

Committee on the Arts and Humanities, the program is now being run by the Kennedy Center for the Performing Arts, so, like the garden, this initiative will continue to have a life even if other administrations fail to make it a priority.[17]

In addition to these and other undertakings, Mrs. Obama weighed in (or perhaps first dipped her toe and then began to wade in) on some of the thorniest issues of the day, particularly toward the end of her years as a White House resident. Having learned during the initial campaign that she might need to temper some of her comments, lest she attract that "angry black woman" or "bitter" label again, there were times when her voice was notably absent from certain conversations. For instance, when her husband delivered his beautiful, heartbreaking speech at the vigil for the victims of the Sandy Hook massacre on December 16, 2012, the First Lady was not in attendance. Why, some wondered, was she not by his side?

We may need to wait for *Becoming*, her long-awaited memoir, to learn the answer to that question, but one can only imagine that perhaps the emotions ran too deep after twenty-six people, most of them six-year-olds, were gunned down at a Connecticut elementary school. Although not personally present at the vigil, she did pen a letter to the Sandy Hook families in which she shared her grief and offered condolences at their unimaginable loss. She also hinted at something she perhaps couldn't express out loud at the time. "And I want you to know that this is just the beginning," she wrote in the letter published in the *Hartford Courant* four days after the vigil. "As my husband has said, in the coming weeks, he will use all the powers of his office to engage citizens from across the country to find ways to prevent tragedies like this one."[18]

She stepped into the discussion of gun violence more pointedly the following year in April 2013, when she delivered a speech during a fundraising event for a new $50 million public-private initiative to combat youth violence in Chicago. Noting that, at the time, her husband was working hard "to pass commonsense reforms to protect our children from gun violence," she expressed her firm support for the effort, saying unequivocally, "These reforms deserve a vote in Congress."

Mrs. Obama said she felt compelled to join the conversation after attending the funeral for Hadiya Pendleton, a fifteen-year-old majorette who had performed in her husband's second inauguration and was shot and killed just days later in a city park near her home in Chicago, not far from where Mrs. Obama grew up. "Hadiya Pendleton was me, and I was her," Mrs. Obama said in her speech, explaining that, like the First Lady, Hadiya was an honors student from the South Side of Chicago. "But I got to grow up and go to Princeton and Harvard Law School and have a career and a family, and the most blessed life I could ever imagine. And Hadiya—well, we know that story.

"We can't stop all the violence in the world," she continued. "But if there is even one thing we can do, even one step we can take to save another child or another parent from the grief that's visited families like Hadiya's . . . then don't we have an obligation to try?"[19]

Perhaps that question was a precursor to the even more concrete language she used in a tweet on February 21, 2018, a year and a month after relinquishing the First Lady title. In support of the students from Marjory Stoneman Douglas High School in Parkland, Florida, who were spearheading a massive gun reform campaign after losing seventeen classmates and teachers in yet another horrific school shooting, she wrote, "I'm in awe of the extraordinary students in Florida. Like every movement for progress in our history, gun reform will take unyielding courage and endurance. But @barackobama and I believe in you, we're proud of you, and we're behind you every step of the way."

Later, she and President Obama expressed the same sentiment in a handwritten letter they sent to the Parkland students. Dated March 10, 2018, the letter credited the students with helping to "awaken the conscience of the nation" while also challenging "decision makers to make the safety of our children the country's top priority." The former president and First Lady went on to say that throughout history, "young people like you have led the way in making America better. There may yet be setbacks; you may sometimes feel like progress is too slow in coming. But we have no doubt that you are going to make an enormous difference in the days and years to come, and we will be there for you." It was signed, simply, "Barack Obama" and "Michelle Obama."[20]

Another issue Mrs. Obama grew increasingly vocal about as the 2016 election drew to a close was gender equality and how we treat our women and girls. Several of her initiatives, such as Let Girls Learn and the mentoring program, had focused on allowing young women a seat at the table where, traditionally, they had not been welcome. As the race between Hillary Clinton and Donald Trump neared the final lap, and as news broke about the *Access Hollywood* video in which Donald Trump was recorded making offensive comments about women, Mrs. Obama also began speaking about the need to respect women and girls in the ways we act and speak. In a fiery speech to New Hampshire voters in October, she shared her feelings in no uncertain terms, although without mentioning Donald Trump by name. "The fact is that in this election we have a candidate for president of the United States who, over the course of his lifetime and the course of this campaign, has said things about women that are so shocking, so demeaning, that I simply will not repeat anything here today," she said. "And last week, we saw this candidate actually bragging about sexually assaulting women.

"This is not something we can ignore," she went on to say, telling voters that by electing Hillary Clinton they can repudiate not only that language but the notion that any members of our country are less worthy than others. "On November the 8th, we can show our children that this country is big enough to have a place for us all—men and women, folks of every background and walk of life—and that each of us is a precious part of this great American story."[21]

Of course, we all know that Hillary Clinton, in the end, did not win the election. But somewhere along the line—especially as news broke about other leading figures mistreating women—the Me Too movement gained traction. Started more than a decade earlier by social activist Tarana Burke, Me Too was suddenly everywhere, with women (and some men) across the country speaking and standing up and transgressors stepping down from their positions of power.

Another issue Mrs. Obama seemed to grow more expressive about over time, particularly during her husband's second term, was race. At first, she seemed to stay away from public discussions of race and racism, letting her husband handle some of the testier exchanges, such as the outcry after Henry Louis Gates, the Harvard professor, was arrested in July 2009 while trying to enter his own home, and the president said the police had "acted stupidly." Remember President Obama's beer summit?[22]

But as the end of their White House sojourn approached—and as the Black Lives Matter movement grew in response to shootings of black citizens, many by police officers—the First Lady began to talk about racism and its effect on Americans. During a commencement speech at Tuskegee University, a historically black university in Alabama, in May 2015, she talked to graduates about the grit and resilience that allowed previous generations of Tuskegee students to "soar past obstacles and outrages, past the threat of countryside lynchings, past the humiliation of Jim Crow, past the turmoil of the Civil Rights era." At the same time, she acknowledged that racism still exists and that, at times, she, too, feels its sting.

Recalling the *New Yorker* cover where she was depicted with the assault rifle and large Afro, she said, "Yeah, it was satire, but if I'm being really honest, it knocked me back a bit." Likewise, "the terrorist fist jab" comment bothered her, as did "Obama's baby mama." She found herself worrying about what her daughters would think if they heard what people were saying, but eventually she chose not to dwell on it. "I realized that if I wanted to keep my sanity and not let others define me, there was only one thing I could do—and that was to have faith in God's plan for me," she said. "I had to ignore all of the noise and be true to myself."[23]

A year later, speaking at a graduation ceremony at Jackson State University, a historically black Mississippi school, she revisited the subject. Recalling how difficult it has been at times to "rise above the fray" amid the repeated calls for her husband to produce his birth certificate, she told graduates she understands how trying it can be to live in the "shadows" of lingering racism. She talked about the problem of "driving while black," the fact that many schools are "still separate and very unequal," and that the criminal justice system "doesn't provide truly equal justice for too many." And yet, she urged her audience to remain positive, even though it is tempting to feel discouraged or angry. "The question isn't whether you're going to come face-to-face with these issues; the question is how you're going to respond when you do," she said. "Are you going to throw up your hands and say that progress will never come? Are you going to get angry or lash out? Are you going to turn inward, and just give in to despair and frustration? Or are you going to take a deep breath, straighten your shoulders, lift your head, and do what Barack Obama has always done—as he says, 'When they go low, I go high.'" Most of all, she told her young, largely African-American audience, there was one key way to protect your rights: Register, head to the polls, and vote.[24]

In a speech to graduating students at City College in New York in June, the First Lady introduced another angle to the race discussion. She was talking about the diversity of the student body and how, as a melting pot of students from all walks of life and all countries of origin, "You are the living, breathing proof that the American Dream endures in our time." She then talked about how she and her family are also part of that narrative, that proof of the American Dream. "It's the story I witness every single day when I wake up in a house that was built by slaves, and I watch my daughters—two beautiful, black young women—head off to school, waving goodbye to their father, the president of the United States, the son of a man from Kenya who came here to America for the same reason as many of you: To get an education and improve his prospects in life," she said.[25]

Mrs. Obama took that same image—the "house built by slaves"—to a much wider audience during the 2016 Democratic National Convention. "That is the story of this country," she said, "the story that has brought me to this stage tonight, the story of generations of people who felt the lash of bondage, the shame of servitude, the sting of segregation, but who kept on striving and hoping and doing what needed to be done so that today, I wake up every morning in a house that was built by slaves—and I watch my daughters—two beautiful, intelligent, black young women—playing with their dogs on the White House lawn."[26]

Juxtaposing those few bold, honest words—"a house that was built by slaves," the "lash of bondage," the "shame of servitude," and the "sting of segregation"—with an image of the black First Family living inside the White House, the First Lady had exposed our country's racist history, while also managing to celebrate the progress that has been made. Describing it as an "ongoing narrative," she also left room for more progress to come. Her decision to include that language in her speech drew praise from many quarters and condemnation from others, some of whom accused her of "race-baiting." One thing is sure—she sparked conversation.

Beyond the initiatives she spearheaded and the issues she focused on, there are also the personal accomplishments she made during her years in the White House, and no story about First Lady Michelle Obama would be complete without listing two of them.

The first, of course, is the Obama marriage. By all appearances, Michelle and Barack Obama have a true partnership, a marriage based on mutual admiration and respect. Especially in contrast to the salacious news we hear about other public figures, the Obamas' marriage has never given us anything to talk about, other than a few random glimpses of affection and playfulness. Remember the description of then-Senator Obama teasing his wife at one of the girls' soccer games and her playfully swatting him away? Remember the First Couple dancing to Beyoncé's version of Etta James's "At Last" during the first inauguration? And how about the video message the president shared on October 3, 2017, the couple's twenty-fifth wedding anniversary?

To commemorate that occasion, Mr. Obama recorded a message for his wife, who was out of town attending the Pennsylvania Women's Conference in Philadelphia. Because they were not together, he sent a greeting to be played to those at the conference, including his bride. "The idea that you would put up with me for a quarter of a century is a remarkable testament to what a saintly, wonderful, patient person you are," he said in the video. "Not only have you been an extraordinary partner, not only have you been a great friend, somebody who could always make me laugh, somebody who would always make sure I was following what I thought was right, but you have also been an example to our daughters and to the entire country. Your strength, your grace, your determination, your honesty, the fact that you look so good doing all this, the way in which you've always taken responsibility for your own actions and looked out for the people around you is remarkable. It's no wonder that as people got to know you the way that I got to know you that they fell in love and it is truly the best decision I ever made to be persistent enough asking you out for a date that you finally gave in."[27]

When he was finished, his wife, visibly blushing, turned to Shonda Rhimes, who was interviewing her, and said, "I better get home!"[28]

And then there are the children. If, as they say, the proof is in the pudding, then Michelle Obama was a stellar mom-in-chief for her nuclear family, raising two confident, smart, well-adjusted daughters. Since that July 4, 2008, interview with *Access Hollywood*, our views of Malia and Sasha Obama have been limited to appearances at public functions, with random photos of the family on vacations or the girls out in public. We don't know much about their personal lives, and that is as it should be. We do know, though, that they are strong and accomplished young women, and that, after taking a gap year when she volunteered overseas and then worked in film in New York City, Malia enrolled at Harvard, no small feat. Sasha is nearing her final year at Sidwell Friends and was reported to be touring colleges with her mother. Like her older sister, we hear she is a committed student—so committed, in fact, that she missed her father's farewell address in Chicago so she could study for a big exam the next day.[29]

In one of the most moving moments of that farewell speech, after thanking his wife for taking on "a role you didn't ask for" and making it your own with grace and with grit and with style and good humor," President Obama paid tribute to his daughters. "Malia and Sasha," he said, "under the strangest of circumstances, you have become two amazing young women, smart and beautiful, but more importantly, kind and thoughtful and full of passion. You wore the burden of years in the spotlight so easily. Of all that I've done in my life, I'm most proud to be your dad."[30]

As for the mom-in-chief, what was her guiding principle on the home front? At the Democratic National Convention in 2012, she told her audience that she and her husband had learned about being good parents when they were children. "Barack and I were both raised by families who didn't have much in the way of money or material possessions, but who had given us something far more valuable—their unconditional love, their unflinching sacrifice, and the chance to go places they had never imagined for themselves," she said.[31]

And then, four years later, during her speech at the 2016 Democratic National Convention, she talked about the importance of being a good role model:

> *With every word we utter, every action we take, we know our kids are watching us. We, as parents, are their most important role models. And let me tell you, Barack and I take that same approach to our jobs as president and First Lady, because we know that our words and actions matter, not just to our girls, but the children across this country.*[32]

Others have also weighed in on the powerful example the Obama parents set, not just for their own children, but for children all over the world. In an essay she wrote for *T, The New York Times Style Magazine* just before the Obamas moved out of the White House, Gloria Steinem, feminist icon, summed up the First Lady's manifold contributions this way:

> *Though I'm old enough to remember Eleanor and Franklin D. Roosevelt in the White House—and all the couples and families since—I have never seen such balance and equal parenting, such love, respect, mutuality and pleasure in each other's company. . . . Michelle Obama may have changed history in the most powerful way—by example.*[33]

To the mom- (and dad-) in-chief, thank you.

CHAPTER 14

Michelle Obama's Legacy

How She Made Us Feel

I've learned that people will forget what you said, people will forget what you did, but people will never forget how you made them feel.
—MAYA ANGELOU

WHEN YOU LOOK AT A PERSON AND TRY TO ASSESS HIS OR HER CONTRIbutions to the world, you typically consider a list of concrete accomplishments. Certainly, First Lady Michelle Obama has her own very long list. But an equally important part of a person's legacy is intangible. How did she make us feel?

That is a complicated question, particularly in a country so polarized, and no doubt the answer will vary widely from person to person. But in broad terms, it is accurate to say that most of us felt pretty good about Michelle Obama at the conclusion of her eight years as First Lady. We know this because we have a tool designed to gauge such things: the so-called favorable ratings.

When she left the White House in early 2017, Michelle Obama's favorable rating stood at 68 percent, according to Gallup, meaning that close to 70 percent of the population viewed her favorably. The First Lady's ratings were a full ten points higher than her husband's 58 percent as he prepared to leave office. As First Ladies go, Michelle's final rating wasn't the highest in recent history—that would belong to Laura

Bush, who left the White House with a 76 percent rating (compared to her husband's 40 percent rating at that same time)—but it was a dozen points higher than Hillary Clinton's 56 percent when she left the White House in 2000. And Michelle's ratings were consistently favorable throughout her husband's eight years in office. The only time they dipped below 50 percent was in May 2008, months before her husband was first elected president, back when people really didn't know who she was.[1]

Ratings aside, perhaps the most telling data about how Michelle made us feel came from other quarters. The morning after Donald Trump's unexpected victory, when the world was reeling from the news that he, and not Hillary Clinton, as had been widely predicted, would be our next president, social media was abuzz with another phenomenon. A new hashtag, #Michelle2020, was trending.

"Dear @MichelleObama," read one tweet. "I know you wanted to be done with the White House but we're going to need you to run for president in 4 years."

"MICHELLE IF YOU RUN FOR PRESIDENT 2020 I WILL EAT ALL MY VEGGIES AND DO GREAT IN SCHOOL PLEASE @FLOTUS," read another.[2]

Google Michelle Obama 2020 and you will come up with various Facebook groups dedicated to the cause and a whole slew of Michelle 2020 T-shirts to choose from. (I counted at least twenty-five different versions.)

In the weeks and months following the 2016 election, the discussion grew so loud that Mrs. Obama eventually weighed in. During a Q&A session at the American Institute of Architects Annual Conference in Orlando in April 2017, she was asked if she would consider running for office. No, she said, adding that she "wouldn't ask my children to do this again."[3]

Truth be told, the subject had been broached publicly even before she and her husband had moved out of the White House when, during a farewell interview with Oprah Winfrey in December 2016, the talk show host asked the question that had been on everyone's mind. Would she run for office? Michelle's answer was No, with the same stated reason: She wouldn't put her family through it. She also told Oprah that she thinks the people who want her to run are just being hopeful. And then she added, "Hope is good," a comment that may have inspired some #michelle2020 folks to continue to cross their fingers.[4]

So what was it about Michelle Obama that made so many like her so much, to the point of desperately hoping she'd run for president? (To be sure, she also had her detractors who were thrilled to see her gone from the White House—remember the 32 percent who were unfavorable?—we'll address them in a bit.)

Perhaps the greatest tool Mrs. Obama had at her disposal was her remarkable ability to connect with people, whether through a speech from a national stage addressed to the multitudes or during a face-to-face meeting with an audience of one. Her singular, completely authentic voice; her skilled delivery; her message of inclusion; and her genuine warmth moved people and made them feel that she really saw them, really heard them. Or, as Valerie Jarrett, her husband's chief adviser and her longtime friend said just before the First Lady left the White House, "She has this extraordinary ability to meet people where they are. And I think that's hard to do from the lofty perch of the White House. But she has never climbed up on that perch!"[5]

That warmth and that ability to "meet people where they are" translated into action in the Obama White House. One of the first things the president and First Lady did when they moved into their new home was to open its doors to the public. Calling it "The People's House," the First Family welcomed more than six hundred thousand visitors that first year alone, the largest one-year number since the September 11 attacks. Sometimes the president and First Lady—sometimes accompanied by the White House dog, Bo—would drop in, unannounced, to surprise visitors during White House tours, a practice they continued throughout their eight years as residents.[6]

Through her girls' mentoring program, the First Lady invited young women into the White House each month so they could partner with and learn from her colleagues, but also so they could practice walking through the White House door in a literal way, an act that might break down figurative barriers for these young women in the years ahead. She invited children to work with her in the White House Kitchen Garden, to prepare State Dinners, to attend musical and theatrical events.

To Michelle, the house she and her family called home for eight years really belonged to the entire country. Here she is in a welcome message when she unveiled a new a virtual tour of the White House's public rooms: "The White House isn't simply a home to First Families or meeting space for world leaders. It's also known as 'The People's House,' a place that should be open to everyone. . . . So, go ahead, look around, enjoy the history and the beauty of the rooms. Because, after all, this is your house, too."[7]

The warmth and openness Mrs. Obama exuded made others feel warm toward her, too. Remember the video of the First Lady meeting the Queen of England? The media, and particularly the British press, went practically apoplectic when they saw the footage of Queen Elizabeth II with her arm around Michelle Obama's waist and the First Lady responding in kind. Many observers found the First Lady's action, namely touching the Queen, to be a breach of protocol. But what got the British royal watcher Charles Mosley, author of *Blood Royal*, exercised wasn't Mrs. Obama's action. Rather, it was what his famously remote queen did. Speaking on CNN's *American Morning*, Mosley said:

> *What is astounding is the picture of the queen with her arm around Michelle Obama, and Michelle Obama's arm around the queen, too. But the queen made the first move. This is the most astounding thing, because the queen is not known for being touchy-feely. Indeed her son, Prince Charles, complained on one occasion that he wasn't given enough affection when he was a child. . . . It's a very significant gesture. . . . For all I know this is a breach of White House protocol.[8]*

Mrs. Obama was even welcoming when she might have preferred not to be. Perhaps nothing expressed that graciousness quite so much as when President-Elect Trump and Mrs. Trump arrived at the White House on Inauguration Day in 2017 for the obligatory First Couples' greeting and photo op before the official ceremony at the US Capitol. When the Trumps' motorcade arrived in front of the White House, the soon-to-be president exited the car and began ascending the steps without waiting for his wife to join him, an oversight which set off a small media storm. *Town & Country* ran an article headlined, "Donald Trump Is the Only Recent President Who Didn't Escort His Wife Into the White House," assembling videos of previous presidents-elect arriving at the White House on Inauguration Day. Every one of them waited for their wives before walking together, arm in arm, up the White House steps to meet the outgoing president and First Lady.[9]

The Daily Mail also criticized the way Trump handled his entrance into the White House after the photo with the Obamas. The president-elect "barreled through the front door, leaving Melania to be escorted by the former President and First Lady," the British newspaper reported.[10]

But President and Mrs. Obama barely skipped a beat, stepping up to take the arm of the soon-to-be First Lady when her husband didn't. When Mrs. Trump extended her hand to shake Mrs. Obama's, the outgoing First Lady leaned in to embrace the incoming one, kissing her on both cheeks. That graciousness is even more remarkable when you consider that Donald Trump had been one of the biggest promulgators of the rumor that President Obama was not born in America, only one of several actions the outgoing president and First Lady might have taken objection to. But as Mrs. Obama said so often—and showed repeatedly—"When they go low, we go high."

The vision of the incoming and outgoing First Ladies, Melania Trump in her powder blue dress with matching, powder blue gloves and Michelle Obama in her belted, red Jason Wu dress, standing side by side, arms around each other's waist for the "handover" photo op, brings up another way Mrs. Obama connected with us. As mundane as it sounds, clothing, accessories, and hairstyles drew people to her—and in many cases made them want to emulate her. As Leah Bourne wrote in "7 Indisputable Ways Michelle Obama Changed the Way You Dress," published in *Glamour*, "What truly made Obama such a powerful style icon during her time in the White House . . . was the wink her clothes made to women everywhere: *You too can look this good.*"[11]

For the companies that designed and distributed the clothing Mrs. Obama chose to wear, that "wink" could be worth a small fortune. In a study for *Harvard Business Review*, David Yermack, a professor of finance at New York University's Stern School of Business, examined 189 outfits Mrs. Obama sported between November 2008 and December 2009. At the same time, he tracked publicly traded stocks from the companies who made the clothing, and his findings were pretty astonishing. "It was truly remarkable how much more effect Mrs. Obama had on the commercial industry than almost any other celebrity you could find in any other commercial setting," Yermack said. "This would be a very permanent thing. The stocks would not go down the next day. So to put a number on it for just a generic company at a routine event, it was worth about $38 million to have Mrs. Obama wear your clothes."[12] Mrs. Obama's sense of style—and the fact that people wanted to emulate it—led to other business boons as well. During her years in the White House, she helped sell countless magazines that chose to put her image on their cover, and her fashion flair was the subject of at least four books: *Everyday Icon: Michelle Obama and the Power of Style* by Kate Betts; *Michelle Obama: First Lady of Fashion and Style* by Susan Swimmer; *Commander in Chic: Every Woman's Guide to Managing her Style like a First Lady* by Mikki Taylor; and *Mrs. O: The Face of Fashion Democracy* by Mary Byun.

A change in hairstyle could create a frenzy at hair salons across the country, as happened when the First Lady appeared at her husband's second inauguration sporting what quickly became known as "Obama Bangs." Likewise, she almost singlehandedly sparked a renaissance in sleeveless sheath dresses, brought cardigan sweaters back into style, and made the "belted look" popular. She often opted for flats over heels, and she favored "statement jewelry," such as a string of large beads setting off a monochromatic dress (not that she didn't also rock the patterns). Perhaps most of all, she invited women to embrace their bodies and to take care of them, setting an example by getting up early each morning, sometimes at 4:30 or 5, to work out before helping her daughters get ready for school. Her commitment to fitness and to her workout routines was emulated by women across the country, who, again, wanted to look like their First Lady. (Her legendarily toned arms were, as we know, a particularly sought-after quality, and you can find any number of Michelle

Obama "arm workouts" online.) The women who sought to emulate her were all shapes, sizes, ages, ethnicities, and creeds.

It is ironic, then, that it was the way the First Lady looked—and not so much the things she did—that seemed to really ignite her detractors. Although First Lady Jacqueline Kennedy wore her share of sleeveless sheath dresses during her White House years, when Michelle Obama did the same thing forty years later, it sparked outrage. "The conservative media went crazy, writing stories about the First Lady's arms," observed Tanisha C. Ford in "She Slays," one of the essays from *The Meaning of Michelle: 16 Writers on the Iconic First Lady and How Her Journey Inspires Our Own*. Her arms were called "too muscular and too masculine," and detractors were "appalled by seeing the health-conscious Obama doing pushups in public to promote her anti-childhood obesity campaign, Let's Move!" According to Ford, Mrs. Obama's strength and height made her seem "stronger and larger than life, threatening even," and the focus on her arms opened conversations "about the whole of her body and the ways in which it was out of place in the White House."[13]

There were many other looks-related slights. In one memorable one, the director of a nonprofit in Clay, West Virginia, called Mrs. Obama "an ape in heels" on Facebook. Eventually the woman, Pamela Taylor, was fired from her job—but only after the town's mayor commented that she had "made my day" with the post. The mayor, Beverly Whaling, ended up resigning.[14]

Conservative talk show host Rush Limbaugh called her "Michelle My Butt," and others "likened her to a character from *Planet of the Apes*, a Star Wars Wookiee and a gorilla, a racist slur with a particularly long and ugly history," Peter Slevin wrote in the the *Washington Post*.[15]

And of course, it wasn't just her looks that made her a target. When Mrs. Obama made her comments about race to students at Tuskegee, Laura Ingraham, the conservative talk show host "saw a litany of victimization," Slevin wrote. "Media comment boards filled with talk of a 'tirade' and an 'America-hater' and an 'angry woman who has no appreciation for the many gifts our country has bestowed on her.' Someone wrote, 'Can she or her husband ever just be Americans? Why do they always have to focus on their skin color? Repulsive.'"[16]

Asked by her pal Oprah Winfrey during an interview the summer before leaving the White House how she handles "the haters," Michelle responded that she doesn't pay attention. Rather, she focuses on her own to-do list:

When it came to this role, I just said, let me just be First Lady. Let me wake up every day and work hard to do something of value and to do it well and to do something consequential and to do something that I care about and then let that speak for itself. And that would shut up the haters, because I would have a whole portfolio of stuff that defined me because it's what I did, not what you called me.

"Good work" is the "best revenge," Mrs. Obama said. "You don't have to say anything to the haters. You don't have to acknowledge them at all. You just wake up every morning and be the best you you can be, and that shuts them up."[17]

To commemorate the conclusion of her time as First Lady, the *New York Times' T Magazine* asked four writers and/or public figures to write thank you notes to Mrs. Obama, "who spent the past eight years quietly and confidently changing the course of American history." As we saw in the previous chapter, Gloria Steinem wrote about the way the First Lady and her husband modeled love, respect, and partnership. Author Chimamanda Ngozi Adichie wrote about how Mrs. Obama had "called herself mom-in-chief, and cloaked in that nonthreatening title, done what she cared about" while making the title First Lady "mean a person warmly accessible, a person both normal and inspirational and a person many degrees of cool." Presidential historian Jon Meacham wrote about how the First Lady managed to not just "withstand the scrutiny of the spotlight," but to "prevail" over it. She did so, he said, "by finding . . . that most elusive of things: balance," cultivating "her own garden," and "leaving the White House a strong and popular figure with a lifetime of good will and great reservoirs of capital on which to draw as she and her husband write their next chapters."

Finally, actress and writer Rashida Jones wrote that Michelle Obama speaks to and for women everywhere:

If feminism's goal is equal opportunity and choice, Michelle makes me feel like every choice is available. You can go to Princeton and Harvard, you can rap with Missy Elliott, you can be a mother and a lawyer and a powerful orator. You can champion the Lilly Ledbetter Fair Pay Act, while also caring about fashion. You can dance with Ellen and also fearlessly remind people, on live television, of the reality of your position. . . . You can be your husband's partner and supporter, and also use your cultural and political capital to campaign for Hillary Clinton, unflinchingly standing up to her "locker room talk"-ing bully of an opponent with the battle cry "enough is enough!"—eloquently putting into words what a lot of people, myself included, had been feeling.

Jones said Michelle Obama "will have her own legacy, separate from her husband's," and that legacy will be "that she was the first First Lady to show women that they don't have to choose. That it's okay to be everything."[18]

Here's one last, rather unorthodox example of the way Michelle Obama, First Lady, made us feel. In late March 2018, an Instagram photo began circulating online. It showed the side of a man's head with a face shaved onto it. It turns out the owner of the head, Nolan Beck, a visual designer in Cleveland, had gone to Nick Castellanos, LeBron James's hairstylist, and asked to have his favorite photo of Michelle Obama "carved" onto his head.

"I chose Michelle because she is one of the most elegant and sophisticated people in the public eye," he told *Marie Claire* magazine. "She's strong, so smart, and hilarious, and an inspiration." Beck added that he had always been a fan of the Obamas, admiring their "poise and resilience" as "they handle everything with grace and a sense of humor . . . two qualities I try to emulate every day." Plus, he joked, the photo he selected, and the way Castellanos replicated it on his head, "kinda looks like she's whispering in my ear."[19]

Although, unlike the "Obama Bangs" phenomenon, it's a pretty safe bet to think we won't see too many Michelle Obama–inspired hairstyles like Mr. Beck's, we imagine he's not alone in hoping the former First Lady will continue whispering in his ear for months and years to come.

CHAPTER 15

What's Next?

The Single Most Important Thing

THE "WHISPERING" FROM MRS. OBAMA MAY HAVE FELT FAIRLY FAINT during that first post–White House year. After all, it is customary for departing presidents and First Ladies to disappear from the spotlight for a while, giving their successors time and space to adjust to their new reality. It's also an opportunity for the departing First Couple to take a well-deserved vacation from life under a microscope, not to mention their colossal, unrelenting responsibilities.

We knew things would be quiet because Mrs. Obama told us so. At 5:13 p.m. on Inauguration Day, while the Trumps were presumably getting primped for the Inaugural Balls, @michelleobama tweeted this: "After an extraordinary 8 years, I'll be taking a little break. Will be back before you know it to work with you on the issues we care about."[1] And then the now-former First Lady headed off with her husband, the now-former president, on a series of globe-trotting adventures, starting with a few days in Palm Springs, California, followed by a visit to the British Virgin Islands.

Over the course of the next several months, the Obamas were sighted on an array of islands across the world, from Indonesia to French Polynesia to Hawaii, and other exotic locales, interspersing their travels with time at home in their new house in the Kalorama section of Washington, DC. We followed their adventures mostly through photos and videos—for instance, a Tahiti television station gave us a glimpse of Michelle

Obama paddleboarding in French Polynesia,[2] while videos and photos of her husband kite surfing in the British Virgin Islands went viral.[3]

Every so often, the former First Lady's actual voice would reach us as well, usually when she returned to a stage in the United States to—in her words—"work with you on issues we care about." There was her speech at the American Institute of Architecture's annual conference in April 2017, followed by appearances at the Partnership for a Healthier America Summit in May, the Women's Foundation of Colorado's 60th Anniversary celebration in July, the Pennsylvania Conference for Women in October, and the Obama Foundation Summit in November.

She also returned to Twitter, giving us periodic, brief glimpses into her activities. The first tweet, shared on February 14, was accompanied by a photo of two pairs of feet—presumably those of the former First Lady and president—on a sandy beach, with the following message: "Happy Valentine's Day to the love of my life and favorite island mate, @barack obama. #valentines."[4] A few weeks later, in honor of Black History Month, she posted a photo of herself under a sign that said "Colored" talking to a young woman under a sign that said "White." "Remembering those who made possible the dreams of today," she tweeted. "Will never forget. Will never stop honoring their legacy. #BlackHistoryMonth."[5] Five days later, the former First Lady made a surprise visit to a Washington, DC, classroom, and tweeted, "Always love visiting DC schools. Thank you for hosting me today @BallouSTAY. Stories of students #reaching higher continue to inspire me."[6]

If you missed seeing or hearing from the former First Lady in a regular or more substantive way, you weren't alone. Even before the Trump inauguration, *The Guardian* newspaper published an editorial called "The Guardian View on Michelle Obama: Missing Her Already."[7] Scarymommy.com, a popular parenting site, published "9 Reasons I'm Already Missing Michelle Obama,"[8] and exactly one year after she and her husband left the White House, *Essence* ran an article called "We Miss Michelle Obama: Here Are All the Times We Caught a Glimpse of the Former First Lady in 2017."[9]

But even as we missed seeing Michelle Obama day in and day out, she reminded us that she'd be back. In keeping with her Inauguration

Day tweet, she made a promise at the Partnership for a Healthier America Summit in May: "We're not gone—we're just breathing, y'all. We've got to get our new lives set up."[10]

Given what we've learned about Michelle Obama over the years, we should have realized that "just breathing" and "getting our new lives set up" probably meant more than simply kicking back on the beach at a succession of remote islands, returning periodically to check on things at home. For one thing, both the former president and First Lady had a major assignment on their to-do lists during their island idylls (which must have been anything but idle): writing his and hers memoirs.

As we learned in March 2017, the Obamas had signed a two-memoir deal with Crown, a Penguin Random House imprint. According to the *Financial Times*, the winning bid for the joint memoirs was a whopping $65 million, although other sources have put the figure in the tens of millions of dollars. In any event, it's a handsome sum, with publishers betting that readers all over the world are clamoring to hear the unfettered story directly from the horses' mouths.[11]

Almost a year later, presumably with a lot of writing under her belt, Michelle Obama took to Twitter to announce the imminent arrival of *Becoming*, her memoir, scheduled to appear on shelves in November 2018. "Writing BECOMING has been a deeply personal experience," the former First Lady tweeted on February 25. "I talk about my roots and how a girl from the South Side found her voice. I hope my journey inspires readers to find the courage to become whoever they aspire to be. I can't wait to share my story."[12]

Apparently the world can't wait either; as of mid-April, her *Becoming* post had been retweeted 27,457 times and liked almost 150,000 times. Expectations are high that, without the constraints of the First Lady title, Mrs. Obama will be able to speak out a little more, in her own, inimitable voice, about both the highs and lows of her eight years in the White House. What was it like to have to bite her tongue about issues she cared deeply about but which were "too divisive" to discuss publicly? How did she and her husband really feel on January 20, 2017, when they had to hand the White House—and the country and their hard-won achievements—over to their successors?

The Obamas reportedly plan to donate some of the proceeds from *Becoming* and whatever the former president decides to call his memoir, which will come out at a later date, to nonprofits. According to *Vanity Fair*, one million copies of *Becoming* will be donated to First Book, an educational nonprofit that supports access to reading materials for low-income families. The Obamas are also expected to donate "a significant portion" of the proceeds from both memoirs to the Obama Foundation, which was founded in 2014 with a very Obama-esque mission: to "inspire and empower people to change their world."[13]

In addition to writing about their own personal journeys, the Obamas are finding ways to use new media to amplify other people's voices. In May 2018, former President Obama announced the creation of "Higher Ground Productions," a multiyear production deal with Netflix that will allow the former First Couple to produce television shows and films to be streamed online.[14]

"President and Mrs. Obama have always believed in the power of storytelling to inspire," said Eric Schultz, a senior adviser to the former president. "Throughout their lives, they have lifted up stories of people whose efforts to make a difference are quietly changing the world for the better. As they consider their future plans, they continue to explore new ways to help others tell and share their stories."[15]

With some 118 million subscribers around the world, Netflix will provide a global platform for the former president and First Lady to continue to advocate for the ideas and causes they care so deeply about. It could also provide an opportunity to counteract some of the misinformation that news delivery in the age of the Internet has enabled.[16]

In a statement issued when the Netflix deal was announced, the former president said one of the "simple joys" of life in public service has been having the opportunity to hear people's stories. "That's why Michelle and I are so excited to partner with Netflix," he said. "We hope to cultivate and curate the talented, inspiring, creative voices who are able to promote greater empathy and understanding between peoples, and help them share their stories with the entire world."[17]

The Obamas will also continue to make their presence felt through the work of the Obama Foundation. "From leaders who are already making an impact, to people who are interested in becoming more involved, but don't know where to start, our goal is to make our programs accessible to anyone, anywhere," the Obama Foundation says on its website. "We'll equip civic innovators, young leaders, and everyday citizens with skills and tools they need to create change in their communities."[18]

The day they left the White House, the outgoing president and First Lady shared a video farewell in which they thanked citizens for "giving us this incredible privilege of serving the country that we love." They also invited their fellow Americans to join them in their work with the Obama Foundation, asking citizens to send "your ideas, your hopes, your beliefs about what we can do together." "The work of perfecting our union is never finished," the former president said, "and we look forward to joining you in that effort as fellow citizens."[19]

On October 31 and November 1, 2017, the Obamas hosted the first Obama Foundation Summit, welcoming 500 civic leaders from around the world to Chicago, where the Obama Presidential Center is being constructed on the South Side, Michelle's home turf. Incorporating the ideas that others had shared with them, they used the summit to discuss an array of topics, from how to inspire young people to participate in civic engagement to the ways in which technology might be used to create equitable and inclusive communities. They also used the occasion to reignite hope, with the culminating concert—featuring Andra Day as the opening act with her rousing anthem, "Rise Up," followed by an all-star lineup including Chance the Rapper, Common, Lin-Manuel Miranda, Brandi Carlile, Gloria Estefan, and Nas, among others—leading one attendee to write, "In a time when hope and logic and kindness seem to be dwindling, we all felt lifted up last night. . . . The Summit proved there are such good people and programs and communities working together for our future. For our kids future. I want to be a part of that."[20]

That was the point. At a conference for a Japanese nonprofit in Tokyo five months later, the former president spoke about what he has learned since leaving the White House, as he has worked alongside his wife to shape the Obama Foundation. "After I left office, what I realized is that the Obama Foundation could potentially create a platform for young, up-and-coming leaders, both in the United States and all around the world, to come together, meet together, create a digital platform where they could exchange information," he said. "If I could do that effectively, then I would create a hundred, or a thousand, or a million young Barack Obamas or Michelle Obamas."[21]

As it happened, the Tokyo conference took place on March 25, one day after the youth-led movement against gun violence inspired more than one million people—and perhaps as many as three million—to participate in the March for Our Lives in Washington, DC, or its sister events across the globe.[22]

Obama paid homage to the students at Marjory Stoneman Douglas High School who spearheaded the movement and to those who followed their lead. "This is all because of the courage and effort of a handful of 15- and 16-year-olds, who took the responsibility that so often adults had failed to take in trying to find a solution," he said. "I think that's a testimony to what happens when young people are given opportunities, and I think all institutions have to think about how do we tap into that creativity and that energy and that drive."[23]

During the various Marches for Our Lives, you could almost imagine the student leaders, speakers, and attendees channeling Michelle Obama. When Emma Gonzalez, a senior at Marjory Stoneman Douglas, bravely took to the podium at the DC gathering, she read off the names of the seventeen classmates and teachers who lost their lives in the massacre at her school, and then she stood silently, tears streaming down her face, for an excruciating four minutes and twenty-six seconds—the time it took the gunman to take those lives in his violent rampage. Imagine the courage and determination she had to summon. How much easier would it have been to curl up in a fetal position? Remember Michelle Obama's final words before leaving the White House? *So don't be afraid. You hear me, young people? Don't be afraid. Be focused. Be determined. Be hopeful. Be empowered. Empower yourselves with a good education. Then get out there, and use that education to build a country worthy of your boundless promise. Lead by example with hope. Never fear.*

In one of eight hundred March for Our Lives sister events, held near my hometown in Connecticut, a brave, young friend was one of the four featured youth speakers. She was the last to speak, and the youngest, being all of nine years old. Taking the stage—or rather, the makeshift stage for the event, a wooden picnic table—as a small group of protestors across the street used a megaphone to shout, "Build that wall" and "Trump," this four-foot-tall powerhouse told her audience she wanted to talk about three things: how student activism has "always been a part of every major social movement and push for equality" in our country; how, as a fourth grader, she doesn't remember a time when she wasn't doing safety drills and lockdowns at school; and how "black people and people of color are at greater risk of being killed in gun violence by people who are supposed to protect us."[24]

My friend, who is black, brought up the example of Ruby Bridges, who "was only six when she stepped into an all-white racist school to integrate it." At six years old, she said, Ruby "became a student activist. Everyone in the world was watching her." She then described how the parents of white students took their children out of school because they didn't want them to "learn alongside a little black girl—a little black girl like me." She spoke about how Ruby persisted, and how over time other black and brown children have led the way in the fight for racial and social justice, in places like Ferguson, Baltimore, and Houston.

"Unfortunately," she continued, "people haven't recognized all students' voices equally, and adults don't always pay attention to things they don't want to hear." My small but mighty friend then paused, turning slightly on her picnic table perch, and gestured at the people across the street, eliciting a cheer from her audience and prompting a loud "Build that wall!" from the other side of the road.

She didn't skip a beat, continuing her talk, speaking about the deaths of black children and black adults by gun violence, often at the hands of police, and ending with a call for her almost exclusively white audience to join her by committing to support black children and other children of color. "After today will you remember that black children are not adults?" she asked. "Will you fight for black people and people of color too? Will you take direct action so that black children like me can grow up free?"

"Yes!" her audience roared in response, their applause and cheers drowning out the "Trump" chants. Watching this nine-year-old speak her truth, even in the face of opposition armed with megaphones, how could you not think of Michelle Obama and her journey? Remember the speech she delivered a full ten years before, the one at Benedict College in South Carolina, when she urged her largely black audience to aim high and take chances? The one that began, "We are confronted with doubters, people who tell us what we can't do" and ends with the line: "You know, every time somebody told me, 'No, you can't do that,' I pushed past their doubts and I took my seat at the table." Is my little friend, standing on that picnic table at the East Haddam, Connecticut, March for Our Lives event, not exactly who and what Michelle Obama was talking about?

In his Tokyo speech the day after March for Our Lives, the former president made a very simple, but deeply profound statement. After serving as the "leader of the free world" for eight years, Obama said this: "The single most important thing I can do is to help develop the next generation."[25]

The *Single Most Important Thing*. Barack Obama, the former commander-in-chief, was beginning to sound a lot like his wife, Michelle Obama, the mom-in-chief, who had been saying as much for a decade.

Again, her words from the official unveiling of the White House garden in October 2016:

> *This garden has taught us that if we have the courage to plant a seed, just be brave enough to plant it, then take care of it, water it, tend to it, invite friends to help us take care of it, weather the storms that inevitably come, if we have the courage to do that, we never know what might grow.*[26]

Your garden is growing, Michelle Obama. Your whispers are being heard.

Acknowledgments

Writing a book about a national figure in a few short months—and then updating it ten years later to reflect what had occurred in the intervening decade—is a daunting task, and it wouldn't have been possible without assistance from many quarters.

First, heartfelt thanks to my dear friend, Georgiana Goodwin, whose idea it was to suggest me as an author for the Michelle Obama biography.

Second, many thanks to Tom McCarthy, senior editor at Globe Pequot, who decided to take a chance on me. Thank you for both the opportunity to tell this compelling story and your guidance. Thanks as well to senior production editor Meredith Dias, for her keen eye and close reading.

Thank you to all the friends and acquaintances who helped with research and/or introductions.

Thank you to my colleagues at school, who were gracious enough to allow me some flexibility.

Thank you to my parents, Dick and Judy Lightfoot, for, like Marian and Fraser Robinson, making your children believe they could do anything they set their minds to.

Thank you to my husband, Nick, and children, Graeme, Isabel, Alastair, and Honor, for supporting and encouraging me and for being, as Michelle Obama said in her yearbook, "the most important things in my life."

Finally, thank you to Michelle and Barack Obama for providing such an inspiring story. May we all continue to say "Yes We Can" and work toward a "world as it should be."

NOTES

Preface: How This Book Came to Be

1. Michelle Obama, interview by Larry King, *Larry King Live*, CNN, Feb. 11, 2008.
2. E-mail from Michelle Obama at info@barackobama.com, Feb. 6, 2008.
3. E-mail from Michelle Obama at info@barackobama.com, Feb. 6, 2008.
4. Jessica Curry, "Looking Up to Mrs. Obama," *New York Times*, Mar. 12, 2018.
5. Hanna Kozlowska, "Michelle Obama Brought Herself and Everyone Around Her to Tears with Her Final Speech as First Lady," *Quartz*, Jan. 6, 2017.

Introduction

1. Michelle Obama, interview by Larry King, *Larry King Live*, CNN, Feb. 11, 2008.
2. Paul Begala, interview by Larry King, *Larry King Live*, CNN, Feb. 11, 2008.
3. Jamal Simmons, interview by Larry King, *Larry King Live*, CNN, Feb. 11, 2008.
4. Michael Medved, interview by Larry King, *Larry King Live*, CNN, Feb. 11, 2008.
5. Tim Hutchinson, interview by Larry King, *Larry King Live*, CNN, Feb. 11, 2008.
6. warking27, comment posted after watching YouTube video of Feb. 11, 2008, *Larry King Live* interview with Michelle Obama. Available at YouTube.com/watch?v=py Bc33UjvDU.
7. 12totok, comment posted after watching YouTube video of Feb. 11, 2008, *Larry King Live* interview with Michelle Obama. Available at YouTube.com/watch?v=py Bc33UjvDU.
8. Michelle Robinson, "Princeton-Educated Blacks and the Black Community" (thesis, Princeton University, 1985, 2).
9. Michael Powell, "Following Months of Criticism, Obama Quits His Church," *New York Times*, June 1, 2008.
10. Christopher Hitchens, "Are We Getting Two for One?" *Slate*, May 5, 2008, www .slate.com/id/2190589.
11. Barack Obama, interview by Robin Roberts, *Good Morning America*, ABC, May 19, 2008.
12. Kate Harding, "Michelle Obama Watch," Broadsheet, *Salon*, June 13, 2008, www .salon.com/mwt/broadsheet/2008/06/13/michelle_obama/index.html.
13. Andy Sullivan, "Laura Bush Defends Michelle Obama," Tales from the Trail blog, June 9, 2008, http://blogs.reuters.com/trail08/2008/06/09/laura-bush-defends-michelle -obama.
14. John McCain, interview by Dana Bash, CNN, June 13, 2008.

15. Roland S. Martin, "The Shameful Sliming of Michelle Obama," Creators Syndicate, June 13, 2008, www.creators.com/opinion/roland-martin/the-shameful-sliming-of -michelle-obama.html.

16. "Barack Obama and America's Moment," *Times* (London), June 4, 2008.

17. "Obama's Victory Stirs Hope from Abroad," *USA Today*, June 6, 2008.

18. Ibid.

19. Frank Rich, "How Obama Became Acting President," *New York Times*, July 27, 2008.

20. Michelle Obama, interview by Larry King, *Larry King Live*, CNN, Feb. 11, 2008.

21. Christi Parsons, Bruce Jasper, Bob Secter, "Barack's Rock: Michelle Obama," *Chicago Tribune*, Apr. 22, 2007.

22. Richard Wolffe, "Barack's Rock," *Newsweek*, Feb. 25, 2008.

Chapter 1

1. *The Colbert Report*, Comedy Central, Apr. 15, 2008.

2. Ibid.

3. Jay Newton-Small, "Michelle Obama Finds Her Voice Too," *Time*, Jan. 24, 2008.

4. David Mendell, *Obama: From Promise to Power* (New York: Amistad, 2007), 65.

5. Barack Obama, *The Audacity of Hope* (New York: Three Rivers Press, 2006), 331.

6. Linda Lowen, "Profile of Michelle Obama," About.com: Women's Issues, http:// womensissues.about.com/od/influentialwomen/p/MichelleObama.htm.

7. Peter Slevin, "Her Heart's in the Race," *Washington Post*, Nov. 28, 2007.

8. Ibid.

9. Ibid.

10. Susan Saulny, "Michelle Obama Thrives in Campaign Trenches," *New York Times*, Feb. 14, 2008.

11. Rosalind Rossi, "The Woman Behind Obama," *Chicago Sun-Times*, Jan. 20, 2007.

12. Lauren Collins, "The Other Obama: Michelle Obama and the Politics of Candor," *New Yorker*, Mar. 10, 2008.

13. Karen Springen, "First Lady in Waiting," *Chicago Magazine*, Oct. 2004.

14. Rossi, "The Woman Behind Obama."

15. Judy Keen, "Michelle Obama: Campaigning Her Way," *USA Today*, May 11, 2007.

16. Saulny, "Michelle Obama Thrives."

17. Rossi, "The Woman Behind Obama."

18. Whitney M. Young Magnet High School, "About WMYHS," www.wyoung.org/ about_wymhs.jsp?rn=3760502.

19. Collins, "The Other Obama."

20. Rossi, "The Woman Behind Obama."

21. www.wyoung.org, "About WYMHS."

22. Collins, "The Other Obama."

23. Rossi, "The Woman Behind Obama."

24. Whitney Young High School Press Release, "Whitney Young Celebrates 30 Years of Academic Excellence," Aug. 16, 2005.

25. Richard Wolffe, "Barack's Rock," *Newsweek,* Feb. 25, 2008.

26. Mendell, *Obama,* 96.

27. Wolffe, "Barack's Rock."

28. Newton-Small, "Michelle Obama Finds Her Voice."

29. Saulny, "Michelle Obama Thrives."

30. Slevin, "Her Heart's in the Race."

31. Associated Press, "Michelle Obama Vows First Job as First Lady Is Mother to Her Daughters," Aug. 5, 2008.

32. Obama, *The Audacity of Hope,* 330.

33. Ibid., 350.

34. Michelle Obama, interview by Suzanne Malveaux, *Anderson Cooper 360,* CNN, Apr. 30, 2008.

35. Obama, *Audacity of Hope,* 331.

36. Leslie Bennetts, "First Lady in Waiting," *Vanity Fair,* Dec. 27, 2007.

37. Ibid., 332.

38. *Colbert Report,* Apr. 15, 2008.

Chapter 2

1. Evan Thomas, "Alienated in the U.S.A.," *Newsweek,* Mar. 13, 2008.

2. Sally Jacobs, "Learning to Be Michelle Obama," *Boston Globe,* June 15, 2008.

3. Ibid.

4. Princeton University, "Princeton Establishes New Center for African American Studies," news release, Sept. 18, 2006, www.princeton.edu/main/news/archive/S15/85/91C70/index.xml?section=topstories.

5. Kelly Lack, "First African-American Alumni Remember Journey to Integration," *Daily Princetonian,* Feb. 18, 2008.

6. Massachusetts Foundation for the Humanities, "First African American Graduate of Harvard Born, Jan. 30, 1844," Mass Moments, www.massmoments.org/index.cfm?mid=35.

7. "At Yale, a Multicultural Society of Friends," *College Digest,* www.collegedigest.com/The%20colleges/yale.html.

8. Lisa Birnbach, *The Official Preppy Handbook* (New York: Workman Publishing, 1980), 85.

9. F. Scott Fitzgerald, *This Side of Paradise* (New York: Scribner, 1920), 37.

10. Ibid., 43.

11. Sarah Brown, "Obama '85 Masters Balancing Act," *Daily Princetonian,* Dec. 7, 2005.

12. Jacobs, "Learning to Be Michelle Obama."

13. Lauren Collins, "The Other Obama: Michelle Obama and the Politics of Candor," *New Yorker,* Mar. 10, 2008.

14. Lisa Robinson, interview with author, July 24, 2008.

15. Rebecca Johnson, "Michelle Obama Interview: I'm Nothing Special," *Telegraph,* July 26, 2008.

16. Jacobs, "Learning to Be Michelle Obama."

17. Michelle Obama Interview, "Michelle Obama's Passions: Wife, Mother, Intellectual, American Woman," ABC News, July 7, 2008.

18. Brown, "Obama '85 Masters Balancing Act."

19. Collins, "The Other Obama."

20. Ibid.

21. Richard Wolffe, "Barack's Rock," *Newsweek,* Feb. 25, 2008.

22. Brian Feagans, "Georgian Recalls Rooming with Michelle Obama," *Atlanta Journal-Constitution,* Apr. 13, 2008.

23. Ibid.

24. Ibid.

25. Ibid.

26. Ibid.

27. Jacobs, "Learning to Be Michelle Obama."

28. Ibid.

29. Feagans, "Georgian Recalls Rooming with Michelle Obama."

30. Wolffe, "Barack's Rock."

31. Ibid.

32. Michelle Robinson, "Princeton-Educated Blacks and the Black Community" (thesis, Princeton University, 1985), iv.

33. Collins, "The Other Obama."

34. Robinson, "Princeton-Educated Blacks," 26.

35. Ibid., 2–3.

36. Ibid., 2–3.

37. Ben Macintyre, interview with author, July 13, 2008.

38. Lisa Robinson, interview with author, July 24, 2008.

39. Ibid.

40. Ibid.

41. Louise Ambler Osborn, interview with author, July 18, 2008.

42. Ibid.

43. Lauren Robinson-Brown, interview with author, July 31, 2008.

44. Michael Juel-Larsen and Josh Oppenheimer, "Professors Vote for Obama with Wallets," *Daily Princetonian,* Jan. 21, 2008.

45. Lauren Robinson-Brown, interview with author, July 31, 2008.

46. 1985 Princeton University yearbook.

47. Lauren Robinson-Brown, interview with author, July 31, 2008.

48. Juel-Larsen and Oppenheimer, "Professors Vote for Obama with Wallets."

49. *Princeton: Defining Diversity* (Princeton: Office of Communication, Princeton University, 2007), 44.

50. Ibid., 18.

51. Admissions office information session, July 25, 2008.

52. Princeton University, "Princeton Establishes New Center."

53. Ibid.

54. Robinson, "Princeton-Educated Blacks," 58.
55. Princeton University, "Princeton Establishes New Center."
56. *Princeton: Defining Diversity,* 24–25.
57. Robinson, "Princeton-Educated Blacks," 1–2.
58. Robinson, "Princeton-Educated Blacks," 64.
59. Louise Ambler Osborn, interview with author, July 18, 2008.
60. Barack Obama, *Dreams from My Father* (New York: Three Rivers Press, 1995).
61. Jacobs, "Learning to Be Michelle Obama."
62. Ibid.
63. Wolffe, "Barack's Rock."
64. Rosalind Rossi, "The Woman Behind Obama," *Chicago Sun-Times,* Jan. 20, 2007.
65. Susan Saulny, "Michelle Obama Thrives in Campaign Trenches," *New York Times,* Feb. 14, 2008.
66. Chris Szabla, "One Month to Go, Obama's Profs Rally for Victory," *Harvard Law Record,* Oct. 9, 2008.
67. Wolffe, "Barack's Rock."
68. Charlayne Hunter-Gault, book jacket, *Dreams from My Father* by Barack Obama.

Chapter 3

1. Rebecca Johnson, "Michelle Obama Interview: I'm Nothing Special," *Telegraph,* July 26, 2008.
2. Dan Slater, "Campaign '08: Michelle Obama's Sidley Austin Years," *Wall Street Journal* Law Blog, June 23, 2008, http://blogs.wsj.com/law/2008/06/23/campaign-08 -michelle-obamas-sidley-austin-years.
3. Ibid.
4. Peter Slevin, "Her Heart's in the Race," *Washington Post,* Nov. 28, 2007.
5. Ibid.
6. Johnson, "Michelle Obama Interview."
7. Slevin, "Her Heart's in the Race."
8. Michelle Robinson, "Princeton-Educated Blacks and the Black Community" (thesis, Princeton University, 1985), 10.
9. Johnson, "Michelle Obama Interview."
10. Ibid.
11. Ibid.
12. Don Terry, "In the Path of Lightning," *Chicago Tribune,* July 27, 2008.
13. Ibid.
14. Ibid.
15. Rosalind Rossi, "The Woman Behind Obama," *Chicago Sun-Times,* Jan. 20, 2007.
16. Slater, "Campaign '08."
17. Ed Hornick, "Obama Highlights Plan for National Service," www.CNN.com/ 2008/POLITICS/07/02/obama.service], July 2, 2008.
18. Ibid.
19. Ibid.

20. Jill Lawrence, "'Community Organizer' Slams Attract Support for Obama," *USA Today,* Sept. 4, 2008.

21. "Experts Praise Barack Obama's National Service Plan," in Obama's News and Speeches, BarackObama.com, Dec. 5, 2007.

22. Ibid.

23. Ibid.

24. Ibid.

25. Slevin, "Her Heart's in the Race."

26. Rossi, "The Woman Behind Obama."

27. Slevin, "Her Heart's in the Race."

28. Rossi, "The Woman Behind Obama."

29. Ibid.

30. Ibid.

31. Slevin, "Her Heart's in the Race."

32. Rossi, "The Woman Behind Obama."

33. Ibid.

34. University of Chicago Hospitals, "Michelle Obama Appointed Vice President for Community and External Affairs at the University of Chicago Hospitals," news release, May 9, 2005, www.uchospitals.edu/news/2005/20050509-obama.html.

35. Ibid.

36. Johnson, "Michelle Obama Interview."

37. Lynn Sweet, "Michelle Obama Quits Board of Wal-Mart Supplier," *Chicago Sun-Times'* The Scoop from Washington blog, May 22, 2007, http://blogs.suntimes.com/sweet/2007/05/sweet_column_michelle_obama_qu.html.

38. Associated Press, "No Ifs or Buts, Michelle Obama Anticipates Life as 'Mom-in-Chief,'" Aug. 4, 2008.

39. Michelle Obama, interview by Katie Couric, "Michelle Obama on Love, Family & Politics," *CBS Evening News,* CBS, Feb. 15, 2008, www.cbsnews.com/stories/2008/02/15/eveningnews/main3838884.shtml.

40. Ibid.

41. Ibid.

42. Ibid.

43. John McCormick, "Michelle Obama, Alice Waters Talk Food," *Chicago Tribune's* Swamp blog, July 28, 2008, www.swamppolitics.com/news/politics/blog/2008/07/lunch_and_with_michelle_obama.html.

44. Carrie Dann, "Michelle Obama Talks Fatherhood," MSNBC's First Read blog, July 10, 2008, http://firstread.msnbc.msn.com/archive/2008/07/10/1193601.aspx.

45. Ibid.

46. Suzette Hackney, "Michelle Obama Has Plans for America, Too," *Detroit Free-Press,* July 10, 2008.

47. "Barack Obama's Plan to Support Working Women and Families," pamphlet.

48. Hackney, "Michelle Obama Has Plans for America, Too."

49. Ibid.

50. Scott Helman, "Michelle Obama Revels in Family Role," *Boston Globe,* Oct. 28, 2007.

Chapter 4

1. Barack Obama, *The Audacity of Hope* (New York: Three Rivers Press, 2006), 328.
2. David Mendell, *Obama: From Promise to Power* (New York: Amistad, 2007), 93.
3. Kevin O'Leary, "Why Barack Loves Her," *US Weekly*, June 30, 2008.
4. Obama, *Audacity of Hope*, 328.
5. Michelle Obama, interview by Katie Couric, "Michelle Obama on Love, Family & Politics," *CBS Evening News*, CBS, Feb. 15, 2008, www.cbsnews.com/stories/2008/02/15/eveningnews/main3838884.shtml.
6. Obama, *Audacity of Hope*, 328.
7. Ibid., 329.
8. Ibid., 329.
9. Michelle Obama, interview by Katie Couric, Feb. 15, 2008.
10. Obama, *Audacity of Hope*, 329.
11. Michelle Obama, interview by Katie Couric, Feb. 15, 2008.
12. Ibid.
13. Ibid.
14. Ibid.
15. Melinda Henneberger, "The Obama Marriage: How Does It Work for Michelle Obama?" *Slate*, Oct. 26, 2007, www.slate.com/id/2176683.
16. Ibid.
17. Mendell, *Obama*, 100.
18. Andy Katz, "Brown Coach Robinson Coaching Brother-in-Law Obama, Too," ESPN.com, Sept. 13, 2007, http://sports.espn.go.com/espn/print?id=3009012&type=story.
19. Ibid.
20. Ibid.
21. Ibid.
22. Ibid.
23. Scott Fornek, "15th Wedding Anniversary/Obamas Recall First Date, Proposal that 'Shut Up' Michelle," *Chicago Sun-Times*, Oct. 3, 2007.
24. Lauren Collins, "The Other Obama: Michelle Obama and the Politics of Candor," *New Yorker*, Mar. 10, 2008.
25. Obama, *Audacity of Hope*, 332.
26. Michelle Obama, interview by Katie Couric, Feb. 15, 2008.
27. Mendell, *Obama*, 94.
28. Fornek, "15th Wedding Anniversary."
29. Collins, "The Other Obama."
30. Ibid.
31. Fornek, "15th Wedding Anniversary."
32. Ibid.
33. Michelle Obama, interview by Rachael Ray, *Rachael Ray Show*, CBS, Apr. 29, 2008.
34. Ibid.
35. O'Leary, "Why Barack Loves Her."
36. Obama, *Audacity of Hope*, 336.
37. Ibid., 340.
38. Ibid., 340–41.

39. Cassandra West, "Her Plan Went Awry, But Michelle Obama Doesn't Mind," *Chicago Tribune,* Sept. 1, 2004.

40. Associated Press, "Michelle Obama: Barack's Book Sales Paid Off Our Student Loans," Apr. 9, 2008.

41. Mendell, *Obama,* 144.

42. Ibid., 99.

43. Ibid., 151–52.

44. Sandra Sobieraj Westfall, "The Obamas Get Personal," *People,* Aug. 4, 2008.

45. Ibid.

46. Ibid.

47. Obama, *Audacity of Hope,* 327.

48. Michelle Obama, interview by Rachael Ray, Apr. 29, 2008.

49. Peter Slevin, "Her Heart's in the Race," *Washington Post,* Nov. 28, 2007.

50. Susan Saulny, "Michelle Obama Thrives in Campaign Trenches," *New York Times,* Feb. 14, 2008.

51. Associated Press, "Obama's Wife Attends Rallies in Indiana," Apr. 16, 2008.

52. Joy Bennett Kinnon, "Michelle Obama: Not Just the Senator's Wife," *Ebony,* Mar. 2006.

53. Lynn Norment, "The Hottest Couple in America," *Ebony,* Feb. 2007.

54. Tonya Lewis Lee, "Your Next First Lady?" *Glamour,* Sept. 2007.

55. Ibid.

56. Michelle Obama, interview by Katie Couric, Feb. 15, 2008.

57. Carly Zakin, "Michelle Obama Plays Unique Role in Campaign," MSNBC, July 30, 2007, www.msnbc.msn.com/id/20041755.

58. Maureen Dowd, "She's Not Buttering Him Up," *New York Times,* Apr. 25, 2007.

59. Ben Macintyre, interview with author, July 13, 2008.

60. Jill Lawrence, "Michelle's Homemaker Side," *Chicago Sun-Times,* July 1, 2008.

61. Ibid.

62. Lewis Lee, "Your Next First Lady?"

63. "Pool Report," *Wall Street Journal,* reported by Lynn Sweet, "Obama's Saturday in Chicago," *Chicago Sun-Times'* The Scoop from Washington blog, June 29, 2008, http://blogs.suntimes.com/sweet/2008/06/obamas_saturday_in_chicago_hit.html.

64. O'Leary, "Why Barack Loves Her."

65. Norment, "The Hottest Couple in America."

66. Ben Macintyre, interview with author, July 13, 2008.

67. Michelle Obama, interview by Katie Couric, Feb. 15, 2008.

68. Lewis Lee, "Your Next First Lady?"

69. Bennett Kinnon, "Michelle Obama."

70. Michael Wolff, "It's the Adultery, Stupid," *Vanity Fair,* June 2008.

71. Ibid.

72. Mendell, *Obama,* 259.

73. Ibid.

74. Ibid.

75. Interview by Larry King, *Larry King Live,* CNN, Feb. 11, 2008.

76. Shaila Dewan, "Obama's Wife Evokes Dangers of Campaign," *New York Times*, Jan. 15, 2008.
77. Christi Parsons, Bruce Japsen, and Bob Secter, "Barack's Rock: Michelle Obama," *Chicago Tribune*, Apr. 22, 2007.
78. Barack Obama, interview by Ellen DeGeneres, *The Ellen DeGeneres Show*, Feb. 28, 2008.
79. Obama, *Audacity of Hope*, 346.
80. Liam Ford, "Obama's Church Sermon to Black Dads: Grow Up," *Chicago Tribune*, June 20, 2005.
81. Jeff Long and Christi Parsons, "Obama in Father's Day Sermon Reminds Dads That Parenting Doesn't End at Conception," *Chicago Tribune*, June 15, 2008.
82. Mendell, *Obama*, 382.
83. Obama, *Audacity of Hope*, 226.
84. "Ohio Gov. Strickland Declares Obama Next President at Senior Forum on Retirement Security in Columbus," ePluribus Media, Ohio News Bureau, June 15, 2008, http://discuss.epluribusmedia.net/node/1889.
85. Lewis Lee, "Your Next First Lady?"
86. Jeff Zeleny, "Q&A with Michelle Obama," *Chicago Tribune*, Dec. 24, 2005.
87. Jennifer Loven, "Obama and Family Spend Fourth of July in Montana," Associated Press, July 5, 2008.
88. Ibid.
89. Michelle Obama, convention speech at the Democratic National Convention, transcript from National Public Radio, Aug. 26, 2008.
90. Loven, "Obama and Family Spend Fourth of July in Montana."
91. Ibid.
92. Daryl Paranada, "Future First Lady: Cindy or Michelle," *Huffington Post*, June 10, 2008.
93. Jenna and Laura Bush, interview by Ann Curry, *Today Show*, NBC, Apr. 22, 2008.
94. Sheri and Bob Stritof, "Barack and Michelle Obama Marriage Profile," About.com, http://marriage.about.com/od/celebritymarriage/p/barackobama.

Chapter 5
1. Monica Langley, "Michelle Obama Solidifies Her Role in the Election," *Wall Street Journal*, Feb. 11, 2008.
2. Shipman, Rucci, and Yacus, "Michelle Obama's Passions."
3. Sandra Sobieraj Westfall, "The Obamas at Home," *People*, Aug. 4, 2008.
4. Ibid.
5. Ibid.
6. Ibid.
7. "The Barack Obama Workout," Train Like a Warrior blog, http://trainlikeawarrior.blogspot.com/2008/03/barack-obama-workout.html.
8. Jill Lawrence, "Michelle Obama Has Busy Summer Ahead," *USA Today*, June 29, 2008.
9. Shipman, Ricci, and Yacus, "Michelle Obama's Passions."

10. Kevin O'Leary, "Why Barack Loves Her," *US Weekly*, June 30, 2008.

11. Tribune Wire Reports, "Maria Menounos, Obama Family Interview," *Chicago Tribune*, July 14, 2008.

12. Malia Obama, interview by Maria Menounos, *Access Hollywood*, Fox, July 7, 2008.

13. Barack Obama, interview by Rachael Ray, *Rachael Ray Show*, CBS, Apr. 29, 2008.

14. Michelle and Barack Obama, interview by Maria Menounos, *Access Hollywood*, Fox, July 7, 2008.

15. Tribune Wire Reports, "Maria Menounos, Obama Family Interview."

16. Ibid.

17. "Michelle Obama: Sarah Palin's Children are 'Absolutely' Off Limits," USMagazine .com, Sept. 4, 2008.

18. Tim Harper, "Obama Regrets Kids' Television Appearance," Reuters, July 12, 2008.

19. Westfall, "The Obamas at Home."

20. Tribune Wire Reports, "Maria Menounos, Obama Family Interview."

21. Andrew Sullivan, "The Hubris of Obama?" *Atlantic*'s Daily Dish blog, July 10, 2008, http://andrewsullivan.theatlantic.com/the_daily_dish/2008/07/the-hubris-of-o.html.

22. Ibid.

23. Barack Obama, *The Audacity of Hope* (New York: Three Rivers Press, 2006), 341.

24. Robin Abcarian, "Is There a Goldendoodle in the Obamas' Future?" *Los Angeles Times*' L.A. Unleashed blog, June 9, 2008, http://latimesblogs.latimes.com/unleashed/2008/06/every-once-in-a.html.

25. Tony Barboza, "PETA to Obama: Wanting a Purebred Dog Is Elitist," *Los Angeles Times*' L.A. Unleashed blog, July 29, 2008, http://latimesblogs.latimes.com/unleashed/2008/07/peta-to-obama-i.html.

Chapter 6

1. Ted Koppel, *Nightline*, Mar. 26, 1992.

2. "A Brief History of Hillary Clinton's Body Politic," *New York*'s Daily Intel blog, Oct. 30, 2007, http://nymag.com/daily/intel/2007/10/a_brief_history_of_hillary_cli.html.

3. Joan Vennochi, "Make Over Old Views, Not Political Wives," *Boston Globe*, June 29, 2008.

4. "That Again? *Washington Times* Repeats False 'Scumbags' Rumor," Media Matters for America, Oct. 1, 2004, http://mediamatters.org/items/200410010010?f=s_search.

5. David Paul Kuhn, "Mrs. Kerry to Reporter: 'Shove It,'" CBSNews.com, July 26, 2004.

6. "Heinz Kerry Apologizes for Remark," CNN.com, Oct. 21, 2004, www.cnn.com/2004/ALLPOLITICS/10/20/theresa.apologizes.laura/index.html.

7. Program description for *Eleanor Roosevelt*, American Experience, PBS, www.pbs .org/wgbh/amex/eleanor/filmmore/description.html.

8. Laura Bush, interview by Jonathan Karl, *Good Morning America*, ABC, June 9, 2008.

9. Michelle Malkin, "Michelle Obama's America—And Mine," Townhall.com, Feb. 20, 2008.

10. Barack Obama, interview by Robin Roberts, *Good Morning America*, ABC, May 19, 2008.

11. Mosheh Oinounou, "McCain Uncomfortable with TN GOP Anti-Obama Release," Fox Embeds blog, Feb. 27, 2008, http://embeds.blogs.foxnews.com/2008/02/27/mccain-uncomfortable-with-tn-anti-obama-release.

12. Reuters, "Clinton Faces Kenyan Cattle Fine Over Obama Photo," Feb. 29, 2008.

13. Carrie Budoff Brown, "Michelle Obama Becomes GOP Target," Politico.com, June 12, 2008.

14. Reuters, "No Slack for Michelle Obama from Cindy McCain," June 19, 2008.

15. Barack Obama, interview by Robin Roberts, May 19, 2008.

16. Ibid.

17. Michelle Obama, interview by Robin Roberts, *Good Morning America*, ABC, May 19, 2008.

18. Michelle Obama, interview, *The View*, ABC, June 18, 2008.

19. Lynn Sweet, "Obama Fights Smear: Michelle Obama and the 'Whitey' Rumor," *Chicago Sun-Times'* The Scoop from Washington blog, June 13, 2008, http://blogs.suntimes.com/sweet/2008/06/obama_fights_smear_michelle_ob.html.

20. Ibid.

21. Margaret Talev blog, "Obama Launches Rumor Response website," "Hot Off the Trail," *McClatchy Trusted Voices,* June 12, 2008.

22. "The Truth About Michelle," Fight the Smears, my.barackobama.com.

23. Sweet, "Obama Fights Smear."

24. Ibid.

25. Michael Powell and Jodi Kantor, "Michelle Obama Looks for a New Introduction," *New York Times,* June 18, 2008.

26. E. D. Hill, on *America's Pulse,* Fox News, June 6, 2008; "Fox Anchor Calls Obama Fist Pound a 'Terrorist Fist Jab,'" *Huffington Post,* June 9, 2008, www.huffingtonpost.com/2008/06/09/fox-anchor-calls-obama-fi_n_106027.html; "'Terrorist Fist Jab' Anchor Gets Canceled," *Chicago Tribune's* Swamp blog, June 12, 2008, www.swamppolitics.com/news/politics/blog/2008/06/ed_hill_apologies_loses_show.html.

27. "Palin Says Obama 'Palling Around with Terrorists,'" Associated Press, Oct. 5, 2008.

28. Johanna Neuman, "Bush Does the Obama Power Fist Bump," *Los Angeles Times'* Countdown to Crawford blog, July 2, 2008, http://latimesblogs.latimes.com/presidentbush/2008/07/bush-does-the-o.html.

29. M. J. Stephey, "A Brief History of the Fist Bump," *Time,* June 5, 2008.

30. Barack Obama, interview by Brian Williams, *NBC Nightly News,* June 4, 2008.

31. Don Frederick, "Fox News in Trouble Again Over Obama Smear: 'Baby Mama,'" *Los Angeles Times'* Top of the Ticket blog, June 12, 2008.

32. Public Relations Problems and Cases blog, College of Communications at the Pennsylvania State University, http://psucomm473.blogspot.com/2007/04/downfall-of-john-kerrys-2004.html.

33. "Kitty Dukakis," Wikipedia, en.wikipedia.org/wiki/Kitty-Dukakis (accessed July 16, 2008).

34. Holly Bailey, "In Search of the Real Cindy McCain," *Newsweek,* June 30, 2008.

35. Ibid.

36. Ibid.

37. Nancy Collins, "Cindy McCain: Myth vs. Reality," *Harper's Bazaar*, July 2007.

38. Bailey, "In Search of the Real Cindy McCain."

39. Cindy McCain, interview, *Today Show*, NBC, May 8, 2008.

40. Mark Hosenball and Michael Isikoff, "Obama: Can't 'Swift Boat' Me," *Newsweek*, Apr. 28, 2008.

41. Powell and Kantor, "Michelle Obama Looks for a New Introduction."

42. Carla Marinucci, "Candidates' Wives Under Media Microscope," *San Francisco Chronicle*, June 29, 2008.

43. Ibid.

44. Vennochi, "Make Over Old Views, Not Political Wives."

45. Marinucci, "Candidates' Wives Under Media Microscope."

46. Ann Althouse and Robin Givhan, bloggingheads.tv, bloggingheads.tv/diavlogs/122 01?in=00:18:32&out=00:27:17.

47. Jcdemtl, comment on "On *The View*, Michelle Obama Makes Pantyhose Confession," *Chicago Sun-Times'* The Scoop from Washington blog, comment posted June 18, 2008, http://blogs.suntimes.com/sweet/2008/06/on_the_view_michelle_obama_mak.html.

48. "Pool Report," *Wall Street Journal*, reported by Lynn Sweet, "Obama's Saturday in Chicago," *Chicago Sun-Times'* The Scoop from Washington blog, June 29, 2008, http:// blogs.suntimes.com/sweet/2008/06/obamas_saturday_in_chicago_hit.html.

49. Emma Cowing, "Although a Woman Won't Be in the Oval Office After the Presidential Election, There Will Be One Behind the Throne," *Scotsman*, June 9, 2008.

50. Ibid.

51. Ibid.

52. "Michelle Obama Doesn't Need to Fight Bill Clinton—That's What You Are For," *New York*'s Daily Intel blog, Jan. 24, 2008, http://nymag.com/daily/intel/2008/01/ michelle_obama_doesnt_need_to.html.

53. Karen Springen, "First Lady in Waiting," *Chicago Magazine*, Oct. 2004.

54. Michelle Obama, interview by Katie Couric, "Michelle Obama on Love, Family & Politics," *CBS Evening News*, CBS, Feb. 15, 2008, www.cbsnews.com/stories/2008/02/ 15/eveningnews/main3838884.shtml.

55. Springen, "First Lady in Waiting."

Chapter 7

1. Amy Fine Collins, interview with author, Aug. 2, 2008.

2. "Flash: It Girl Michelle Obama Lights Up the Campaign Trail, Proving That She Is a Fashion Force to Be Reckoned With," *Vogue*, Apr. 2008.

3. Guy Trebay, "She Dresses to Win," *New York Times* Style section, June 9, 2008.

4. Ibid.

5. Jesse Oxfeld, "Fashion Fist Bump! *Bazaar* Tribute," *New York*'s Intelligencer blog, Aug. 3, 2008, http://nymag.com/news/intelligencer/48938.

6. Trebay, "She Dresses to Win."

7. Jill Lawrence, "Michelle Obama Has Busy Summer Ahead," *USA Today*, June 29, 2008.

8. Ann Sanner, "Michelle Obama Describes Duty as Mother-in-Chief," Associated Press, Aug. 4, 2008.

9. Kate Linthicum, "Michelle Obama Is *Vanity Fair*'s 'Best-Dressed,'" *Los Angeles Times'* Top of the Ticket blog, July 29, 2008, http://latimesblogs.latimes.com/wash ington/2008/07/michelle-obama.html; Cynthia Nellis, "Definition of a Sheath Dress," About.com: Women's Fashion, http://fashion.about.com/cs/glossary/g/bldefsheath.htm.

10. Amy Fine Collins, interview with author, Aug. 2, 2008.

11. Ben Macintyre, interview with author, July 13, 2008.

12. Robin Givhan, "Dressing to Impress Upon Memory," *Washington Post*, June 8, 2008, www.washingtonpost.com/wp-dyn/content/article/2008/06/05/AR2008060502012 .html.

13. "The Color Purple," Wikipedia, http://en.wikipedia.org/wiki/The_Color_Purple (accessed Aug. 9, 2008).

14. Pam Adams, "America Is Colored Purple," *Peoria Journal Star*, July 2, 2008.

15. Michelle Obama, interview by Katie Couric, "Michelle Obama on Love, Family & Politics," *CBS Evening News*, CBS, Feb. 15, 2008, www.cbsnews.com/stories/2008/02/ 15/eveningnews/main3838884.shtml.

16. Eric Wilson, "Across the Political Spectrum," *New York Times*, July 31, 2008.

17. Ibid.

18. Ibid.

19. Tony Allen-Mills, "Michelle Obama Fuels Frock Fashion Frenzy," *Sunday Times*, June 29, 2008.

20. Leonard Doyle, "Obama by Versace: Candidate Inspires Donatella's New Style," *Independent* (UK), June 24, 2008.

21. Ibid.

22. Michelle Obama, interviewed on *The View*, ABC, June 18, 2008.

23. Ibid.

24. Ibid.

25. "America's New Jackie O Is Called Michelle, Supporters Say," Agence France-Presse, June 19, 2008.

26. Michelle Cottle, "The Softening Has Begun," *New Republic*'s Plank blog, June 18, 2008, http://blogs.tnr.com/tnr/blogs/the_plank/archive/2008/06/18/the-softening-has -begun.aspx.

27. Megan Garber, "The Sisterhood of the Traveling Pantyhose," *Columbia Journalism Review*'s Campaign Desk blog, June 19, 2008, https://archives.cjr.org/campaign_desk/ the_sisterhood_of_the_travelin.php.

28. Helen Kennedy, "While Michelle Obama Has Been Front and Center, Cindy McCain Is a Mystery," *US News and World Report*, June 23, 2008.

29. Holly Bailey, "In Search of the Real Cindy McCain," *Newsweek*, June 30, 2008.

30. Cindy McCain, interview by John King, "Spotlight on Cindy McCain," CNN, June 19, 2008.

31. Kennedy, "While Michelle Obama Has Been Front and Center."

32. Wendy Donahue, "That Obama Dress," *Chicago Tribune*, June 23, 2008.

33. Cheryl Lu-Lien Tan, "Michelle Obama: Fashion's New Darling," *Wall Street Journal*, June 19, 2008.

34. Cathy Horyn, "Conspicuous by Their Presence," *New York Times,* June 19, 2008.

35. Alessandra Stanley, "Michelle Obama Shows Her Warmer Side on *The View,*" *New York Times,* June 19, 2008.

36. Ibid.

37. Ibid.

Chapter 8

1. Kevin Merida, "Hill, Yes! O., No!" *Washington Post,* June 27, 2008.

2. "Tucker on Sen. Clinton . . . ," Media Matters for America, Mar. 20, 2007, http://mediamatters.org/items/200703200013.

3. Katharine Q. Seelye and Julie Bosman, "Media Charged with Sexism in Clinton Coverage," *New York Times,* June 13, 2008.

4. "After Vowing Not to Underestimate Clinton . . . ," Media Matters for America, Jan. 9, 2008, http://mediamatters.org/items/200801090008.

5. Seelye and Bosman, "Media Charged with Sexism in Clinton Coverage."

6. "Confronted on *GMA* . . . ," Media Matters for America, May 30, 2008, http://mediamatters.org/items/200805300010.

7. "Does Our Looks-Obsessed Culture Want to Stare at an Aging Woman?" Rush Limbaugh, *Rush Limbaugh Show,* Dec. 17, 2007, www.rushlimbaugh.com/home/daily/site_121707/content/01125114.guest.html.guest.html.

8. "Media Hall of Shame: 2008 Election Edition," National Organization for Women, www.now.org/issues/media/hall_of_shame/index.html (accessed Aug. 9, 2008).

9. Seelye and Bosman, "Media Charged with Sexism in Clinton Coverage."

10. Ibid.

11. Ibid.

12. "Baby Mama," Wikipedia, http://en.wikipedia.org/wiki/Baby_mama (accessed Aug. 9, 2008).

13. Gene Stout, "Hip-Hop Star Nas Protests Fox News 'Obama Smears,'" *Seattle Post-Intelligencer's* Big Blog, July 22, 2008, http://blog.seattlepi.nwsource.com/thebig blog/archives/144082.asp.

14. "Media Hall of Shame: 2008 Election Edition"; Lars Larson, on *Verdict with Dan Abrams,* MSNBC, June 18, 2008, www.msnbc.msn.com/id/25264764.

15. "Media Hall of Shame: 2008 Election Edition"; Cal Thomas, on *Fox News Watch,* Fox News, June 14, 2008, www.foxnews.com/story/0,2933,367601,00.html.

16. Cal Thomas, on *Fox News Watch.*

17. Roger Stone, interview by Geraldo Rivera, *Geraldo at Large,* Fox News, June 1, 2008.

18. E. D. Hill, on *America's Pulse,* Fox News, June 6, 2008; "Fox Anchor Calls Obama Fist Pound a 'Terrorist Fist Jab,'" *Huffington Post,* June 9, 2008, www.huffingtonpost .com/2008/06/09/fox-anchor-calls-obama-fi_n_106027.html; "'Terrorist Fist Jab' Anchor Gets Canceled," *Chicago Tribune's* Swamp blog, June 12, 2008, www.swamp politics.com/news/politics/blog/2008/06/ed_hill_apologies_loses_show.html.

19. "O'Reilly: 'I Don't Want to Go on a Lynching Party . . . ,'" Media Matters for America, Feb. 20, 2008, http://mediamatters.org/items/200802200001.

20. "Hip Hop Artist Nas to Join Protest of Fox Race-Baiting and Obama Smears," Colorofchange.org media advisory, July 23, 2008, http://colorofchange.org/foxobama/delivery.html.

21. "Michelle Obama's America," *The Economist,* July 3, 2008.

22. Ruben Navarrette, "Michelle Obama's Under Fire, But for No Good Reason," *Sacramento Bee,* June 23, 2008.

23. Ibid.

24. "Magazine Mavens Discuss Covering Michelle Obama," *Tell Me More,* NPR, June 25, 2008.

25. Ibid.

26. Ibid.

27. Ibid.

28. Ibid.

29. Ibid.

30. Earnest Harris, "Cal Thomas's Scary Angry Black Michelle," *Huffington Post*'s Off the Bus blog, July 2, 2008, www.huffingtonpost.com/earnest-harris/cal-thomass-scary -angry-b_b_110588.html.

31. Ibid.

32. Ibid.

33. "Is Barack Obama's Wife His Rock or His Bitter Half?," *The Economist,* July 3, 2008.

34. Ibid.

35. Ibid.

36. Ibid.

37. "Michelle Obama: Questions About Husband Being 'Black Enough' Silly," Feb. 1, 2008, CNN.com/2008/POLITICS/02/01/michelle.obama/index.html.

38. Rupert Cornwell, "Out of America," *The Independent,* June 22, 2008.

39. Ibid.

40. Ibid.

41. Ibid.

42. Ibid.

43. James L. Taylor, "The UnAmerican Americans: Or, Why Michelle Obama Is 'Fair Game'" NPR Political Positions blog, June 25, 2008, www.npr.org/blogs/newsandviews/2008/06/the_unamerican_americans_or_wh.html.

44. Ibid.

45. Ibid.

46. Ibid.

47. Clarence Page, "Why the Obama Cartoon Cover Bombed: Is It Funny? Is It True? Is the Target Worth It?" *Chicago Sun-Times,* July 16, 2008.

48. Joe Garofoli, "*New Yorker* Editor Defends Obama Cover," *San Francisco Chronicle,* July 15, 2008.

49. Mark S. Allen, comment on "Come On, Laugh," *Chicago Tribune*'s Vox Pop blog, comment posted July 15, 2008, http://newsblogs.chicagotribune.com/vox_pop/2008/07/did-the-the-new.html.

50. Chuck-in-Wichita, comment on "Is the *New Yorker*'s Muslim Obama Cover Incendiary or Satire?" *Los Angeles Times'* Top of the Ticket blog, comment posted July 13, 2008, http://latimesblogs.latimes.com/washington/2008/07/obama-muslim.html; James Rainey, "Barack Obama Magazine Flap Shows an Irony Deficiency," *Los Angeles Times,* July 15, 2008.
51. "Obama Cartoon Insult to Muslims," AlJazeera.net, July 16, 2008.
52. Barack Obama, interview by Larry King, *Larry King Live,* CNN, July 15, 2008.
53. Ibid.
54. Garofoli, "*New Yorker* Editor Defends Obama Cover."
55. Ibid.
56. Bill Carter, "Want Obama in a Punch Line? First, Find a Joke," *New York Times,* July 16, 2008.
57. Rainey, "Barack Obama Magazine Flap."
58. Garofoli, "*New Yorker* Editor Defends Obama Cover."
59. Joe Murray, "*Newsweek* Poll Shows Obama Gains over McCain," *Bulletin,* June 23, 2008.
60. Ibid.
61. Ibid.
62. "Michelle Obama: I've Got a Loud Mouth," *Good Morning America,* ABC News, May 22, 2007.
63. Ibid.
64. Carter, "Want Obama in a Punch Line? First, Find a Joke."
65. Alessandra Stanley, "On 'SNL' It's the Real Sarah Palin, Looking Like a Real Entertainer," *New York Times,* Oct. 20, 2008.
66. Bill Carter, "An Election to Laugh About," *New York Times,* Oct. 9, 2008.
67. "McCain Cracks Age Jokes on *SNL,*" CNN's Political Ticker blog, May 18, 2008, http://politicalticker.blogs.cnn.com/2008/05/18/mccain-cracks-age-jokes-on-snl.
68. Ibid.
69. Ibid.
70. Associated Press, "So How Old Is John McCain?," June 13, 2008.
71. Mike Allen, "John McCain Goes Online," Politico.com, July 13, 2008.
72. Things Younger than McCain, www.thingsyoungerthanmccain.com.
73. Ricardo Alonso-Zaldivar, "Born Before Computers, McCain Is 'Too Old' for Some," Associated Press, July 15, 2008.
74. Michelle Tsai, "How Smart Is Grandpa? How Much Can You Expect from a Septuagenarian Brain," *Slate,* Apr. 26, 2007.
75. Alonso-Zaldivar, "Born Before Computers."
76. Ibid.
77. "Sarah Palin Presidency Would be 'Really Terrifying Possibility,' Warns Matt Damon," *Telegraph* (UK), Sept. 11, 2008.
78. Mackenzie Carpenter, "Michelle Obama Wows Them at CMU," *Pittsburgh Post-Gazette,* Apr. 3, 2008.
79. "Cindy McCain, Michelle Obama Speak Out," Political Intelligence, Oct. 9, 2008. www.boston.com/news/politics/politicalintelligence/2008/10/cindy_mccain-mi.html.

Chapter 9

1. Brian Stelter, "The Facebooker Who Friended Obama," *New York Times*, July 7, 2008.
2. E-mail from David Plouffe at info@barackobama.com, July 17, 2008.
3. Stelter, "The Facebooker Who Friended Obama."
4. Ibid.
5. "Over One Million Supporters on Facebook," Post from Chris Hughes' Blog, mybarackobama.com, June 17, 2008.
6. Stelter, "The Facebooker Who Friended Obama."
7. Ibid.
8. Jessica Guynn, "Growing Internet Role in Election: Videos, Fundraising Among Many Uses Candidates Employ," *San Francisco Chronicle*, June 4, 2007.
9. Ibid.
10. Stelter, "The Facebooker Who Friended Obama."
11. Gina Barreca, "A Childish Stunt That Only Shocks and Offends," *Hartford Courant*, July 20, 2008.
12. Irene Papoulis, "Cover Makes Us Squirm, But It Forces a Discussion," *Hartford Courant*, July 20, 2008.
13. Adam Nagourney and Megan Thee, "Poll Finds Obama Isn't Closing Divide on Race," *New York Times*, July 16, 2008.
14. Felicia Lee, "CNN Trains Its Lens on Race," *New York Times*, July 23, 2008.
15. Ibid.
16. "Jesse Jackson Apologizes for Crude Obama Remarks," http://elections.foxnews.com/2008/07/09/jesse-jackson-apologizes-for-obama-remarks, Fox News, July 9, 2008.
17. Allison Samuels, "At Arm's Length," *Newsweek*, July 21, 2008.
18. Kevin Merida, "Left on the Sidelines After a Pioneering Career," *Washington Post*, July 20, 2008.
19. Ibid.
20. Ibid.
21. Ibid.
22. Sophia Nelson, "Black. Female. Accomplished. Attacked." *Washington Post*, July 20, 2008.
23. Ibid.
24. Ibid.
25. Ibid.
26. Ibid.
27. Merida, "Left on the Sidelines After a Pioneering Career."
28. Louise Ambler Osborn, interview with author, July 18, 2008.

Chapter 10

1. Foon Rhee, "All Michelle Obama, All the Time," *Boston Globe*'s Political Intelligence blog, Aug. 7, 2008, www.boston.com/news/politics/politicalintelligence/2008/08/all_michelle_ob.html.
2. E-mail from Michelle Obama at info@barackobama.com, July 29, 2008.
3. Ibid.

4. Maureen Dowd, "Mr. Darcy Comes Calling," *New York Times,* Aug. 4, 2008.

5. Kate Linthicum, "Michelle Obama: Cover Girl Cover Girl Cover Girl," *Los Angeles Times'* Top of the Ticket blog, Aug. 7, 2008, http://latimesblogs.latimes.com/washing ton/2008/08/obama---ladies.html.

6. Ibid.

7. Ibid.

8. Michelle Obama, interview by Robin Roberts, *Good Morning America,* ABC, Aug. 7, 2008.

Chapter 11

1. Roger Cohen, "American Stories," *New York Times,* Oct. 30, 2008.

2. Michelle Obama, convention speech at the Democratic National Convention, transcript from NPR, Aug. 26, 2008.

3. Carrie Budoff Brown, "Michelle Obama Focuses on Military Spouses," CBSNews .com, Oct. 20, 2008.

4. Byron York, "Michelle Obama's Two Americas," *National Review* online, Aug. 26, 2008.

5. Patrick Healy, "Debate Audience Members Talk About the Candidates," The Caucus, *New York Times,* Oct. 8, 2008.

6. Caller into *Talk of the Nation,* NPR, Oct. 14, 2008.

7. David Brooks, "Thinking About Obama," *New York Times,* Oct. 17, 2008.

8. Michelle Obama, interview with Larry King, *Larry King Live,* CNN, Oct. 8, 2008.

9. Bonna Johnson, "Roundtable: Palin Heats Up Discussion," *Tennesseean, USA Today,* Sept. 15, 2008.

10. Katherine Q. Seelye, "Michelle Obama Dismisses Criticisms," The Caucus, *New York Times,* Oct. 9, 2008.

11. "Michelle Obama Tells McCain to End Insults," *Times* online (UK), Oct. 9, 2008.

12. Alessandra Stanley, "On 'SNL' It's the Real Sarah Palin, Looking Like a Real Entertainer," *New York Times,* Oct. 20, 2008.

13. Jeff Zeleny, "Donation Record as Colin Powell Endorses Obama," *New York Times,* Oct. 20, 2008.

14. Colin Powell, interview with Tom Brokaw, *Meet the Press,* NBC, Oct. 19, 2008.

15. *Chicago Tribune,* Oct. 17, 2008.

16. "Top of the Ticket," *Los Angeles Times* blogs, Oct. 20, 2008.

17. "Obama Testy with Media on Halloween," Associated Press, Oct. 31, 2008.

18. Kristin Wyatt, "Michelle Obama: Thank Barack Obama's Grandmother," Associated Press, Nov. 3, 2008.

19. Nedra Pickler, "Bittersweet Election Eve for Obama," Associated Press, Nov. 3, 2008.

Chapter 12

1. E-mail from Stephen Danenberg to Liz Lightfoot, Sept. 24, 2008.

Chapter 13

1. Michelle Obama, convention speech at the Democratic National Convention, transcript from NPR, Aug. 25, 2008.

2. Michelle Obama, convention speech at the Democratic National Convention, transcript from NPR, Aug. 25, 2008.

3. Meera Dolasia, "Malia and Sasha's First 100 Days in the White House," DOGOnews.com, Apr. 29, 2009.

4. Michelle Obama, *American Grown* (New York: Crown Publishers, 2012), 9.

5. Remarks by the First Lady at the White House Kitchen Garden Dedication, Office of the First Lady, The White House, Oct. 5, 2016.

6. "America's Move to Raise a Healthier Generation of Kids," Let's Move, Obama Whitehouse Archives.

7. Kelly Miterko, "In Review; First Lady Michelle Obama's Top 10 Let's Move! Moments," Obama White House Archives.

8. "Achievements," Let's Move, Obama Whitehouse Archives.

9. Remarks by the First Lady at the White House Kitchen Garden Dedication, Obama White House Archives, Oct. 5, 2016.

10. "USDA Publishes School Meals Rule, Expands Options, Eases Challenges," US Department of Agriculture Press Release, Nov. 29, 2017.

11. Scott Horsley, "Michelle Obama's Kitchen Garden Will Keep Blooming, Even After She Leaves," WNPR, Oct. 6, 2016.

12. Helena Bottemiller Evich, "Melania Trump Embraces Michelle Obama's Vegetable Garden," Politico.com, Sept. 22, 2017.

13. Helena Bottemiller Evich, "Michelle Obama Sets Her Garden in Stone," Politico .com, Oct. 6, 2016.

14. Remarks by the First Lady at the White House Kitchen Garden Dedication, Obama White House Archives, Oct. 5, 2016.

15. "Michelle Obama," About the White House, Whitehouse.gov.

16. Colleen Curtis, "Michelle Obama Talks About Being a Mentor," Obama White House Archives, Feb. 2, 2012.

17. Turnaround Arts, Kennedy Center website, kennedy-center.org.

18. "Michelle Obama's Letter to Newtown: 'Holding You in Our Hearts,'" *Hartford Courant*, Dec. 20, 2012.

19. Philip Rucker, "Michelle Obama on Gun Control: 'These Reforms Deserve a Vote,'" *Washington Post*, Apr. 10, 2013.

20. Betsy Klein, "Obamas: Parkland Students 'Helped Awaken the Conscience' of US on Gun Violence," CNN Politics, March 21, 2018.

21. Michelle Obama's Speech on Donald Trump's Alleged Treatment of Women, WNPR, Oct. 13, 2016.

22. Helene Cooper and Abby Goodnough, "Over Beers, No Apologies, but Plans to Have Lunch," *New York Times*, July 30, 2009.

23. Remarks by the First Lady at Tuskegee University Commencement Address, Obama White House Archives, May 9, 2015.

24. Remarks by the First Lady at Jackson State University Commencement, Obama White House Archives, April 23, 2016.
25. Remarks by First Lady at City College New York Commencement, Obama White House Archives, June 3, 2016.
26. Michelle Obama's Prepared Remarks for Democratic National Convention, NPR, July 26, 2016.
27. Barack Obama video, YouTube, Oct. 3, 2017.
28. Tierney McAfee, "See Barack Obama Crash His Wife's Conference with Gushy Anniversary Tribute That Made Her Gasp, 'I Better Get Home!'" *People*, Oct. 30, 2017.
29. Hilary Weaver, "Where Was Sasha Obama During the President's Farewell Address?" *Vanity Fair*, Jan. 11, 2017.
30. President Obama Farewell Speech—transcript, *Time*, Jan. 11, 2017.
31. Michelle Obama Convention Speech, Transcript, NPR, Sept. 4, 2012.
32. Michelle Obama, Convention Speech, Transcript, *Washington Post*, July 7, 2016.
33. Chimamanda Ngozi Adichie, Gloria Steinem, Jon Meacham, Rashida Jones, "To the First Lady, With Love," *New York Times*, Oct. 17, 2016.

Chapter 14

1. Justin McCarthy, "President Obama Leaves White House with 58% Favorable Rating," Gallup, Jan. 16, 2017.
2. Megan McCluskey, "The Internet Really, Really Wants Michelle Obama to Run for President in 2020," *Time*, Nov. 9, 2016.
3. Daniella Diaz and John Couwels, "Michelle Obama Says She Won't Run for Office," CNN, Apr. 27, 2017.
4. "Does Michelle Obama Plan to Run for Office?" Oprah Special, Oprah Winfrey Network, Dec. 19, 2016.
5. Jonathan Van Meter, "Michelle Obama: A Candid Conversation with America's Champion and Mother in Chief," *Vogue*, Nov. 11, 2016.
6. "Michelle Obama, Bo Surprise Visitors," *Huffington Post*, Jan. 20, 2010.
7. "In Review: How the White House Has Engaged With the American People Online," The Obama White House, Medium.com.
8. First Lady's Surprising Hug from the Queen of England, CNN video, CNN video (YouTube.com), Mar. 26, 2012.
9. Sam Dangremond, "Donald Trump Is the Only Recent President Who Didn't Escort His Wife into the White House," *Town & Country*, Jan. 25, 2017.
10. Anna Hopkins, "First Ladies First: Why Didn't Trump Wait for Melania at Their Car When They Arrived at the White House to Meet the Obamas . . . Unlike Barack, George and Bill Did with Their Wives?" *Daily Mail*, Jan. 27, 2017.
11. Leah Bourne, "7 Indisputable Ways Michelle Obama Changed the Way You Dress," *Glamour*, Jan. 20, 2017.
12. Karen Grigsby Bates, "Mrs. Obama Saves the Cardigan: 'The Obama Effect' in Fashion," NPR, May 14, 2016.

13. Tanisha C. Ford, "She Slays," *The Meaning of Michelle: 16 Writers on the Iconic First Lady and How Her Journey Inspires Our Own*, edited by Veronica Chambers (Picador, New York), 124.

14. Ian Simpson, "West Virginia Official Who Called Michelle Obama 'Ape in Heels' Fired," Reuters, Dec. 27, 2016.

15. Peter Slevin, "How Michelle Obama Became a Singular American Voice," *Washington Post*, Dec, 12, 2016.

16. Ibid.

17. Video of Michelle Obama interview with Oprah Winfrey at the United States of Women Conference, Obama White House, June 20, 2016.

18. Adichie, Steinem, Meacham, and Jones, "To the First Lady, With Love."

19. Lindsay Robertson, "The Story of a Guy Who Got Michelle Obama's Face Shaved into His Head Last Night," *Marie Claire*, Mar. 29, 2018.

Chapter 15

1. @michelleobama, Twitter, Jan. 20, 2017.

2. *"Michelle Obama a rejoint son mari au fenua,"* TNTV News, Apr. 9, 2017.

3. Rebecca Shabad, "Watch Obama Kitesurf with Richard Branson in the British Virgin Islands," CBS News, Feb. 7, 2017.

4. @michelleobama, Twitter, Feb. 14, 2017.

5. @michelleobama, Twitter, Feb. 23, 2017.

6. @michelleobama, Twitter, Feb. 28, 2017.

7. Editorial, "The Guardian View on Michelle Obama: Missing Her Already," *The Guardian*, Jan. 6, 2017.

8. Lisa Sadikman, "9 Reasons I'm Already Missing Michelle Obama," ScaryMommy .com.

9. Danielle Kwateng Clark, "We Miss Michelle Obama: Here Are All The Times We Caught a Glimpse of the Former First Lady in 2017," *Essence*, Dec. 20, 2017.

10. Tierney McCafee, "Michelle Obama on Life with Barack Today and What's Next: 'We're Not Gone, We're Just Breathing, Y'all,'" *People*, May 12, 2017.

11. Krissah Thompson, "The Obamas Just Signed a Jumbo Book Deal: Here's Why a Publisher Is Betting Big on Them," *Washington Post*, Mar. 1, 2017.

12. @michelleobama, Twitter, Feb. 25, 2018.

13. Emma Stefansky, "Michelle Obama's Must-Read Memoir Hits Shelves This Fall," *Vanity Fair*, Feb. 25, 2018.

14. Michael D. Shear, "Coming to Netflix: The Obamas Sign Deal to Produce Shows," *New York Times*, May 21, 2018.

15. Michael D. Shear, Katie Benner, John Koblin, "Obama in Talks to Provide Shows for Netflix," *New York Times*, Mar. 8, 2018.

16. Shear, Benner, Koblin, "Obama in Talks to Provide Shows for Netflix."

17. Shear, "Coming to Netflix: The Obamas Sign Deal to Produce Shows."

18. Obama Foundation website, www.obama.org/mission.

19. "What's Next from Barack and Michelle Obama," YouTube video, Obama Foundation, Jan. 20, 2017. www.youtube.com/watch?v=ODVxuN6m6E8&list=LLArcv6aB35 UQ7AVwqu6DBdQ.

20. Katy [last name unknown], "I Got to Go the Obama Foundation Summit Concert and All I Got Was This Hope, Inspiration, and Gratitude," *I Got a Dumpster Family!* blog, Nov. 2, 2017.

21. Clare Foran, "Obama Hopes to Create 'A Million Young Barack Obamas or Michelle Obamas,'" CNN, Mar. 26, 2018.

22. Kanisha Bond, Erica Chenoweth, and Jeremy Pressman, "Did You Attend the March for Our Lives? Here's What It Looked Like Nationwide," *Washington Post*, Apr. 13, 2018.

23. Paul Owen, "Obama Wants to 'Create a Million Young Michelle and Barack Obamas,'" *The Guardian*, Mar. 25, 2018.

24. Emerson Chontos, speaking at March for Our Lives at Two Wrasslin' Cats, East Haddam, Connecticut, Mar. 24, 2018.

25. Foran, "Obama Hopes to Create 'A Million Young Barack Obamas or Michelle Obamas.'"

26. Remarks by the First Lady at the White House Kitchen Garden Dedication, Obama White House Archives, Oct. 5, 2016.

INDEX